GiRL ON A LEASH

The Healing Power of Dogs

a memoir

BETTY LiM KiNG

Sanctuary Press

Published by Sanctuary Press

King, Betty Lim, 1949-
     Girl on a Leash : The Healing Power of Dogs : a memoir
/Betty Lim King. ~ 1st ed.
     p. cm.
     Library of Congress Catalog Card Number : 98-96447
     ISBN : 0-9665954-0-8

     1. Dogs~Therapeutic use. 2. Human-animal relationships.
3. King, Betty Lim, 1949- 4. Dogs~Anecdotes. 5. Pet owners~
Biography. 6. Chinese-American women~Biography. I. Title.

RM931.D63K56 1998   636.7'088
                            QB198-1081

Printed in the United States of America

CONTENTS

N.B. *Words and terms in Chinese, except those in Fujian, are in Pinyin. Some Wade-Giles versions are retained for their familiarity.*

Acknowledgments

This book would not have been possible without the help and support of Dr. Ruben Santos Cuyugan, my husband and editor. I cannot count the number of hours we spent debating all issues and aspects of the book in the manner of Socrates and his fellow-seekers of the correct and true, in the company of our four-legged boys and their friends. In the end, they still believed in me even when I stopped. To them, I dedicate this book in recompense.

In the production of this book, it has taken a village to make it come into print. I am grateful to Joy Nakrin for her wise and refreshing comments on the draft and, at a tender age, sharing my commitment to animal welfare; Grace King Dols, for her unfailing support and artistic skills; Dr. Teresita L. King for her generosity of long duration; Dr. Mary L. King & Dr. James Nash for patiently reading the draft and offering many helpful suggestions; Dr. Andrew S. Nakrin for his thoughts on an early manuscript; Dr. Rosemary L. King & Dr. Horner C. Chen, Jr. for their steadfast encouragement; Katie, Jenny-Beth, and Chet Dols, for their growing love of animals.

My special thanks to Thomas Yueh, for his helpful suggestions and cover design; Jeff Nakrin for his incisive comments on a draft; Vince & Linda Cuyugan, Myrna & Renato Livas, Carolyn Hamby, Cathy Eller, Fides S.C. Asensio for giving me a shoulder to cry on; Inang & Roy Gonzales, Fulvia Rand, Marcelle Navannec, Stephen Mills, Lisa Annas, Mely Nicolas, Janine Brookner, Peggy Carter, Shizuko & Terry Melton, Anna Mae McElveen, Mary Bruce, Mike Slaughter, Kurt Yahn, Sigrid Hice, Sue Davis, Neni Sta. Romana-Cruz, Ed Minnick, Cleofe Verzola, Carmina & Joe Segovia, Ada & Philip Mabilangan, Linda & Burgess Walker for their friendship.

I am grateful to all those who have dedicated their lives to increasing public awareness about a range of animal issues.

And last but not the least, I must thank my parents for what I am and am not.

N.B. Part of the proceeds of this book shall go to charities that directly benefit animals.

PROLOGUE

*A*ll my life I was on a leash.

I lived in three regions of the world: Asia, Europe, and America. Each was a phase in my life. In each I was on a leash, a leash that was transmuting in magical ways, affecting me profoundly. Whoever was at the other end guided and shaped my thoughts, desires, and purposes; gave joy or sorrow, healed my injuries ~ and filled my life.

As I traversed the world I made an inner journey from torment and destructive fixation on self to empathic rapport with other selves. Dogs became a salve for psychic wounds, the leash a conduit for strength and sustenance for the spirit.

My earliest recollections were of being tightly reined in by an iron code of inflexible rules. The Confucian leash was taut, unyielding. It gave a sharp tug with the slightest deviation or dissent, much as in the non-Confucian China of today. In the Chinese family that is a given. It is its virtue, and its flaw. Faced with modernity, the family retreats and assumes a rearguard defense mode, becoming even more intolerant.

Much as the code maintains stability, it also promotes backwardness. It is a social order that stifles rather than fulfills. All too often, it causes pain and unhappiness.

Schooled in the liberating ideals of democracy, I could not reconcile *yin* and *yang* contradictions in the family. I was a misfit, a maverick. As such I suffered unbearable inner conflict. Before me stretched the prospect of a slow, wrenching slide toward the edge and oblivion.

Fortunately, one gentle being after another came into my life and turned me around. They tugged me out of limbo onto a new existence, calmed my torment, and straightened out my life purposes and aspirations.

The leash now carried a positive emotional charge, and began to convey joy. At last I had a constant companion by my side. Together we were a binary star system, Sun revolving around Sun, one reaching out to the other in ineffable and mysterious ways. Krishna came in many guises: from Poodle to Borzoi to Jack Russell ~ and mutts.

The murder of a beloved Borzoi jolted me up a notch in the primordial sharing of sentiencies between species. His wanton and senseless killing opened my mind's eye to other killing fields. It snatched me out of my comfortable but limited existence to a more acute awareness of animal issues and a greater rapport with all of creation. A defining moment came when I advanced towards a new plane of existence, where mutualism between different species gave insight into self, and taught me to be at peace with myself as well as with those who had caused me pain. A sense of quiet bliss ultimately took over. From the crucible of this tragic loss I emerged with a clearer sense of purpose: who I was, where I wanted to go.

From tether, the leash transformed into lifeline.

These are stories of such enthrallments: what dogs meant to me and I to them. Through these stories I retrace my three-fold path through life in the company of dogs. Each dog is a hyperlink to my life experiences at different periods and places, each contributing to the healing of my dysfunctions. What I say about dogs is something in me that I see in them, just as what I see in them is something I see in society, or something missing in that society.

Writing about pets is writing about self, but more than that it is writing about the human condition. How we treat animals says much about our communities and ourselves. Living in three different cultures has made me conscious of how differently each culture regards and treats pets, revealing much about those who make up those societies.

Yet, despite wide differences, how remarkably alike dogs respond to humans! Dogs may be tortured, eaten, kicked around, totally neglected; or pampered and loved to death. However treated, they are steadfast in their loyalty and devotion to our species. We have snatched them away from their wolf mothers, and made them part of us; they have never left our side. It is we humans who waver. Just before dying in a research laboratory, a suffering and mutilated dog licked the hands of the technician who was causing his death. How superbly can they teach us about being humane!

In these stories, I begin by re-living the private agonies of my past. Dogs trigger memories whose meanings I could not apprehend at the time. Remembrance of pets past and present brings clarity and wholeness to the bits and pieces that make up the collage of a bewildering life.

I was the second of five sisters in an expatriate Chinese family in the Philippines, in the *Nanyang* or Southeast Asia, where throughout history Chinese were an underdog minority living a precarious, roller-coaster kind of existence..

After getting married I lived in Paris, France, where my husband was a Director at Unesco. Upon his retirement we moved to the United States to be near my family of origin in a milltown in western North Carolina. By this time, my entire family ~ fearful of racial incidents in which ethnic Chinese are often the primary targets ~ had all moved out of Asia. With the exception of Eldest Sister who lived in England all of us, including parents, were in America.

We were a perfectly normal, dysfunctional Chinese family hanging on together, trying to keep up with change in a non-Chinese milieu. Both my parents had uprooted themselves from a disintegrating China. As sojourners they lived in the midst of what Chinese regarded as an inferior, barbarian culture. The ensuing culture shock deepened already existing dysfunctions in the family. Adopting a policy of minimal personal engagement, my parents dealt with the host culture in the only way they knew, through their five daughters. The pressures bore heavily on the shoulders of Eldest Sister and mine. For me, they became truly unbearable.

Growing up in Asia built up an inner distress the causes of which at that time I had no clue. For some reason conflicts came to a head in me more than in any of my sisters. I felt trapped, suffocated. Everyone kept telling me what to do, what not to do, but nobody knew a way out of the morass in which I was mired. I began to hit out angrily, blindly and was told I was worse than a wild animal, needing to be tamed the Chinese way. I needed to be kept not only on a tight leash, but with a choke collar to keep me in line.

Now I know why I was in such turmoil. A Western education had made me completely dysfunctional with respect to the rigid code in the family. Immersion in Roman Catholicism made me feel awash in sin and headed for eternal roasting in hell. My Buddhist and Confucianist origins and antecedents constantly nagged my conscience. The exaggerated sense of guilt and shame built up a head of steam in me that eventually exploded into a full-blown neurosis. Clueless, I was told I alone was the willful source of all the turbulence in the family.

Every overseas Chinese family is a fortress unto itself, besieged, walling in its contradictions. An intolerant code of obedience and deference chained us up the generational and age hierarchy and glued us to a sticky web of kin. It was a chain-link fence that shut us in as it shut out the world. But such an ethos did not make for peace and harmony. In our family there were maelstroms of conflict, not social order.

For centuries Confucius has meant order in the family and harmony in society through a *clearly defined pecking order*. Children obey parents *without question*, wife submits to husband, inferiors kow-tow to superiors, women to men, younger to older. The code demands blind obedience to those above, magnanimity and benevolence to those below. Look over your shoulder, not ahead; look back to ancestors, not descendants; look to the past, not the future. The spoils, as it were~comfort, health, happiness, long life~belong to the *older*, to *men*, to *superiors*. The younger generation sacrificed for the sake of the older. Youth gets a fair shot only when the older generation disappears.

In the society in which we were growing up, the legitimacy of feudal, authoritarian ways was under fire. We sisters were exposed ~ by school, peers, and the media ~ to subversive ideas, viz., democracy versus tyranny, equality versus autocracy, individual worth versus group supremacy, equal importance to the *entering* as well as to the *exiting* generation, freedom ~ not suppression ~ of expression. The fortress was under siege. But we were still too young to add our voices to the clamor at the gates, too young to even be aware of such issues.

For us sisters, being Chinese was supposed to erect a wall between us and the non-Chinese, and to be a source of strength and self-identity. But nobody ever made clear, perhaps nobody really knew, what it was to be truly Chinese. Sure there were fleeting references to cuisine, medicinal drugs, language, the looks and ways of the non-Chinese. We were expected to instinctively fill in the blanks ~ about being Chinese. How could we? We were not growing up in a Chinese community. All our parents ever told us was that they had crossed the South China Sea from a great but sad country they called *Chung-guo,* where ancestors lay buried, where relatives lived. Not much else.

Throughout history Nanyang Chinese and their Southeast Asian hosts related to each other in a blow-hot, blow-cold manner. The Chinese quickly became major players in the economy, but otherwise they kept a low profile, shying away from public affairs and local politics. China itself did not count for much in world affairs. When Mao Zedong took over in 1949 (the year I was born), overnight China began to loom sinister. China was becoming a superpower, and it was only 700 miles away.

In history, the Chinese in Southeast Asia had always provoked mixed reactions: they were welcomed, they were reviled. After 1949, they were increasingly viewed with hostility and fear. When the cold war was coldest, even rich Chinese merchants were suspected of being Communists. Material success had its price. Not only were they despised or envied, now they were dangerous, a potential Fifth Column. Memories of Japanese aggression were still fresh. In no time their situation became quite an oxymoron: a threat, if a helpless one. Most felt caught in a vise.

We sisters never felt ourselves in a vise, for ours was a nebulous, shifting Chinese image. We moved at the margins, in-between cultures. We were marginal to mainstream Chinese, to those who lived in Chinatown, spoke only Chinese and sent their children to Chinese schools. To them we were "banana barbarians" ~ yellow on the outside, white inside. To the affluent middle-class Filipinos among whom we lived we were somewhat alien. Chameleons we became, agilely changing colors to suit the situation. We learned to walk a fine line: not too Chinese so that we could blend in, not too native as to incur our parents' ire. Being marginal gave us the best of both worlds, but at a price. Shifting from one mask to another led to nagging self-doubts about one's true identity. Self-esteem was at rock bottom.

Like a dog trying to catch its own tail, we ran in endless circles. Told that being a girl was an opprobrium, bringing disgrace to our parents, making them lose face, each of us overcompensated. Doggedly we tried to prove over and over again that being a girl was better than being a boy. In our zeal we competed against each other to win the prize of parental approval. Competition was fierce, even bitter. It was a single trough from which to feed. Often there was only enough for one. A sister's triumph was always another sister's defeat.

Strangely, the more the collar choked the tighter the ties to parents became, as if in trying to ease the pain of choking we had to get closer rather than farther. One who has never had such a collar can never fully apprehend the excruciating pain it causes the psyche, the damage it inflicts on family interactions, the friction it causes between family and kin. No one can ever imagine its power to control, to keep a member in bondage.

Fortunately, as far back as I can recall, there were always dogs in our home. In history, dogs were always a part of Chinese life. In Imperial China, they were court favorites, to while away the idle hours of bored concubines, or prized as gastronomic items for the Chinese table. They were in practically every house and village. In the recent past, Mao Zedong tried vainly to extirpate them from Communist society, along with all other "decadent" vestiges of capitalism. But dogs survived him. Today they are back. Big-character poster signs proclaim "Raise dogs. Get rich."

Among us sisters dogs had much value: they provided protection, entertainment and diversions. They were our dolls to cuddle and play with, to daydream and kindle our fantasies with, to order about. They were furniture and decor in our house, like chattel. To our parents breed was important. Breed dogs were for showing off our affluent lifestyle, boosting family prestige, and sometimes, selling for profit. Father went for a variety of pedigrees: Alsatian, Dalmatian, Great Dane, Chow Chow, Chihuahua, French toy and miniature Poodles. He fussed about purity of blood and AKC papers. We became pretty snobbish about pedigrees. They projected class, success, and sophistication.

In the beginning dogs did not really take up much of my personal life-space. I was too busy preparing myself to contribute to the family coffers, an inescapable duty. Time off assigned tasks was always vetoed.

Even friends were considered a frivolous diversion. Luckily, I had a personal dog, Kenneth, with whom I sneaked many a happy hour alone.

That was the first phase.

Growing up in an adoptive country meant moving from one crisis to another, day after day. It finally got to me. I began to internalize every conflict, unable each time to reconcile thesis and antithesis, unable to achieve a synthesis. The result: I began to suffer severe psychic impairments. Unlike my sisters I had not set up any coping mechanisms. I found myself all twisted up in knots, defiant, hypersensitive, and verbally aggressive. Inside I was eating myself up. Pushing dangerously close to the edge, I was about to crash. Fortuitously, I managed to withdraw into a state of denial. A kennel-full of dogs helped me escape from an all-too-painful reality. A personal pet was an intimation of what dogs would eventually mean to me.

In Paris a mutt began the process of pulling me back from a freefall as he dragged me along on the sidewalks and gardens of Paris, in this the second phase of my life. He rid me of snootiness about dogs and concern with class. How could I not drop all pretence, with this throwaway pup snuggling its way into my life?

He was ugly as sin, but as irresistible as French dark chocolate. He was *déclassé*, a street gamin. For the first time a dog was neither a commodity nor a possession, but a living, breathing, sentient being. He was not a wind-up toy, not a surrogate human; not an "it," but a persona, a "he." He took center stage; we tuned into each other's moods and impulses; we encouraged rather than inhibited each other. He introduced me to the underworld of mongrels and took over my life as no other dog had ever done. It transformed my life in Paris as a diplomat's wife into one high adventure after another. I was happy to be leashed to him. The leash underwent a dramatic qualitative change; it no longer constricted, indeed it liberated.

He became my *copain*, my sidekick. We conspired, played games in which we both knew the stakes. In Paris, a *petit chien* ~ no matter what breed ~ was an ever-valid passport into society. He opened doors and unlocked gates. Pulling me along, he conned me into prowling gardens and alleys I would never have dared enter alone. Provoking attention, he could extract a smile or affectionate comment from the dour Parisian. I came to know more about the *riverains* ~ the locals ~ this way. By playing his part he could get things for me, as well as for himself, that without him I could not have gotten. He knew exactly what I had in mind, but only he could execute the plan and get away with it, with the atrocious *sang-froid* of a trickster. I realized the French regard you as human ~ that is, more French ~ if you came with a pet. Somehow a pet completes you and makes you deserving of attention. Without one, you're merely a foreigner to ignore. Just another barbarian.

This cunning rascal of a foundling did much more. He purged me of a neurosis that grew out of a tangled web of family relationships. It no longer rankled. He gave me a password to a new identity, making me aware of what it meant to be alive in Paris. My world just simply exploded into a myriad scintillant facets. The leash became a magician's wand.

It was all too soon over. Coming from Paris to live in America near my parents and two sisters was stepping back in time. Even if two other sisters lived very far from us, it was like a sustained flashback in which we resumed where we left off, as if nothing had changed. But the contingencies of living away from Asia tore sharp, jagged gashes in the interpersonal fabric of the expanding family. The feverish climb up Gold Mountain revived old internal discordances and activated many new ones. Culture clashes waxed to white-hot levels, fueled by a new element: interracial marriages. Powerful centrifugal forces countervailed the centripetal; fissures began to crack wide open. Remarkably, a state of denial still persisted. This in itself masked an underlying dysfunction.

We were grown-up and married, but the juvenile turbulence was still there. Worse, new value-conflicts and cross-allegiances surfaced. Clashing personal agendas ran out of control. Recent infant arrivals ~ young Chinese-Americans ~ added their burgeoning, unfamiliar demands to the discordant babble. By this time, we were all women of independent means. However, reaching the pinnacle of success did not break us free from our Confucian leash. That leash was alive and well. All of us continued to be like unweaned puppies jockeying for the choicest teats. Even when some of us tried to cut loose from the family umbilical cord, that is, to grow up, emotional booster shots were craftily administered to quickly bring us sharply back to a state of infantile dependence.

In America people hate to run in vicious circles. If you must run, go straight forward. Don't keep circling back. In a misguided but futile attempt to redefine the family by giving equitable status to the young Chinese-Americans among us, I ran full tilt into a stonewall. It was *déjà-vu* except that this time blockbuster force backed infantile impulses. Money became a "nuking" weapon. I found myself completely marginalized. Tagged as a dissident, I was virtually banished ~ for six years.

At the start of this period of exile a magnificent Borzoi named Chornley became a member of my family. He was a kindred soul who himself needed succoring. For a glorious while I had a pack of three dogs that sustained me in my isolation. They expanded my sensibilities and released my suppressed capabilities. They were a crutch and a refuge while I tried to put together the scattered jigsaw pieces of my life.

Three years went by, then one day a neighbor's son shot and killed Chornley, afterwards disposing of his body without giving me a chance to grieve and to bury him. This wanton, senseless act of violence became for me, an act of the community itself, by virtue of its stony indifference to my pleas and grief. I read the message ~ I was not one of the "good ol' boys." To my entreaties even the criminal justice system threw up its hands in seeming helplessness. Given all the illusions I had about America, the experience was shattering.

Anguish shortly turned to anger when I became convinced it was more than just a random act of violence. The evidence was clear: the killing was deliberate as it was symbolic. It was another message. I was painfully reminded of the signs on buildings and parks at Western enclaves in old China that read: NO DOGS OR CHINESE ALLOWED.

When total strangers started to leave dogs at my doorstep ~ when my grieving became known ~ I thought it a subtle way of telling me it was "just an animal." It can be replaced. Maybe they felt helpless in the ugly face of violence, but in my bitterness I sensed a discomfiture, a knee-jerk sticking of head in sand.

There was another equally disturbing message: pets are disposable, like toys or paper plates. It conveyed the sense that their right to life is less important because they are different; their right to life rests on whim or prejudice. If people shrug off evidence of endemic violence against women, children, minorities, the aged, the handicapped, homosexuals, AIDS victims, why should anyone be concerned with a victim that is, after all, " *just an animal?*"

One shocking experience after another jolted me to the realities of American society: the racial undertones, the cultural narrowness, the legal attitude towards animals, the positive linkage between human violence and animal abuse, the impact of local culture on law enforcement and the judicial system.

This was a major turning point, the start of the third phase of my life in the company of dogs.

Stirred to action, I looked into the extent of abandonment, abuse and neglect of pets. It was appalling. To vindicate partly my illusions about America and to complete the grieving process, I turned proactive, an unchinese role for a Chinese in a southern American suburbia. This time, I was not going to put tail between legs and slink off somewhere to sulk. Somebody had to hold up a mirror so everyone could see the nature of the beast. Turn a bad thing into a good thing.

Thus began a crusade ~ to rescue abandoned, "useless" dogs and re-integrate them into the community as therapists, teaching aids, guardian angels, or life companions. I thought of ways to relight the fire of love for, and sense of oneness with, the four-footed victims of our throwaway society, in the hope that an act of social CPR could breathe back love.

The leash was undergoing a quantum change. From tether the leash was transmuting into a lifeline.

Chornley's life enriched my spirit, his death expanded my consciousness to a wide range of animal issues. I felt the presence of all my former pets acting in unison to affirm our karmic connection, empowering me, opening my mind's eye to new, expansive vistas.

That animals could heal, teach, reconfigure perceptions, and enhance our "soul-essence" was a eureka experience. Maybe they are better attuned to life on this planet, more privy to its secrets. By attuning ourselves to them we can share in some of these secrets. Among sentient beings, nothing is more natural than a Gaia act of sharing, engaging in amazing mutualisms with one another.

Witness the remora fish and the shark, the egret and the water buffalo; the puny bird that picks the teeth of an open-jawed crocodile; the symbiosis among ants, trees, other creatures, between the animal and plant species; the wondrous partnership between bees and flowering plants, the mutual affection and care between dolphins and humans, between whales and ~ would you believe it? ~ dogs. Even the ancient hunter and the animal he hunted for food had a spiritual bond between them, a covenant. The hunter asks for forgiveness and expresses his profound gratitude for the animal that is sacrificing itself. We even fantasize the blending of species such as the sphinx, centaur, minotaur, mermaids. The ancient Egyptians depicted the blending of the falcon with a human to represent a person's individuality and character that survived death, hovering as *Ba* over the dead body, its original home.

There must be more to mutualism than just understanding one another. I was convinced that it is the helping of each other that matters ~ the healing, the nurturing, and the caring. We all have a glimpse of a common point origin, an intimation of a common end when everything comes together again. The "bush-soul," an animal or plant, is part of the soul of a primitive man, making that animal a "brother" to the man, essential to his identity. Being separate species does not belie the commonality that makes one a latent if not actual healer of the other's psychic dysfunctions.

Creatures who injure one another can also heal one another. Throughout evolution, humans have had this dual affinity with animals. If animals are the *Ba* of deities as the Egyptians postulated, they have a special significance for humankind, for they embody the spirits of gods. Animals are on earth indeed to help humans in their spiritual evolution; so that at death the human individuality and character, enhanced by contact with animals, survives. All animals can help this way if we but let them.

Impelled by the idea that animals can heal, I converted the survivors of my pack into canine social workers. They took to their new role as though they were to the manner born. My "Heinz-57" mutt was a hit with the senior citizens in the nursing and retirement homes. My Jack Russell terrier proved adept at assisting children with attention-deficit hyperactive syndrome (ADHD). Curiously, they related differently to the elderly as against the young.

Health workers at these institutions reported that petting my dogs ~ indeed their mere presence ~ lowered blood pressures and pulse rates, including the staff's. Stress levels dropped. My dogs charmed, provoked smiles, and elicited verbal responses from the silent and the lonely. Some cried, as long-lost memories of love and youth came flooding back. Even those who suffered from dementia started reminiscing with nostalgia about their own pets. The muscle-impaired eagerly sought tactile contact with their pet therapist, something they would not do with their human therapist. Cold science may simply ascribe the effect to endorphins ~ the brain's chemical fuel for re-stoking capacity for pleasure. For me the wonder of it all is the way the wagging of a tail and licking by a wet tongue can produce endorphins ~ this science does not explain.

Challenged, I immersed myself in studies on the therapeutic effects of animals on people. While many animal lovers had long known about it, only recently did scientific studies begin to provide evidence. The Harvard Health Letter (December 1993) reported two studies that showed the benefits of having a pet over a period of time.

The physiological impact of a pet on a human is to lower blood pressure, cholesterol and triglyceride levels regardless of socioeconomic status, diet, exercise, smoking habits, height, weight. A pet's nurturing friendship strengthened the human immune system by lowering the level of stress hormones.

The socio-psychological impact was the heightening of a sense of security, lessening the need for attention by health care providers. During stressful life-events, those who owned pets made fewer doctor visits. Pets' acute sensitivity to human feelings and moods makes them useful to those with psychiatric and neurological disorders such as multiple sclerosis.

The third phase brought a flood of insights. I realized the human condition can never be made whole without the living presence of animals who share this planet with us. The plethora of joy they endow our existence is enough raison d'être for Noah's Ark.

America's soul   was in disarray as much as mine was. Dysfunction and dissonance had become as American as apple pie. America had not yet come to terms with its growing diversity, the differences that made for dynamism and prosperity. America had yet to build bridges between communities.

I realized I had a great gift in my hands with which to rebuild a bridge to family and community. Dogs were no longer just a crutch, a refuge, a blessed relief from a disingenuous way of life. With their natural ability to break through barriers of age, gender, race, religion, and politics, dogs helped me connect to my own kind. I had to become as sensitive to human gestures, facial expressions, mannerisms, and cues as dogs superbly are. And as tolerant. Their ability to dissipate the murk with which humans surround themselves taught me to go behind masks humans use to obfuscate, not communicate, feelings and thoughts.

Unlike others, I did not turn to Valium, Prozac, and Ritalin. I did not have a shrink, counselor, Zen master or guru. Instead I had my dogs, and my dogs had me. They did for me what humans could not and would not do, asking nothing in return. For me their presence dredged up more insights into my infirmities than any sage or healer could ever have done.

If dogs can do these, are they not worthy of being considered therapists, albeit unlicensed? Don't they do what psycho- or socio-therapists do? Can't we say they are *natural* therapists, achieving without cost what it takes MD's and Ph.D.'s years of studying to do? Should they not be considered alternative healing resources?

After six years living at the foot of a small mountain by ourselves, an unexpected event suddenly brought me and my original family back together. Mother suffered a stroke that nearly paralyzed her entire left side. Going to meet with them after all these years, I was sure of one thing: much had changed in me, even if nothing else had. That is exactly what I found. As the French say, *plus ça change plus est la même chose.* Only this time I had what I needed to cope with all vicissitudes. I now had the gift of the healing power of dogs.

After three years the effects of Mother's cerebral stroke and diabetic condition were reversed. She had run the gamut of therapies: from conventional to natural to unconventional. The most important were the ministrations of family's pet therapists - five dogs, two cats, and a ferret.

Mine is a karmic debt I can only begin to repay by awakening the mind to a deeper awareness of how animals can enrich human existence. Then Noah's efforts will not have been wasted. And this planet will continue to flourish in diverse splendor. In larger unity.

PHASE ONE: ASIA & THE PACIFIC
(1949-1975)

1

YAMA

Milagros took a double take at the kitchen clock and ran in panic up the stairs.

Stepping awkwardly over the big furry heap sprawled on the floor between twin beds, she stood, chest heaving. Gasping, she shook both girls by the legs, gently but insistently, with sawdust-brown hands.

"Get up! Get up, you two! It's late *na!*" Milagros knew she would be blamed if we were late.

Yama lay unconcerned as the *major domo* anxiously moved from bed to bed. Finally she got up heavily from the scatter rug and shook herself. Ears pricking up, black eyes glinting, long sabre-like tail twitching slightly, she watched Milagros wax frantic as the seconds ticked by.

"Yama, out of the way," the *major domo* said, irritated, as she vainly tried to push the dog aside with her legs. Twenty-five inches at the shoulder, Yama was simply too bulky to be easily pushed around.

Three hours earlier I had been wide awake, laboriously scratching out my homework, a calligraphy exercise in English longhand. Yesterday Sister Tionelle called me to the front of the class and thrust the paper into my trembling hands. Eyes unblinking, she said, sternly, someone else had done my homework. She didn't believe I could have done it myself. I had done it all too well, with many flourishes. Third grade teacher insisted an adult had done it, meaning my parents, who else. My parents? All they could write were Chinese characters!

I was to repeat my "punishment" ten times. In a pique I decided to make it exactly like my rejected masterpiece, down to the last curlicue. Sister Tionelle couldn't possibly say my parents did my punishment for me. I was even prepared to write on the blackboard the same way.

Eldest Sister ~ older by a year ~ finally got up sighing, and after shaking her mane like a dog, shuffled off to the shower. I too got up and busied myself with my uniform laid out the night before. A few minutes later Eldest Sister emerged and without a word put on the long-sleeved, white-cotton shirt and navy-blue, pleated poplin skirt. She tied a matching blue bow around her collar and, posing before a large oval mirror, pivoted her head on a broad neck. Carved dragons and other celestial animals framed her image in the mirror. Then she plumped down on the *palo-china* dresser stool, pulled on white cotton-ribbed socks and, with a groan, squeezed her fat toes into shiny black-patent shoes.

Brushing down her jet-black hair and then slipping on a velvet headband, she quickly got up and tucked away her *shantung* pajamas. Always the neat and orderly one, she was now ready to go downstairs.

"Itchy!" I said, petulantly, ripping off the white shirt in exasperation. "I told you I don't like starched shirts." The convent school made no concession to the heavy, muggy air of the tropics. It didn't seem to bother Eldest Sister.

"*Dios ko!*" Milagros said under her breath, fidgeting nervously. "*Hala*, I'll tell you to your mother. Don't you know she told the *labandera* all your shirts must be starched so they don't crease?"

Mention of Mother took all the starch out of me. I quietly crumpled and rubbed the armsleeves to soften it.

Eldest Sister moved her books around on the study table, impatience and disapproval all over her face.

At last I was ready. We all started down in silence.

Father was in the dining room, already eating. There was none of the usual bustle and clatter, the talking loud when a Chinese family sat down to a meal. Today there was no joy; only the elemental act of eating. Something vital was missing.

Father was, as is his wont, absent-mindedly shoving pieces of bean curd from the celadon bowl into his mouth with red-lacquered chopsticks. But he showed no pleasure; rather, he looked pre-occupied. I couldn't see his eyes. It seemed he wanted to avoid looking at us.

As the aging German Shepherd came forward, Father's face relaxed a bit. "Yama, you want to go out?" he asked, speaking softly and slowly as to a child. She bowed as if in answer, her tail swishing from black splotch to another on her brown flanks. Father had raised Yama himself and allowed no dog except her to come into the house.

Eldest Sister and I sat facing each other across the wide, mahogany table. Father was at one end. Five-year-old Third Sister fretted at the other end. She had just started kindergarten. Silently we dug into our steaming bowls of oatmeal gruel and sipped our hot Ovaltine.

All of a sudden Third Sister wailed "MAMAaaa...!" Another maid quickly came running up, took her arm and walked her out.

Eldest Sister then asked in Fujian, her voice quivering, "Father, when will Mama come home?" I was afraid to ask myself.

He stood up and glowered at us. Unusually bulky and tall for a southern Chinese, with his thick eyebrows, full lips and moon face, he looked just like a warlord. The blazing tropical morning sun made his bald pate shine. He was not naturally bald but took pains to have a barber come to the house to shave him twice a week.

In China during the war he had malaria. Not only did he get the village barber to shear off his coarse, heavy mane; he had him shave his pate clean. He kept it that way after he got well, saying that hair stank; shaving it off kept the scalp clean and smelling good. After all, did not Buddhist monks who sought a pure, austere life first shave their heads?

Peering at us through thick rimless glasses, he did not answer Eldest Sister's query. Instead he growled, his nose flaring. "Hurry up, *Xiao Swat!* Seven-thirty already. You'll be late." He was always hurrying us along.

"Crazy girl demon..." Father had called Eldest Sister by her ugly nickname, chosen to ward off the *gwei*, the devil spirits. Being the eldest, even though a girl, she required special protection from evil spirits lurking in the dark, disguised as a shadow, smoke, fog, or cloud, ready to snatch away a favored child. Curiously enough I needed no such protection.

Last night was the crisis. It was a hot muggy night in 1956. Although just in her seventh month, Mother started to have contractions. Only twenty-nine, she was going to deliver her sixth. The fifth had been a caesarian. Every delivery posed the risk of toxemia. As she was being carried out on a stretcher, her delicate frame hidden in linen, I saw a silver spoon sticking out of her mouth, and asked about it. I got no answer. Later, Milagros explained, "Your mother was starting to bite her tongue."

At the private hospital the obstetrician said it might take another twenty-four hours. As Mother lay in pain, a maid leaned over, fanning her face with a woven-leaf *pai-pai*. The sticky air and the pain in her abdomen brought beads of perspiration to Mother's brow. With a damp towel the maid dabbed at Mother's alabaster forehead. On a side-table stood a two-foot statuette of Our Lady of Lourdes. It had a rosary-necklace of dainty, white tropical *sampaguita* and pastel-orange *ylang-ylang* flowers exuding a rich, heady fragrance. At its foot, votive candles in tiny glass bowls burned at all hours.

Mother was not just beautiful, she was strikingly patrician. And she knew it. She was Aphrodite rather than *Kuan-Yin*.

To Dr. Garcia she gasped out in halting Tagalog: "A boy this time, Doctor.... please!"

"Now, now," he said gently, "Better rest, not time yet... just one finger," he said. He then palpated her distended abdomen, intently. He had warned her against having a sixth baby.

To the Chinese a woman's body was worthless until it brought forth a son. A woman was supposed to dedicate herself to this task, even if it meant losing her life. The son belonged not to the wife's lineage but to her husband's. A son kept it going, and affirmed its hierarchy, the backbone of Confucian tradition. The wife was only an instrument. Her filial duty was to his parents, not to her own. She owed obedience and loyalty to her husband and his clan, all the way up to its patriach; she paid tributes to his ancestors, not her own. That was the way it was in China. That is the way it always has been.

Without a son the hierarchy collapsed, the clan fell apart. Because Mother had not produced a son, my paternal grandmother had offered to buy Father a second wife to give him a son who would perpetuate the family name and add to the ancestral tablets. Father refused; he loved his wife too much.

As girls we were just tolerated, not really wanted. Mother had to tell everyone, in my presence that when she was pregnant with me everyone was overjoyed thinking I was a boy. I was so heavy she was in labor for twenty hours. When finally I came, thirty minutes into the day after Christmas, she cried for days, because even though I weighed eight pounds I was *merely* a girl, another daughter! On my first birthday (a Chinese baby is one year old the day she is born) there were no red-dyed eggs. Instead Father's mother cursed that I was one more useless mouth to feed. Better that I be drowned or abandoned in a garbage dump.

Growing up, I was bewildered and then resentful that my birthdays were glossed over, unlike those of my sisters. Often there were no long noodles to wish me long life, or hard-boiled eggs to insure my fertility. I felt I was the least wanted among five unwanted daughters.

Was it because my birthday happened also to be Mao Zedong's birthday? Or that, on the year I was born, Mao marched with his Communist hordes into Beijing and took over China? To the Fujianese, Mao was a particularly hideous demon, not because he was the Communist ringleader, but because he had "magnanimously" offered our province ~ across from Taiwan ~ to the Americans as a target for their atom bombs. It was a heinous offer that would have put Stalin to shame. But truly Machiavellian; if the Americans ever dropped a bomb on Fujian, it would so infuriate the Chinese people all over the world that it would turn them into a mighty weapon against America. What did Mao care about our ten million relatives and neighbors in the province? Like any Emperor in antiquity, he thought nothing of laying waste the coasts of China, creating many new hungry ghosts to roam the countryside and threaten those who neglect to offer them food.

Grandmother on Father's side fervidly despised us for being girls. When we were small we lived with them in the big ancestral house. Eldest Sister was a real crybaby. One day she began to bawl non-stop. In a fury Grandmother Abu snatched her up and smacked her smartly on the chin with one hand where the middle finger bore a heavy emerald ring. Eldest Sister's cries rose in crescendo and became an ear-shattering scream. Glaring at her, curses and spittle issuing from her red-painted mouth, Grandmother Abu fished out a discarded tin can lid from the trash can and deliberately gouged my sister's face with it. Even that didn't stop Eldest Sister's wails. As her forehead bled, Grandmother Abu screeched through gold teeth: "*Si tsabo kuwe!* Death to young devil girls! Why didn't your father dump you between the graves in La Loma Cemetery! In China they would have thrown you into the baby tower for the vultures!"

Gritting her 24-karat gold-plated teeth, she plunked down my distraught sister onto the floor and hobbled back ~ on tiny clogs that elevated her inches above the ground ~ to where she had been sitting. Fancying herself the Empress Dowager, she liked to sit and survey her "empire," her long, sharp fingernails curling around the armrests of the rosewood chaise lounge. She had made it her throne with the character *Luung*, meaning dragon, our ancestral family name, carved on its back, and had it studded with semi-precious stones, in the design of a phoenix ~ the fabled dragon's consort.

No one dared utter a word. Father could only silently strike his fist into his palm. To this day the scar on Eldest Sister's forehead, near the hairline, is still there. It left a scar on her spirit too, I know, but she bears it stoically, hidden from view. Unlike me. I wear my scars on my sleeves.

Grandfather called his wife a goddess, with magical powers to have produced so many sons ~ nine in all. Father was the sixth son. In gratitude, Grandfather gave her emeralds to detect poison, a glowing ruby ring to be worn on her left finger to repel bad dreams, and an amulet to change color if an enemy approached. She wore a huge red coral bracelet around her fat wrist to protect her from madness (it didn't work, I guess) and stuck a jade hairpin ~ the expensive variety ~ in her thinning hair to bring her good luck (that worked).

Father's mother also had four daughters, but they didn't count. Only her sons would be allowed, and expected, to honor her grave. I never knew any of my four aunts, although I met three of them fleetingly during a grand *lauriat*, a feast given in honor of a favorite grandson, the son of Fourth Uncle. The oldest aunt, I heard, was sent to a mental institution after she tried defending herself from a philandering husband who beat her up to accept his liaison with a nurse-employee. I used to hear Father's brothers blame their sisters when their husbands strayed or became abusive. A few years ago I inadvertently overheard Father talk about how a sister had put on her best dress and jewelry before arraying herself in bed to fall into a final sleep.

On our obligatory visits, Grandmother Abu often startled Eldest Sister and me by the way she appeared in public. Believing that the image of a perfect circle repels evil, she often painted a big red 0 around her mouth with vermilion lipstick, which made her look like she was always pouting. We would come upon her as she soaked her bound feet in a broth of monkey bones. We girls were expected to serve her hand-and-foot. As she got up, Father signalled us to hold her up by the arms on each side and guide her as she staggered to the dresser. There she put on a flowing silk mandarin gown, hiding the flab of a self-indulgent body. She was proud of her bound feet; it was an emblem of wealth. To me, it was a grotesque, stinking ball of flesh, arched like a quarter moon, four inches long, an inch wide. The four lesser toes were folded back under the sole and the front of the foot was drawn back toward the heel where the instep seemed to have collapsed. Now she was ready to preside over the Clan of Luungs.

Manila, where I grew up, is the capital of a country of many islands on the South China Sea across from Vietnam, Laos, Cambodia, and Thailand. Mainland China is only a few hundred miles to the northwest. Immediately south are the islands of Indonesia and Malaysia. The Chinese call the region Nanyang, or South Seas. For a thousand years millions of Chinese migrated there. Today more than thirty million Chinese count it their home.

The climate is monsoonal, tropical, with only two seasons: hot and dry, wet and not so hot. Filipinos are the same people as Malays and Indonesians. With them, they had close cultural and trade ties until the intolerant Catholicism of the Spanish shut off all connections between the Philippines and its other island neighbors. Spain named the country after one of their kings, Philip II. After four hundred years of Spanish misrule and fifty years of American occupation, Christianity had become the dominant faith. The Catholics make up 85% of the population, the Protestants 7%; the rest are Muslim, Buddhist, animist and polytheist.

The use of English is widespread, much more so than Spanish which only a few of the native aristocrats picked up. The lifeways, material culture, and social values are, on the surface, more Hispanic and Anglo-American than Asian. The better-educated layers of the population are a racial mix of Malay-Indonesian, Spanish, Chinese, and (White) American elements. In addition to a few terms borrowed from the Chinese, the native languages contain a sprinkling of Indian (Sanskrit) and Islamic Arabic terms and concepts.

The school system follows American models. English is one of three official languages, the other two being Spanish and Tagalog. Literacy is relatively high, about 80%, but poverty is widespread. One hesitates to call Manila an Asian city. Under Spanish rule, and even after the Americans took over, it had a distinct Hispanic flavor, but gradually North American influences became pervasive. Manila began to be called the westernmost suburb of the United States in the Pacific, consumers of more Coca-Cola, Hershey's, Max Factor, Motown records than any other Asian city. Like its neighbors, it has an old Chinatown, where the poorer and more traditional Chinese live. To many a Chinese refugee or migrant from the mainland, Manila was one of the few places where one could continue to be in Asia and live in the West at the same time.

The driver looked at his watch. It said 7:27. Quick, before the school gates shut.

The school bell was stridently ringing when the car pulled up. Eldest Sister and I hurriedly scrambled out with our heavy bags and slipped unnoticed into the line, just as the national anthem started blaring raucously from the public loudspeaker. We made sure we were in our proper places. St. Theresa nuns were persnickety about our lining up in the courtyard with the shortest in front and the tallest at the rear. I was in the middle, I knew exactly who was in front and behind. As soon as the anthem grated to a finish we marched in parallel lines two flights up to the classrooms.

"No holding hands!" Sister Tionelle sharply slapped my wrists as I walked hand in hand with a classmate. In heavily accented Flemish English, she chided: "How many times you must, I tell: good girls never hold hands!" Then, darkly, "Mortal sin!" she hissed with clenched lips, her permanently ruddy face growing redder. I felt shame.

School was always stressful. Not only were the nuns no-nonsense teachers, they were joylessly authoritarian, but not mindlessly so. For they had a purpose. They were always breathing down our necks because the school was competing with other exclusive girls' schools: for academic honors and reputation. The aim was to snare the daughters of the *crème de la crème* of society.

To us sisters, this pressure was not really needed. We did not need anyone to push us. We had a built-in nag, an inner voice ~ imperious, demanding, implacable ~ egging us on. We had to be the best of the best in the best school. We competed not for the sake of the school, but for our parents' approval.

Unlike Eldest Sister who seemed so self-assured, I was always on edge. I envied her. When taunted by our non-Chinese classmates, she would say they're just jealous. We made better grades than they did. But beneath the surface, a clear sense of "us" and "them" lurked, ready to pounce. An occasional jeer brought it out snarling.

"What's that you're eating? Soy sauce sandwich?" Guffaws and giggles. They had chicken-breast sandwiches slathered with dripping mayonnaise, or hot dogs drowning in catsup or mustard ~ typical fare of rich families immersed in Hollywood movies and American magazines. I was different. I carried my own drink in a thermos bottle; I never bought anything from the school canteen Giving an allowance was not done in our family. I did not tell them what they called soy sauce was Bovril, or Marmite, an expensive vegetable-yeast import from England. I doted on it. It did look like soy sauce.

I did not react. I smiled to myself, exulting in my enjoying something beyond their reach. But ridicule made me retreat deeper into my private world. Yet I was ambivalent ~ I wanted to be, and not to be, part of their world.

Coming home was a relief. I looked forward to it each time. Home was a sanctuary behind iron gates and massive adobe walls, eight-foot high, glass shards sticking out their top. It meant being with sisters and dogs. Eldest Sister and I often lay prone on the Bermuda grass in the lingering warmth of many an afternoon, under the coconut palm heavy with bulbous nuts. We watched Yama, the dominant female, take precedence at the water basin, noisily lapping up water with her tongue while Einstein, an albino bitch, waited her turn, her bushy tail dipping low. Mozart, a black male Alsatian, smaller than Yama, stood aloof, on the lawn, tongue lolling, impatient for Einstein to return so the two could resume their romp. Yama was their mother; they deferred to her.

"Yami! Come here!" I commanded.

"No, Yama! Come here to me," Eldest Sister would counter.

Caught in a contest of wills, Yama grunted but did not make a move. I quickly got up to where she lay and plumped my head down on her warm belly. Her panting made my head bob up and down. She groaned, not making a move to get up.

Father named her after General Yamashita, the "Tiger of Malaya," who commanded the fearsome Japanese force the Americans chased out of Manila and annihilated in the mountains during Liberation, before I was born. The name ended with an "a." In Spanish, it sounded feminine. Anyway Father never considered the sex of a dog relevant except for breeding. But naming her after a ferocious Japanese General executed for war crimes? To honor him? I should say not. Or maybe to insult him by calling a dog after him. Maybe it was Father's way of expressing outrage at Japanese atrocities in China and the Philippines, or simply to show the Chinese contempt for the "dwarf devils."

A hated name for a favorite dog? It did not sound right to me. Was Father paying tribute to a fellow Asian who dared defy the white imperialists? I doubted it. Father never bothered with politics. Besides, the Japanese were the worst imperialists. Father's actions were always ambiguous. Whatever his motive, Yama was the exact opposite of her fierce namesake. She endeared herself to all of us by her gentle ways.

Maybe Father had in mind, the Chinese General Yama: *Yanluo Wang*, King of the Demons in the Chinese Hades. Many Chinese expect their fates in the other world to be decided by General Yama, and his twin sister Yami. He boasts an army of 80,000 animal-headed demons. Two ferocious four-eyed dogs act as his emissaries, to summon people at the hour of their death. Could Yama be both the General and one of his dogs? Father was not always politically correct. Yama was, after all, not Chinese but Hindu. He was the Indian Lord of Death whose guard dogs had to be bribed with kidneys of a sacrificed goat, a funeral offering placed in the hands of the dead.

The Chinese were not about to let race or national origin influence this decision. They were just too happy to count Yama among their deities and give him a Chinese face. One more Demon made for a richer this-world and a livelier other-world.

Nonetheless, there were practical problems to face, not in the netherworld but here and now. Father kept big dogs for our protection, he said, because everyone wanted a share of the booty from moneyed Chinese. To us girls, however, dogs were playmates rather than sentinels. We led quite isolated lives by parental fiat, even from classmates. We only had each other and our dogs. We related to dogs better than to Filipinos or even to other Chinese.

That afternoon, as soon as we came home from school, Eldest Sister and I hurried to the rock grotto in the garden, a miniature version of the Lourdes grotto in the south of France. Water recirculated up from a small artificial pond to rocks higher up a concrete mound, gurgling out from a simulated spring and flowing gently down a concrete ramp to where jade-white goldfish swam under red-speckled water lilies. On a small concrete bridge across the pond, Yama and her progeny occasionally squatted, watching the goldfish flash by below. As the sun retreated west, its angled rays shone on the figure of Our Lady, causing its reflection on the water to glow like gold amidst the silver of darting fish.

I went down on my knees in front of the blue-and-white robed image. "Holy Mary Mother of God," I cried out, "Please make my mother well soon. I promise I will be a good girl and go to Mass and Communion every day."

Silently reciting the rosary prayers as she fondled each wooden bead, Eldest Sister suddenly blurted out, "Don't you know Mama is not Catholic?"

"Not Catholic? But she prays every night in front of the Crucifix." I shouted, as if talking loud made me right.

"Mama is Protestant. She was never baptized Catholic."

That night I wept in bed, unable to sleep. Sister Rosalie told me only Catholics will be saved.

The phone rang in the middle of the night. It was the hospital. Father had to come quick. In the anteroom, the U.S.-educated obstetrician was grim, unsmiling.

"She's had convulsions and we run the risk of her suffering brain damage. It's eclampsia with hypertension." He looked Father in the eye. "We can even lose her. You must choose between your wife and the baby. I need to do a C-section now or she may never come out of the coma. The baby's lungs are not fully developed yet. We don't have a respirator to keep them open. I must tell you: it's fifty-fifty."

Father stiffened, looking stunned. "Doc, what you mean, fifty-fifty? I.... choose? No! You save both, Doc." Moving close, he said, "Please, I have money. I pay!"

Uneasy, the Doctor, who was quite wealthy, stood swaying slightly, staring past Father. He was thinking about his wife's trip to New York City the next month. No telling how much money she would need. The Manila rich, at the first opportunity, hied themselves off to America on shopping sprees at Berdorf-Goodman or discoing at Regines.

Tears flowed down Father's cheeks. He shook his head. He could not believe he had to make a choice. It was as if he was being punished, or blamed. What had he done? Did his daughters do something bad? Did his wife offend the Kitchen God? Did a business client put a curse on him? Did he do the *tsoi* right before the Buddha... clasp hands, bow low, and chant *Nammu Omi toe hoot* correctly? Did he forget to offer the usual bribe to the *tu-ti*, the nature spirits? Maybe it was just plain bad luck ~ *suwe*.

"Try, try. Doc." Father pleaded. "I have money. I pay. Thank you, thank you." Hands clasped tightly to his chest, he bowed again and again as he spoke, going lower each time. Dr. Garcia held Father by his arms, afraid that Father would end up kneeling before him.

Panicked, Father hurried out of the hospital to the *kongsi* to burn gilt paper money before the ancestral tablets, to "pull strings" with the spirits in the netherworld. Father's parents reminded him that "a wife can be replaced, but not a son."

His mind in a whirl, he agreed: it is the baby who must be saved. True, he needed a son ~ to be filial to his father and maintain his line; a son to obey him and revere him as an ancestor when he dies; a son to take care of him in his old age. He must have a male descendant to offer him food so he would not end up a hungry ghost himself. Yet he was too much in love with his beautiful wife. She was faithful, she took care of him and served him well. Did he not fly her, first class, all the way from China? Dare he again defy the gods, like when he spurned the marriage arranged by his parents, and married the woman he loved? In his heart he knew he could not lose her. He must save her at any cost.

Confused, Father left the clan house and then rushed home to gather together the high-priced ivory religious carvings from Hong Kong he had brought back and stashed for just such an occasion. He must ask the nuns in his daughter's school to intercede for his wife and son's survival.

"You cannot sacrifice the life of an unborn child to save the life of your wife. If you have to choose, it is the child you must save," was the nuns' peremptory command.

"Please. Please ask your God to save my wife and my son," he implored.

"You have to have faith, my son," the Mother Superior piously intoned. "With faith there is hope. Pray. Almighty God in His infinite wisdom is testing you, to see how worthy you are. He gave up his only Son to save all of us. Pray. You must be prepared to make your own sacrifice."

"Yes, yes, thank you," Father got up to leave, bowing low.

We did not see Father for several days. Neither were we allowed to visit Mother in the hospital. Every mealtime we were just by ourselves. Our younger sisters fretted a great deal more and the maids got ruder and crankier. The household was in disarray; no one knew what was going on or what to do.

Eldest Sister and I were frightened, with nothing to take our mind from Mother, except Yama. Retreating to our bedroom, we laid on the shiny narra floor taking turns smothering the aging dog with scented talcum powder. Yama was our cuddly Panda. She was always patient, especially with me. She seemed to sense the moment's vexations. I didn't have to hold back anything from Yama. Voicing out my disquiet was never met with a put-down. Even as children, we were expected to keep things to ourselves

It seemed Mother lay comatose for days. One day, the chauffeur took the five of us to the hospital. We tiptoed in silence into the darkened room with its array of monitors and strange machines. Father was in one corner, his eyes red, his sighs accenting Mother's labored, heavy breathing. We stood about, confused, afraid to speak.

When Mother finally came home she slept for days in a room with drawn blinds. We let Yama peep into the room, Father did not object. When Mother asked for her baby boy, Father said he was still in the hospital in an incubator. Inventing truth anesthesized the spirit and eased the return to reality.

I never understood why we were not told what happened. Nor why our parents still refuse to talk about it till this day. Maybe they don't want to remember the pain. Or maybe they feel shame at losing a son.

Only when I was much older did I learn that my baby brother lived only ten hours. Being staunchly Catholic at the time, I was bothered by Father's decision. But I was also glad he made that choice. I could not imagine life without Mother. In my Catholic mind, Father had sinned, terribly, and faced eternal roasting in hell. But he had not yet become a Catholic, so maybe he was exempted.

One late summer afternoon, Father ordered me to call the veterinarian to come quickly. For days Yama had lain prostrate from acute arthritis, her old ailment. But this time she had stopped eating. The vet came, examined her, and shook his head. After consulting Father, who nodded his head resignedly, he took out a syringe, and injected pentobarbital into a vein.

Yama stubbornly fought off its effects. For several minutes, eyes dimming, she tried to raise her head, maybe to say good-bye before setting out on her final journey. Father moved close and got down on his knees to look intently into her eyes. Then Yama stopped moving. Tears ran down Father's cheeks. Passing his right hand with unusual gentleness over her eyes, he pressed the eyelids shut so as not to leave her staring.

I watched from the kitchen window. Rarely did I see in my childhood a more tender scene. It left in my young mind an indelible imprint. To that moment I trace my life-long affinity to dogs.

The Chinese say a dog dies in place of a master.

For Yama, it was mission accomplished. Now she could go back to rejoin the General.

2

RIKKI

(hristmas in Asia, 1959.

The Philippines celebrates Christ's birth with panache and profligacy. This is the time to loosen purse strings, when the stingy are scorned. Scrooges repent and are welcomed back into society.

Not to be left out, many wealthy Chinese ~ Christian or Buddhist ~ get in the spirit of the season. But there is method in their madness. For them, to spend is to invest. This is the time to reward employees and make the grand gesture to prove one's prosperity and boost prestige. This is the time to spread *guanxi* or gifts to lay the groundwork for the year to come. One must sow better seeds to get a richer harvest.

This year the pharmaceutical consortium of Father's clan, more prosperous than ever, decided to do the spectacular and import an entire circus troupe from Singapore, animals and all.

At the opening, we sisters were, as Mother expected, the cynosure of all eyes. She wanted to make sure we all measured up. What to do?

Her face lit up. Yes! We were to be so many Shirley Temples, curls and all; we needed to be permed. But no one else was to do it except herself. It would save money.

The result was disaster. Our perms were overdone, overcooked, over-burned. Instead of soft curls, they were a kinky frizz. More self-conscious than any of my sisters, I sulked in my room, refusing to go anywhere. It took two maids to drag me out upon Mother's orders. Outside, Father lay in wait to give me a few stinging wallops with his leather belt. Mother stood to one side sternly admonishing me to pay heed to Mencius and Confucius, the revered sages of social order.

"You must observe deference and compliance, follow *li*. Preserve social order by obeying the dictats of correct ritual. This is filial obedience," Mother lectured.

For me to be a Shirley Temple in order to be filial was cruel and unreasonable.

The circus put on a festive show. A majestic fir tree, imported from Taiwan, flecked with cotton wads to simulate snow and bejeweled with multi-colored lights and tinsel, stood tall at the entrance gates. Bing Crosby's "I'm Dreaming of a White Christmas" blared, not crooned, from loudspeakers.

On opening day Father marched us in and perfunctorily installed us in a reserved ringside box, after which he disappeared. He didn't want to be seen with so many Shirley Temples in very unchinese frizz. Besides, he preferred to people-watch all by himself.

It was my very first circus. I had a sensation of being drowned in a charivari of lights, sounds and sights. Entranced, I sat agape as brilliantly flashing banks of lights alternated with rows of multi-colored bunting and Japanese crepe-paper streamers. Rows of gaily-colored pennants and flags with dragon designs and Chinese characters fluttered above. In the ring, trumpeting elephants reared ponderously up on their hind legs. Bengal tigers and African lions leapt snarling through flaming hoops, while gaily costumed gnomes and dwarfs cavorted and tumbled all over the ring, making me squeal with utter delight at every antic. Gymnasts in gorgeous costumes held me spell-bound with their acrobatics. Holding my breath, clutching a cotton-candy stick in a sticky hand, I watched open-mouthed as muscular boys and sinewy girls in clinging tights teetered precariously on a taut highwire above the ring, or, leaping off, soared effortlessly high above on swinging trapezes, flitting from one to another like birds. I thought them the tallest, slimmest and most beautiful Chinese boys and girls I had ever seen.

The show over, Father promptly showed up. From a distance I saw him gesticulating, beckoning us with his lips across the circus ring toward a yawning entrance-exit framed with crimson drapes. Beyond was a sort of holding area. Dutifully we scrambled after him as he disappeared through the door, propelled not by his brusqueness but because my sisters and I did not want to miss anything. Beyond the door we passed two gauntlets: one of odors, from animal excreta and built-up circus detritus; the other of cages filled with fearsome animals. Walking warily past snarling tigers and lions, recoiling from mischievous macaques that, yapping and chirping, snatched at us as we went past, we made it to a row of trailers where the circus performers were eating, chatting and laughing around a make-shift table. At one side, as if to mask the animal smells, aromatic incense curled up from braziers standing on tripods in front of little papier mâché figures of spirit gods.

"*King Hsien Tsai,*" they chorused, standing up and bowing in one motion. For a moment Eldest Sister and I looked at each other in surprise. They were a great deal shorter and punier, close up. "*Mei mei ahh!*" they exclaimed in unison, acknowledging and giving us due deference. They spoke Taiwanese, quite the same as *Fujian.*

"*Cha pung,*" someone sang out in a high voice, gesturing for us to join them. We shook our heads and held back. Then, like puppets on strings, they all moved as one back to their porcelain bowls and bamboo chopsticks, heads and necks bent low, slurping and burping ~ sure signs of a good Chinese meal.

No act is more swathed in tradition than sitting down to eat with kin and kindred. They were not about to let us interrupt. We ignored the invitation. By this time Father had again disappeared.

"What's your name?" asked a middle-aged man who remained standing. Barrel-chested, his bulging muscles fairly popped out of the tights he wore for his tiger act. He passed thick rough hands through my kinky hair. I cringed but was too taken by surprise to protest. I had been taught that the head is sacred and no stranger should be allowed to mess with it. I managed to push his hands away, pouting.

"You should not do that to Mr. Sheum, do not be so impolite," Eldest Sister chided in a low voice. That was her. Even when we were still young she was already old. I wanted to tell her the man was rude and impolite to me. I didn't know he was Sheum Shiong Hok, the flamboyant grand-circus master and owner from Singapore. Fat, lighted cigar in his mouth, Mr. Sheum then took Eldest Sister by the hand and walked her toward a corner of the trailer. I followed, curious. So this was the big, bad man Father had talked about.

Last night Father was quaffing expensive cognac ~ too much of it. He started to get hot around the collar and breathe fire in righteous indignation. I heard the name Sheum.

"Shameless!" Father spat out in colorful Tagalog. This man, he fumed, collects concubines like the Manchu. Father praised Sheum's First Wife for always being subservient to her husband's caprice. Take, for instance, the nubile village girl from Peitou, Taiwan, procured for him by a secret society for a pittance. The girl became a top-drawer trapeze star even as she continued to be one of his concubines, his favorite one at that. First Wife, *Tuabo*, did not complain. Imagine, Father said ~ envy in his voice ~ *Tuabo* even let her share their bedroom!

As he fulminated, his anger spilled over to Mother. Without warning, he started questioning her harshly about the household money. Father must have been looking for cigarette money. Why, he asked, was there so little cash left in the house?

Mother, who was sitting on the bottom step of the stairs, began to weep. Eldest Sister, who was in the adjacent study room with me, heard the commotion, rushed out, and headed straight to the bar console. All of us had the habit of throwing the contents of pockets and handbags into the drawers of the Art Deco import with gawdy brass fittings that stood next to the staircase leading to the second floor. Into its inner nooks and crannies everyone dumped eyeglasses, keys, watches, jewelry, paper bills and loose change. Rummaging through the odds and ends, Eldest Sister frantically collected as many paper bills and coins she could find, counted them, and started sobbing. She had to help Mother.

Father kept on breathing fire and alcoholic fumes, oblivious to the distress he was causing. I suspected his indignation was a put-on, just his way to sneak in something salacious in raunchy language and lurid detail, in order to taunt, as well as shock, Mother. She was dutifully impressed by the stories he wove of his exploits ~ most likely imaginary ~ against the *tufei* (bandits) and the dwarf pirates (Japanese imperialists) in wartime China. She would listen in awe even when history became hyperbole. She reacted only when she became the target of his spleen.

As I followed Mr. Sheum and Eldest Sister through the jumble of circus gear and make-shift lean-tos, without warning a snarling monster came charging down on us. Like a rabbit in panic I jumped and backpedaled in a hurry. It was forty pounds of ferocious menace with a shiny bronze coat. Coarse hair bristled on its back like a razor-back boar, slant eyes blazed, open jaw slobbered, bushy tail arched high. It was truly hair-raising. Luckily a long chain jerked it back. Mr. Sheum screamed an imprecation, grabbed the dog by the muzzle and stared it down. Then he spat on his palm and stuck it out for the dog to lick. The human saliva, he said, acts like a charm on a hostile creature. Then, clutching its leonine ruff, he flipped the dog down on its back, straddled it, then bit across the bridge of its black nose till it began to whimper like a puppy.

Sheum then took firm hold of my wrists. "Not to run. Must remind him I am *Tuatauke*, you know, the big boss!" he laughed, showing his decaying teeth. "Not to be afraid." He looked at both of us. I could smell the putrid aroma of cigar, garlic, and bad teeth.

The dog had turned docile. " See thick fur? Good for coat to wear in winter. See strong bones? Good for pulling sledges. And hunting. Look at tongue," he went on, prying the dog's jaws apart. "Black, sometimes blue. If black, very good, best for dogmeat! Tongue, bones, bile good medicine; give back energy if tired. Chow puppies very delicious; keep body warm in winter. Me, I no eat. I just like keep chow. It one-master dog."

"Yukkh... Eating dogs," I said aloud in English. Suddenly I wanted to go home, away from the odor of sweat and the disgusting thought of eating dogs. How could anyone eat a pet?

Later, I read that humans partook only of the flesh of herbivores, not carnivore animals. In the wild, predators don't eat each other.

Mr. Sheum disappeared behind an enclosure. He came back shortly with something in his hand.

"Ho! This is why bitch so angry," he grinned widely, presenting the furry puppy to Eldest Sister. The puppy, a few weeks old, its fur the color of madras curry powder, lay almost unmoving in Eldest Sister's hands.

That was how we came to have a Chow. Though Chows are a storied and favored breed ~ they are the stone or glazed ceramic lion-dogs guarding the gates of Chinese temples ~ Mother was not too excited about the addition to our pack. She did not like the tongue being black. Mother had this thing about black ~ bad omen, bad luck she would say.

Eldest Sister wanted to name him Elvis, after her idol Elvis Presley. I wanted the name Ricky, after my favorite singer, Ricky Nelson. She argued for Elvis. After all, he had replied to her fan mail, sending her an autographed photo. My idol ignored me completely. I defended my choice. Unlike Elvis, this puppy did not sway his butt whenever he wagged his stump of a tail. I insisted on tossing a coin. I was lucky, I won. I spelled it Rikki.

Rikki was as cuddly as a panda. We fussed over him, powdering his whole body so he smelled like a baby. We took turns manhandling him like a flexible toy dog. Mother complained we wasted our time over Rikki, becoming like "little young Western barbarians."

To avoid our becoming *hsiao yang gwei-tsi*, Mother decided we needed Chinese language tutorials. She hired a Chinese tutor to come regularly to our house every Saturday afternoon, for an intensive three-hour session. As a concession, Rikki could stay in the study room with us. He quickly learned to hide under a table. If nobody knew he was there, he could stay longer.

This Saturday afternoon our Chinese tutor noted a greater than usual inattention on our part. We spun around on swivel chairs, bounced up and down on the leather seats. We clambered up the desks, pulling out volume after volume of the Collier's Encyclopedia from the wall bookshelves, and then scattering them about in the library-study. Helplessly, the tutor looked on. No amount of scolding and cajoling worked. Today we were more like little Empress-Dowagers.

"Licky, no," she pushed the puppy away; it was nibbling at her ankles.

Gales of laughter from us. "R. .R. Ricky, not Licky," I snickered. I urged her to repeat after me, rolling my tongue up and rounding my mouth, the way she always tried correcting my Mandarin.

"L..L..L. Licky, Licky," she repeated.

"No, No. Okay, say Ricky Nelson," Eldest Sister said.

"Licky Nerson."

"NO, NO, NO! You're saying it backward." Raucous laughter. Mock despair. Exasperation. We had little respect for Chinese who were not as westernized as we were. To us they were a lesser breed. Besides, how could a language teacher not correct her own speech defects? Native Chinese speakers often inverted the *l*'s and *r*'s in European languages, saying *l* for *r* and *r* for *l*. I teased Eldest Sister, calling her "Mely."

After dawdling for hours over Chinese lessons, I checked the clock on the wall, and then shouted, "It's time!" We all bolted out of the study, leaving the Chinese tutor and Rikki behind. Standing like little saints under the lattice pergola with its intertwined fuschia and red bougainvilla vines forming a bower over the front door, we expectantly looked down the concrete driveway to the open gate.

Today was the day. We had conspired with the nuns in school for a personal visit to our house by the Diocesan Bishop. It would pressure Mother into becoming a Roman Catholic, like us. Buddhist Father had converted with alacrity after Mother's close brush with death. Convinced that the nun's intercessory prayers saved Mother's life, he became a faithful patron of our school and Church, regularly contributing sacks of fragrant *milagrosa* rice, imported dry goods, rare art pieces to the Mother Superior.

Mother? Headstrong, she braced herself to resist. She was not about to change and adopt new ideas. Educated in a Dutch missionary school in China, she was proud to be a Protestant. No one else in her family was one. They were either Buddhists like Father, or professed no religion. Mother criticized the Catholics, saying they never read the Bible. Virgin Mary, the Mother of God? The Bible was vague about this. Nor did she believe in Confession. Even after she finally agreed to be baptized a Catholic, she obstinately refused to confess to another human being. Confess to sin? To a stranger? Shameful! she said.

At last a chauffeured limousine turned into our gate and drove up to the door. Monsignor Olano alighted resplendent in a flowing purple robe and hat. Just like a wealthy mandarin. We flocked around him, genuflecting to kiss the sacerdotal ring as he extended his hand out to us.

A tall, big-framed, forty-something nun, in a sparkling-white habit was with him. We jostled each other to get as close as we could to this Flemish nun with rosy cheeks and leathery face. The scent of a nun's crisp, starched, freshly-ironed habit and the faint tinkling and rustling of the oversized black-glass rosary beads wrapped around the waist, entranced us.

We were curious to know if she had a shaved head, if she had hair inside the "Flying Dutchman" headpiece wrapped tightly across half of her forehead and pulled down to cover her ears. Or, had all those lugubrious thoughts of sin, contrition, and redemption succeeded in pushing out all the hair and leaving her bald?

She had something else that intrigued us: a formidable bosom that bobbed and heaved every time she moved. We were in awe of such large papayas. Asian women did not have more than raisins. Often we jested ~ when she bathed, did she have to sling up her breasts over her shoulders and knot them behind so she could soap under?

Sister Arthur was Eldest Sister's jovial fifth grade teacher who took her under her wing and steered her to the top of the class. When it came my turn, she taught me to soar like an eagle, too. It was also she who made me want to be a nun. A guilt-ridden youth made me fanatical about religion ~ daily Communion after Confession, constant rosary recital, weekly Stations of the Cross, and so on and so forth. Mother also wanted me to be a nun. She said that if she did not have children she would have become a nun. A Protestant becoming a Catholic nun?

The maids brought out a steaming pot of chrysanthemum tea, and a jug of iced *calamansi* juice, freshly squeezed, and pin-wheel cookies freshly baked. Mother did not usually allow us to eat or sit with visitors. This afternoon she could not shoo us away. On such visits Mother rarely said much. In China, a man could divorce his wife for being garrulous. Wives stayed out of sight. Besides Mother did not like talking to strangers. Father, as usual, did most of the talking: about the family's business, his recent trips to Hong Kong and Taiwan. On and on.

Eager to get on with the purpose of his visit, the Monsignor turned to Mother and spoke gently about the need for a family to share the same religion. "The family that prays together, stays together," he said in English with a strong Spanish accent. "You have a responsibility to your children and husband, Mrs. King." (He pronounced it "responsability.")

Uncomfortable at the attention, Mother smiled in embarrassment, nodding as if she agreed, not saying anything. Nodding was a habit inured by the constant need to appear agreeable without having to agree, or to avoid having to respond. Usually people mistook it for acquiescence.

"So, it is agreed. We must set the date for the Baptism, next month, perhaps? My assistant will arrange catechism lessons." Mother looked at the Bishop blankly. She just sat there, impassive. She was not about to contradict him. It might make him lose face.

"Amen. Glory to God in Heaven!" Sister Arthur intoned the coda, hands clasped prayerfully at her waist, her gaze turned upwards.

Relieved, I now knew Mother would be saved.

"Mrs. King, I want you to have this holy water from Lourdes and this rosary from Fatima. Our Lady of Fatima has worked miracles for many who had faith."

Unlike Father, Mother was leery at receiving gifts. She did not ever want to be obligated. Not to be impolite, she accepted, bowed slightly, and received them with both hands, protesting all the while. She then laid the unopened gifts aside as per custom. She must not unwrap them in their presence ~ that would be bad manners. It might embarrass the giver, or suggest cupidity on her part.

We were pleased. Knowing Mother, she would riposte with a larger and more munificent gift. It was the *li*. We wanted Mother to be as generous as she possibly could, especially toward Sister Arthur. Gift-giving in Asia creates obligations that stay alive from one generation to the next. The one who gave the more valuable gift had the moral advantage.

As the Bishop stood to leave, I rushed forward and grabbed his hands, tugging at them as I pleaded, "Your Holiness, please come and bless our pets."

Mother gave me a sharp, withering look. Usually that was enough to stop me in my tracks. But today I was ready to defy the rules, at least until the Bishop had left.

"Of course I will, my child. They are also God's children."

I led him to the backyard, where we kept in separate cages a husk of twelve rabbits ~ white, black, grey ~ and a cete of three guinea pigs, of which a black one was mine. Mumbling a prayer, he sprinkled holy water over all of them. Strangely, a week later all the rabbits and guinea pigs died, one by one. I blamed myself. Was I being punished? Eldest Sister tried to console me by saying they couldn't wait to see God after being blessed.

As Rikki grew older and bigger he became quite a problem, because of his temper and fierce loyalty. At night he was let out to do guard duty, remaining outside until morning. A new maid often was not aware he was still out and not yet put back in his cage. The result was many a frantic encounter, with the maid screaming bloody murder as she ran for her life.

Poor Rikki. His fate was ordained by his breed.*

One morning, a maid found him lying dead under the branches of the spreading frangipani tree, near one of the high walls. He had froth in the mouth, an incredible quantity of vomit around him. He lay sprawling as if he had died gasping for breath. Pieces of raw meat lay scattered around his body. Father pronounced a curse on the thief that threw the poison-laced meat over the wall.

Rikki gave up his life, filial to the very end.

*The unflagging devotion to just one master and the breed's unpredictable moods often put the Chow in a bad light. A 1991 Louisiana poll of U.S. veterinarians cited the Chow as the worst family dog to have because it was so intractable. In some animal shelters in North Carolina, strays with a bit of Chow such as a black tongue are immediately destroyed.

3

WINCHESTER & HAMLET

The news shook Chinatown to its core. It was 1965.

500,000 CHINESE MASSACRED IN INDONESIA ~ screamed the headlines of Manila newspapers.

The Government in neighboring Indonesia accused the local Communist Party (PKI) of complicity in a coup that assassinated more than a dozen Army Generals. It charged that behind the PKI were local Chinese. Suspected of being either Communists or Communist sympathizers, they were accused of instigating the coup upon instructions from Beijing.

Cities, towns, and villages exploded in vengeful fury against both native Communists and Chinese, Communists or not. Flaming graffiti on walls and shops owned by Chinese merchants in the capital city of Jakarta urged: DRIVE OUT THE CHINESE NOW. Others directly threatened the Chinese: YOU WILL BE BEHEADED IF YOU DO NOT LEAVE.

Fearful that the events in neighboring Indonesia might spill over to the Philippines, Father's clan urgently met at the *kongsi* headquarters in Binondo, Chinatown. Opulent ~ from ebony furniture to marble floors to cinnabar red pillars ~ the place now made everyone uneasy. The clan elders worried about the thriving pharmaceutical business founded by its patriarch, my grandfather. It had become a far-flung empire with connections throughout Southeast Asia. They knew that to flaunt wealth was to provoke not only discriminatory laws against the Chinese but also schemes to wrest it from them. Worse, it could rekindle the hatred and passions that brought ruin and death in former times.

The Nanyang Chinese who emigrated to Southeast Asia in the 19th Century ~ part of the exodus that scattered southern Chinese as far as America ~ regarded themselves as temporary visitors or sojourners, huachiao. *Mostly from village farms, they now preferred to cluster in urban ghettoes and to engage in business and trade. Their goal was simple: to rapidly amass a fortune and return home rich so as to distribute largesse to kin, retire and be buried in their ancestral graveplots, wreathed with prestige and honor. Most never returned to their home villages. Some Filipinos felt their wealth came from exploiting the country and its resources. Others, however, recognized their vital contribution to the nation's growth.*

They became traders, artisans, and manufacturers, setting up many business enterprises. They had no interest in becoming rulers, colonizers, and missionaries. Neither did they show much inclination to be artists or scholars, with a few notable exceptions. Material profit was what moved them ~ not so much for immediate consumption but to be hoarded or sent home.

Most Chinese followed tradition and did not assimilate into what they considered inferior and barbaric – the host culture. China was Chungguo – the Kingdoms of the Central States – and Dian Xia – the land under Heaven. China was the center of civilization. Japan, Korea, and all of Southeast Asia were just borrowers and imitators.

Unhappily, the land under heaven was becoming more hell than heaven. Governments and rulers were oppressive, anarchy prevailed, the soil was less and less fertile, the country more and more crowded with an increasingly fractious and rebellious population. After enduring much hardship and fearing for their lives, countless numbers of Chinese decided to leave the land under heaven. They brought with them survival skills of a high order, giving them a decided advantage over the simpler, easy-going people among whom they resettled.

Inner demons drove them relentlessly toward the amassing of wealth. They built enterprises and made them prosper. Secret societies honed their ability to organize and cooperate, an ability that was passed on to progeny. The results of intermarriages with native women were the Chinese mestizos. Many of them climbed high up the ladders of status and of power. Both the huachiao and their descendants found niches in society nobody else could fill, eventually achieving commanding roles in trade and finance, industry, manufacturing, retailing and wholesaling.

Success, however, caused envy and resentment to grow against them. It did not help that they hoarded their wealth and seldom plowed any of it back to the host community. Just as minorities in Europe and elsewhere suffered envy, hatred and persecution, the Nanyang Chinese became convenient scapegoats for any disaster, economic shortfall, or blunder of the colonial government, not always without justification.

They could expect no help from the Chinese government. Under Manchu rulers, overseas Chinese were considered renegades and traitors. But if their hosts were hostile the homeland was even more so. Thus they had no one to turn to but themselves.

They had to tackle a two-fold problem: how to escape sanctions and discrimination, at the same time open up greater opportunities for themselves. The solution: play games with the powers-that-be, riding on the cupidity of native officialdom. These were useful both as patrons and as protectors. It was easy to collude and scheme with such officials to achieve mutually beneficial goals, a symbiotic relationship. Possessing power but no wealth, ambitions but no skills, natives not only provided protection but also opened doors to more lucrative business and bigger fortunes, expecting, of course, a juicy share of the returns. As a result, the Chinese came to develop an image, among others, of an easy source of tong, "squeeze."

It was a gamble with high stakes, but Chinese were born gamblers anyway. Doing business was like gambling. One could end up rich beyond the wildest dreams, or go from disaster to ruin. Adversity had its uses; it steeled the mind to pick up the pieces and start anew. But there was another risk: the greater the success, the higher the profile. The tallest trees in the forest are the first to topple in a typhoon. Therefore one must do a balancing act between getting involved in public life, or keeping aloof. The trick was to find the golden mean: appear neutral, keep a low profile. This required much artful wheeling and dealing with the right people - the powerful, the corrupt and unscrupulous.

It was much the same skill they deployed back in China. Bribing, "gifting," was standard practice, so was that of backing all contending parties. Dissembling, putting on two faces, was well practiced; one had to appear to be a sincere player to both sides. Of course, one's patron and co-conspirator could turn out to be a tormentor or prosecutor. Money was a crucial factor. It could lubricate, but it could also ignite; it could be a blessing as well as a curse; it could save your neck or cause you to lose it. Money pushed many buttons. The job was to find the right ones.

If the gamble failed or - the other side of the coin - it was too successful, repercussions could be fatal. That happened in Indonesia under Sukarno in the '60's and under Suharto in the '90's, as well as in the race riots in Malaysia in the late '60's.

Unlike the Jews in Europe, the huachiao had a homeland to go back to. But for some time after the Communists took over in 1949, this avenue itself was fraught with great personal danger, if not altogether closed. In 1959 the Communist government decided to change the old policy and lure back overseas Chinese with their wealth and valuable foreign exchange. The door now opened a crack; many who were afraid came trickling back. Ironically, the return often proved disastrous, ensnaring many of them in the deadly coils of Qiang Xing and the Gang of Four, or trapping them willy-nilly in the nightmare that was the Cultural Revolution, Mao Zedong's homicidal death-wish ~ to purge China of its past, the modern and the foreign. Mao only served to intensify the alienation of the huachiao. If they chose to become permanent where they were, they had to accept assimilation. If they remained Chinese they found the cards stacked against them.

In the Philippines, the Chinese had to deal not only with the local aristocracy, but also with two successive colonial rulers ~ the Spanish and the American. They took these regime changes in stride. However, when the country moved in 1935 to declare its independence from America anti-Chinese sentiment heated up. Discriminatory laws were enacted. It became extremely difficult and costly to enter the country, stay, or get naturalized ~ even to do business. As the majority of Chinese were in retailing, a law seeking to control and nationalize it became the biggest threat. There was a rush to marry native women in order to get around the law. Informal and illicit arrangements with natives to act as fronts became widespread. The result was petty corruption on a large scale.

Daily living became an exciting but nerve-wracking round of extortions, plots, schemes, investigations, brushes-or deals-with the police, internal revenue, customs, politicians. To be less vulnerable, any ambitious Chinese could, if he was lucky, find a compadre among the high, mighty, and well-born. Originally a religious tie between a godfather and a godchild ~ and his or her parents ~ it evolved into a social relationship with feudal undertones between the adults. The binding tie was a mutual exchange of favors. It gave the Chinese compadre protection and access to more profits, and the native compadre a substantial share of the profits. The native held keys to the backrooms of power and the doors of treasuries, but the Chinese furnished the drive, the imagination, and the know-how.

When Manchu rule fell, China spiraled down into near-total disorder. A nascent republican government dissolved in the acid of misrule, inordinate ambition, power-struggles and corruption at all levels.

A titanic struggle ensued between the republican Guomindang (Nationalists) and the dictatorship Gongjantang (Communists). Utter chaos set in; famine stalked the land, millions died.

Reflecting the fratricidal strife at home, the overseas Chinese acquired an oxymoron image: dangerous as well as hapless. As a hot/cold war erupted between the democracies and Communist countries, Chinese of whatever political affiliation were seen as a potential or actual fifth column, as in Indonesia. The putative threat made them even more vulnerable: targets of suspicion if the image was one of threat; milking cows, if defenseless.

China was a physical fact ~ where ancestors lay buried ~ or as a state of mind, for the huachiao. It never ceased to be a strong emotional pole to them, no matter how much they had "gone native" and to all appearances had lost their Chineseness. But ambivalence in status left many of them in limbo, living a nebulous existence at the margins.

In the case of my family it was not only being marginal to the host society, it was being marginal even to Chinese culture. For us the problem was how to come to terms with marginality itself as a permanent way of life.

Father's parents and nine brothers faced a drastic decision. After hours of bitter wrangling, they agreed it would be safer to place the business under the name of the Filipino wife of Father's Third Brother. Father angrily dissented, but he was alone. They branded him a maverick.

A few years later, company assets mysteriously disappeared, causing tremendous business losses. Father felt vindicated. The resulting discord among the brothers led to the splintering of the clan. The family empire broke up; a few scattered to Canada, Australia, and the United States. Brothers permanently lost contact with each other.

With the break-up, Father moved us out to the suburbs. But nostalgia and the antique charms of his old haunts pulled him back time and again to re-visit Chinatown. The ghetto had many vestiges of the Spanish colonial presence. Cut-stone baroque churches ~ often designed and built by Chinese artisans ~ with twin campaniles housing massive bronze bells, towered incongruously but benignly over squat rows of wooden shops and bustling restaurants. Clangorous streets with Spanish names, such as Evangelista, Luna, and Rosario, displayed a motley assortment of gaily-colored signs in Chinese characters. The atmosphere was like that of any entrepôt on the mainland.

Father loved the noise and hectic activity. This was his turf. He knew everyone, everyone knew him. Always affable, he was gallant to a fault but mostly toward others, even toward total strangers. He was known as *onghitao*, the Chinese Kojak, a ubiquitous presence. Never did he have to carry cash or a checkbook. His credit was good at groceries, hardware stores, shoe shops, haberdasheries, eating places, everywhere. He sealed business deals with a handshake and a smile, sometimes over a bowl of steaming *mami*, a mug of *Pu-erh* tea, a tumbler of *Shaoshing* wine, or a bottle of *San Miguel* beer.

Soon Father realized he could no longer go as often as he did. He now spent more time hanging out with politicians and business partners in coffee shops in the more fashionable sections of the city. No more tasting binges in dumpling shops and noodle bars. No more gorging on sweet-potato pancakes made with freshly shucked oysters and garnished with *ku-tsai*, no more freebie sampling of spiced dried pork, preserved Chinese dates, pickled mangoes, succulent persimmons, cottony-white *masmalu* at the variety store.

I myself never missed Chinatown. Neither was I born there nor did I pal around with such "backward" Chinese. Indeed I hated going there except to eat. I found it chaotic, dirty, noisy, congested. To me there was nothing nostalgic about dank and musty relics or the bedlam of streets. The air was fetid, humid, and dusty. Just a slight breeze stirred up powder-dry horse dung from the street and blew it into my nose, over my dress, my sweating arms, legs, face, stinking up my hair. It was the woeful, scrawny ponies, pulling gaudy high-wheeled *calesa* around Chinatown and neighboring districts, that were distributing their blessings with abandon on the streets. A row of such rigs were always parked on the cobbled streets around the Binondo Church, waiting for corpulent Chinese passengers or doddering hags with bound feet who had to be manhandled up the high carriages. The sight of emaciated ponies ~ dehydrated, almost dead from exhaustion, victims of incessant lashing by the *cochero* driver ~ always made me wince. It was the favored mode of transport of Manila Chinese. I guess it reminded them of the rickshaws back home, pulled by half-starved men with bare feet who could have been their ancestors.

As for Mother, she kept up her forays into Arranque and Divisoria ~ the huge, bustling but grimy public markets in the northern reaches of Chinatown ~ even if it meant being chauffeured several kilometers from our surburban residence. In these open markets fresh farm produce lay strewn in profusion alongside live, squirming Pacific prawns, crabs, *lapu-lapu*. Live pigeons, quails, ducks, chickens were all jammed into woven-cane baskets. Here were all kinds of ingredients essential to Chinese cuisine. Feeding Father was Mother's honorable calling; everything else took a back seat. Unsparing of money and effort in this regard, she was nonetheless frugal to a fault in all other matters. Father was the spendthrift, the *bon vivant*; Mother was the pinchpenny, the bargain-hunter. Mother said that when wife is frugal, husband cannot but behave well. But howsoever Father behaved, she honored without question his princely privileges as paterfamilias.

While Mother dressed modern, she never felt the need to learn the ways of the modern world, including any of its languages. Her daughters would be her go-betweens to the real world.

One day I tagged along on one of her market forays, lured by the prospect of piping-hot mooncakes. The flaky crusts of beef suet and pork fat were filled either with sweetened black beans, or candied wintermelon, lotus seeds, watermelon and sesame seeds, studded here and there with slices of boiled duck's eggs marinated in brine.

"This *lapu-lapu*, no fresh. Two pesos, okay?" Mother addressed a fishmonger. She spoke the patois in pidgin style. Haggling is a reflex act in Asia. Hunting for bargains is not only an obsession; it is a game to enjoy.

"What you mean, no fresh? Don't touch my fish. *Sige*...you don't want it, go away, *intsik beha*, Chinese witch!" the market vendor screeched, fixing Mother with a bristling look. "You *tulo laway*, slobbering wretches with money, you always want things free." Hackles up, she screamed a string of insults, loud and vulgar. "Go back to Red China where you belong!"

Mother was taken aback, visibly upset. Turning to me, agitated, she commanded in Fujian, "Answer her, tell her we do not want things free. Tell her we work very hard for what we have. Tell her!"

I remembered the old Chinese proverb "Under heaven, no parent is ever wrong."

But if I complied, I would get into trouble with this *palenkera* battle-axe. Quickly I walked away from the stall, afflicted with an impromptu attack of deafness. But Mother was not ready to leave. She followed and pulled me to a stop, face flushed, hands quivering.

"Are you ashamed you're Chinese?" she demanded. "Don't be such a coward!"

"Mama-ah. Let us go. There are other stalls. If you want to, tell her yourself," I expostulated, but almost in a whisper.

"We give you everything, and you disobey me, " she scolded. "See, I told your father it was wrong to send you to convent schools where you learn to disobey your parents. Better you go to Chinese schools so you can talk like me, and not question me." She went on. " Pity us, we cannot even visit our ancestors' graves because those Communist demons won't let us. Now even our children don't give us respect."

People around us did not understand of course. I was emboldened to answer back. "Mama, why don't you learn English or Tagalog so you can talk to the *huan-na* yourself?" I said, exasperated that every encounter had to be this emotional.

"You talk like a native. We're Chinese. But your good fortune makes you weak and cowardly," she flung back.

The challenge rankled. At home, after passions had cooled, I asked Mother: "What does being Chinese mean? I cannot even speak Fujian well. None of my friends are Chinese, I have never been to China..." That only served to provoke Mother once more.

"You don't know? I know. Look at your Chinese face," she pulled me to a mirror. "I don't care what you say, but you *are* Chinese! Unfilial, but still Chinese. Why can't you be like your oldest sister?"

Unlike Eldest Sister, I was candid to a fault, especially to my family. I learned at school that to be candid was a virtue, but no one ever taught me to be tactful. When Mother waxed righteous about my lack of filial piety, I would try to reason out. This only served to infuriate Mother.

Eldest Sister seemed to always know what to do. She contrived all sorts of ways to deal with outsiders. But best of all she evolved an effective way to deal with our parents, for in many respects it was harder to please them than outsiders. "Just agree or say nothing," she counseled. Better to withhold the truth from parents if it clashed with their opinions. That way, you don't displease them, you get what you want.

By saying nothing, you say something. There goes *wu-wei* again.

In the face of anti-Chinese agitation, Father and Mother turned more and more to us, to deal with complex situations. Commands grew in number and more often. Unremitting, they kept taking more of our time and energy. Eldest Sister and I had to grow up in a hurry. When the pressures began to overwhelm, I showed signs of resistance. But even the slightest sigh evoked a violent response: how could I be so ungrateful? To be given life by them was a privilege I had to repay the debt. Did I not know girls could be sold like pigs or traded, in China?

There were comic moments. To fend off the collectors, the panhandlers, and con artists who preyed on Chinese, Eldest Sister and I devised a scenario centering on our dogs. She would put on a preppy, collegiate manner while I engaged the predator in talk, diverting attention to our dogs, who by this time were swarming around, over us, over the uninvited. I would launch into a glowing, unending account of our pets' tricks and antics. I would boast about pedigrees and prizes (some imaginary). I usually got carried away myself. In the end, they gave up. Overwhelmed, bored to extinction, and unable to slip in a topic that now seemed impertinent, the intruder excused himself and left. Then we trooped, dogs and all, to Father to report our triumph. He grunted his approval, his moon face brightening up with that wicked grin of his.

This day, Winchester greeted the visitor with arched tail tucked cautiously between hind legs that clumsily supported his cumbersome bulk. Strutting beside him was Hamlet, the jet-black, smooth-coated Chihuahua, scrambling to keep up with Winchester's giant strides. The diminutive five-pounder was self-assured, insolent. *Hamalet* ~ as my parents mispronounced it ~ got her name from Shakespeare we were then reading in middle school. Since gender did not matter, Hamlet seemed right even though *he* was a *she*. She came from a *compadre*, a Filipino lawyer retained by Father to deal with arcane legal and technical requirements in the Kafkaesque government bureaucracy.

"What kind of carabao is that?" the visitor asked, of the 130 pound, 33 inch tall, harlequin Great Dane. "That *damulag* must eat a lot. Where can I get one?"

A powerful giant, with a massive head and a deep chest, the Great Dane had a heraldic presence. In the 19th Century, near the Danube, the Germans developed the *deutsche dogge* for hunting wild boar. It is believed to be a cross between the Irish wolfhound and English mastiff. Why the French later named the breed *grand danois* is not known.

"He's a rare breed, imported from Australia, you know. Named after his kennel, Winchester." I sniffed haughtily, happy to brag. "When we have puppies, you can have one," I promised. (Winchester was male and we didn't have a bitch.)

I hoped the promise was enough to make him leave contented. Freeloaders were all too transparent: happy-go-lucky, frivolous, living from hand-to-mouth. The type who spends his last centavo on the latest denim fashion or import fad, even if it means living off his relatives all year. To support his lifestyle he was not averse to extort at every opportunity. Surely he knew he could never properly care for a Great Dane. But he had seen Winchester; he must have one too.

Hamlet had no appeal for the visitor. He was too small and insignificant. Probably the smallest dog in existence, the Chihuahua was made popular by the American bandleader Xavier Cugat. Known as Techichi among the Toltec Indians of Mexico, the breed dates back to the 9th Century. The custom those days was to bury this dog along with the dead to guide them in the afterlife. Later it was renamed Chihuahua after a Mexican state.

Always wide-awake and noisy, Hamlet was a better watchdog than Winchester, who would rather lie down than stand. The cheeky dwarf dominated the easy-going, good-natured giant. They made an odd couple: one towering, overbearing, the other elfin-like, frisky. They were the best of friends. Like humans, dogs have hard-to-explain preferences. A strange chemistry bonded them to each other, the same way dissimilar humans bond to each other.

They enjoyed each other's company more than with humans. Winchester had the habit of backing his big butt in play into Hamlet's saucy face, making her jerk her tiny head away in disgust. If Winchester persisted, Hamlet would perk up her ears, pop her eyes wide and then in sheer exasperation lunge at him, snapping and scolding.

Hamlet and Winchester were bred to win trophies and awards, incidentally for profit. By symbolizing a rich lifestyle they conferred prestige on the family. They were displayed like fine furniture.

Like Hamlet and Winchester, Eldest Sister and I grew up bonded to each other. In our early teen years, we shared everything, from clothes to crushes to secrets, baring innermost thoughts and feelings to each other, and vicariously sharing each other's adventures. To each other, we spoke bookish English learned from Belgian tutors. Like Stephen Hawking's speech machine, the android Data, or talking computers, we did not elide subject with verb.

Late one evening, as the shimmering moon shone through the sheer bedroom curtains, I sensed Eldest Sister turning and tossing in her sleep. I thought at first Hamlet had sneaked under the bedsheets. I hesitated to shake her awake. (Asians believe that in sleep the soul wanders off. It could be stranded outside if the person suddenly awakened, not giving it enough time to get back into the body.) But maybe she was still awake. I heard her gasping.

"Ahh.. Cannot breathe. My heart, it has stopped beating!" she took several deep breaths, clasping her chest as it heaved.

"Mary," I whispered, irritably. "Stop it. Nothing is wrong with you, you know that. What is eating you?" I tried to shake myself awake. "Is that Hamlet with you?" I thought I smelled talcum powder.

Eldest Sister was a hypochondriac as far back as I remember. She let her worries and fears eat her up inside. Not me, I wear mine on my sleeves.

She sat up, switched on the table lamp, and hastily unbuttoned her nightshirt at the neck as though she was suffocating. Her eyes rolling and disoriented, she reached out to the night table beside her, clumsily pulled out an envelope from a drawer and shoved it to me.

Now fully awake, I made out the words: "Martina Lim."

"Is that not Mother's maiden name?" I did not recognize the writing, although the address was in roman letters. The stamps were unfamiliar. The envelope even smelled strange. At the back it read: Amoy, China. No sender's name. Inside was a two-page letter in

Chinese characters. I stared at it, unable to read beyond the few ideograms I knew.

"I did not know we have relatives in China," Eldest Sister whispered almost inaudibly, as if someone might overhear us. "Shhh.." she shushed herself.

Our eyes met; they locked in fear and confusion. Another crisis. So soon? How come no one ever told us we had relatives in China? And how did this letter get here? There were no diplomatic relations between China and the Philippines. But the letter had been posted. So there had to be mail. Somebody could have read it besides us.

At that time anti-Communist hysteria gripped the United States. Senator Joseph McCarthy was breathing fire and brandishing hate lists of so-called Communists and Leftists. As a former colony the Philippines echoed the paranoia and feeding frenzy. To be seen drinking Coca-Cola with an alleged Communist branded you a Communist. Quack like a duck, walk like a duck...you must be a duck. As Chinese we could not escape getting sucked into the globe-girdling death-struggle between two incompatible political, economic and thought systems. We were automatically suspected of being part of a fifth column of Chinese Communists. Correspondence with relatives in China was enough proof.

"No wonder Mama locks herself up in the library, crying all the time," Eldest Sister said.

"Why is she in touch with them? Sister Rosalie said China is an evil country; people in China are evil. They are Communists and Communists are sinners. Is it not a mortal sin to have relatives in China?" I asked fearfully, terrified more of hell than of any government on earth.

"Shhhh. No one should know. We should never talk about it again. If people find out, they will say we are evil. I read that the only good Communist is a dead Communist."

"I will ask Mother about this," I announced defiantly.

"Why do you want to bring it up and upset her? She cannot do anything about it."

"I just want to talk to her about it."

"That is what is wrong with you," now she raised her voice, and said bitingly, "You are always looking for trouble!"

"I do not want my classmates to turn their backs on me as if I am a leper."

Could I make it to heaven if I had relatives from an evil country? Was I a sinner? Evil? A growing anxiety hovered like a dark cloud over me, that our family secret would leak out, and I somehow would get the blame.

It was around this time that a local Chinese businessman mysteriously disappeared from his home and was never again seen alive. Mr. Ang was a Chinatown resident who started poor and then became prosperous by importing Chinese foodstuffs, like canned lychees, water chestnuts, abalone from the fishermen of Fujian Province through Hong Kong. His Chinese wife and family preferred living in Hong Kong. He had taken a Filipina mistress.

Whenever he came to our house, needing advice on a problem with a government agency, he brought a tribute: a basket-full of imported apples and oranges, Irish soda-cream crackers, Mackintosh toffees; for Father, bottles of Remy Martin, Cutty Sark, and cartons of Winston and Chesterfields. He spoke a funny blend of pidgin Tagalog and English. Rather short and fat, he lived like a coolie, though he probably had more money than we did. Mother made me serve him tea. Absorbed in checking through the contents of a bulging wallet, he reacted irritably to my intrusion. I had the impression what excited him most was the pursuit of money, and counting it was his only physical exercise. What money was for did not much matter except that with it he could make more. Perhaps, I thought, he meant to take it with him to the other side, so he could bribe General Yama, the presiding demon there, into letting him make more.

One fateful day they found him mangled, mutilated, and bludgeoned to death on the vinyl floor of a room in a hotel by the big bayside park in Manila. The Chinese newspapers in Manila were quick to luridly play it up: his eyes had been gouged out, his blood was splattered all over the walls. Apparently he had been kept alive for days, tortured all the while by a hit squad reportedly hired by the rogue son of a prominent congressman from a northern province. The Chinese saw it as a brutal message to all rich Chinese.

"He should just pay *tong*, even two, three times. See what he got hanging on to his money? What use to him, all that money. *Sainya*, those bastards, *che-kao* cheating monkeys!" Father cursed, as he described to Mother, gory details and all, the inglorious end of Mr. Ang. He did not care that Eldest Sister and I were listening with rapt attention.

I had not known any human dying until now. Whenever one of our dogs died, I became hysterical. For me, to die was to be punished. Mr. Ang's gruesome death added to my paranoia. I kept asking myself, over and over again: was he killed because he was a Communist? Was he evil because he traded with China?

Was this the kind of end I could expect as a Chinese?

Dear God, I prayed, when my time comes, let me go like a light bulb switching off. I sprinkled holy water, obtained from church, around my bed before going to sleep, to drive away evil lurking in the dark behind the curtains or under the bed. I could not fall asleep without a maid holding my hands. Once when I went to confession at St. Jude's, I sobbed out the story of Mr. Ang to the priest-confessor, in all its horror. His reaction was simply to mumble: "Father, into Thine hands I commend his spirit."

Mother sat musing as she watched the bloated goldfish milling in the pond in our garden grotto, "Look at them swim, so happy, so quick at snatching up the breadcrumbs. If you catch them and put them on the chopping board, they're still happy." I thought she was making a flippant remark. Now when I think back, I realize why those days she talked with such fatalism, why she chided me when I complained and whined. She was trying to still my fears.

In those crisis-times, there was no one to turn to when neurosis raised the spectre of real or imagined threats from the outside. Home was no longer haven, except that coming home to our dogs and cavorting with them afforded a measure of relief. Unruffled, unconcerned, they were just about the only ones around us without racial or political bias, without hidden agendas.

Hamlet lived ten years. Winchester died much earlier, at age two. He was brought to the veterinary clinic for cosmetic grooming ~ to erect his droopy ears and make them tulip-like for a dog show. The veterinarian, alleging heartworm infestation, administered a bit too much arsenic. How could Winchester have had heartworms, he was asymptomatic. There was no shortness of breath, no deep coughing, no weight loss. Besides, it took years before an infestation manifested itself, and Winchester was only two!

Did the veterinarian do this deliberately to Winchester because we were Chinese?

Our relatives affirmed that his death was to maintain the cosmic balance. It was a surrogate death, a dog's life for someone in the family whom malevolent spirits wanted to snatch away.

In 1969, following the Indonesian incidents, race riots broke out in Malaysia. Many Chinese ~ as well as Malays ~ were killed. In the late 70's the Philippines' economy as well as living conditions under the conjugal dictatorship of Ferdinand and Imelda Marcos took a nose-dive as the couple looted the country wholesale. Throughout, they habitually colluded with rich Chinese, giving and receiving incalculable favors from them. Many of the Marcos cronies were Chinese.

In the late seventies, fearful of a backlash similar to the upheaval in Indonesia and Malaysia, Father made the wrenching decision. We were all to pack up and move out of the country. Our dogs would make that move with us.

The cycle was repeating. Just as their parents had decided to pull up stakes to get away from tyranny, war, corruption, and fear of falling victim to a spreading violence, our parents were for similar reasons uprooting the family to begin life anew in another place of refuge.

Once again it was gambling with life, but one that was worth the stakes. America was a vast gaming table where prizes had no limit. This time they had five loaded dice ~ their daughters, three of them medical doctors. The odds must surely be in their favor.

Life may be a bowl of cherries, but among them was a pair of dice.

1

CINNAMON

October, 1972. "You are invited to the Peoples Republic of China."

The magical summons were the opening words of the letter I was holding in my trembling hands. I cannot begin to describe the joy I felt. It was an official invitation to join a national delegation on a goodwill visit. What a rare chance to cross the bamboo curtain and be an honored guest in the land where my parents were born, the fabled country of the Forbidden City and the Great Wall!

A few courageous college students ~ some I knew well ~ had clandestinely slipped into China. Enamored by a romantic vision of a new socialist world order and a classless society, they defied a ban on travel to China. Fearing arrest if they returned, some stayed on, got married and found employment in China. How I envied them and wished I had made the trip myself. Now, with this official invitation, I could go openly as a student and with approval of both governments. I could not miss this opportunity.

Already, many groups from other countries were crossing the border at Lowu into Canton on Chinese government-approved guided tours. The curtain was lifting now that the Cultural Revolution was winding down. Nixon had just made a historic visit. In the wake of this breakthrough, I would be one of the first *Nanyang* Chinese to visit.

That night I lay awake, too excited to sleep. But first I had Mother's automatic **NO!** to hurdle. Her adamant opposition was itself a bamboo curtain. But was it a ritualistic No, or was she really right in her apprehensions?

I knew precious little about life in China. My parents' lugubrious reports and bitter comments were neither encouraging nor enlightening. At rare moments, I did catch Mother lapsing into nostalgia. So I was sure there must be something wonderful out there despite all the boos and hisses.

Mother was sure if I entered Red China, I would be detained and thrown in prison by the Communists. She loathed them with a passion. Vainly I tried to calm her fears, telling her I would be with journalists, business, civic and academic leaders. Both governments guaranteed our protection. Then I brought in what I thought was the clincher: I did not have to pay for anything except my passage to Hong Kong. NO, she repeated, unmoved.

Mother had never fully grasped the nature of events that made her life in China one turbulent crisis after another. She seemed to still linger in a state of shock. She always waxed bitter about what she saw in and around her village in her youth, and what she heard. To Mother, China was a completely lost cause. She would never agree to her own family having anything to do with the China she remembered.

She was born in the village of Whei-hua, Fujian Province, and went to school on nearby Gulanggu Island in Amoy Bay. Her father was a dashing, middle-aged landowner, her mother his much-younger fourth wife. They lived all together ~ her father, four wives and their numerous children ~ inside a walled-in concrete compound. From infancy her memories were of panic after panic. All around them bandits savaged the villages, contending warlord armies ravaged the countryside in an orgy of violence that seemed to go on and on without end and conclusion.

To make things worse, weakened China fell prey to a rapacious Japanese invading army. She recalled as a child huddling in fear with other children as they listened to stories about villages going up in flames, officials buried alive, captured soldiers blindfolded and propped up on poles as target for bayonet drills. She listened in horror about men decapitated, women repeatedly gang raped, babies impaled on bayonets. She heard about the dwarf pirates slicing through limbs, leaving the victims to die a slow and excruciating death just because they did not bow low enough or humble themselves in front of a Japanese samurai.

She heard about village people dying of hunger. How, in desperation, some of them followed water-buffalo carts passing by with seized sacks of rice, spilling rice on the dusty road. A compassionate patriot slashed a sack with a knife as it went past. They then swept up the precious grains, and boiled them into a watery gruel, adding water again and again. The lucky ones survived on this.

It was a nightmare come alive. All of China was a torture chamber. Crops were destroyed or stolen, livestock confiscated. Local governments imposed forty-four kinds of taxes, eleven types of exactions to aid the military and innumerable ad hoc fees and fines. Women were forced to go into prostitution; children sold into slavery, able-bodied men reduced to idiocy by smoking opium. Thousands died from floods or drought.

It was a time of tyrannical rule and arbitrary laws. As China fell apart within, it was set upon from without; foreign powers dismembered it by slicing out "spheres of influence," humiliating it with unequal treaties. Atrocious living conditions prevailed; filth-borne diseases accounted for three-fourths of all deaths. Half of the population was dead before age 30. Schools shut their doors. Traditions crumbled, and thousands of families broke up. Insanity seemed to have taken over the nation.

Mother's father had succumbed to a heart attack during the turmoil, leaving most of his lands and wealth to her brothers. Father was then living in Manila. His family had already built up a business empire there. After the Japanese surrender and a year before the Communists took over, Father's father ordered him to make a trip to Fujian province. His mission was to deliver *guanxi* to the secret society and to the regional tin-pot bosses who had taken over from the warlords. In Amoy he met Mother by chance in a shop owned by a cousin. Mother was swept off her feet by Father's gallantry. The courtship was swift, cut short by a sense of urgency. Father chartered the Pan-American *China Clipper* to fly Mother to Manila.

Mother brought all her wordly possessions in a heavy teak steamer trunk. The arabic numerals 1947 were crudely incised on its hinged cover, above a heavy brass lock with a carved design of two fish, symbol of a happy marriage. The numbers formed part of a celestial sphere above a globe representing earth. Broad bands radiated from the globe and girdled the chest; dragons and clouds, suggesting abundance, were carved on each band. On the cover bats spread their wings, insuring the happiness of the trunk owner. At the base several *fanchuan* rode the seawaves. On the sides, repeated at the back, were picturesque village scenes with trees and gabled-roof houses. Also on top was a prominent carving of an intimate, filial grouping of two boys and their mother. Here and there were representations of the pilgrims's gourd ~ a Taoist symbol of one of the Eight Immortals ~ and the peach and sacred fungus ~ emblems of immortality.

Shortly after Mother left China, the Communists stripped her family of their land and property. The family scattered. Mother feared she would never see them again. Through occasional letters she learned that a brother had joined the People's Liberation Army. (He was bought as a child in the belief that Mother's mother would as a result produce a son. Shortly after, she did bear a son.) He was subsequently posted to Xinjiang, to a remote frontier outpost bordering Soviet Asia and Afghanistan, near the Lop Nor nuclear testing grounds. Straddling the fabled silk route, the province was practically all desert, and had few inhabitants ~ mostly Moslems who spoke a Turkic-Persian language. Here and in Tibet the Han Chinese were a minority, but dominant. It was by all accounts a desolate hardship post for government and army. Occasionally anti-Chinese riots flared.

To have relatives outside China, meaning us, was to be reactionary in the eyes of the xenophobic Communists. Uncle was lucky to have been able to join the Peoples Liberation Army (PLA).

In the early 60's, Mother's mother and younger sister managed to flee to Hong Kong in a smugglers' junk. The rest of her family remained behind, trapped, virtually under the gun. Pendulum swings in politics, endless court intrigues around Mao Zedong, and the baleful influence of whoever had his ear at the moment ~ for example, Lin Biao and Mao's wife Xiang Qing ~ made life terribly insecure and dangerous.

"When elephants fight, the ants get trampled," Mother pontificated. "Why do you want to visit the elephants?"

Desperate, I turned to Father who was sitting on the capacious rosewood settee, his feet up on the cloisonné coffee table, watching the smoke from his *Kings* curl up to the ceiling. On the table within arms' reach was a crystal goblet of cognac. I looked at him with a plea in my eyes and anxiously awaited his intervention. Although Father was autocratic, it was to him I could turn; he was more flexible and amenable to entreaty than Mother. I knew he relished being conspiratorial where he was the star. Mother was adamantly negative; rejecting anything that to her was left-radical, untraditional, licentious, liberal, or unfilial. It would lose us our Chineseness, make us immoral, she insisted.

"Okay, okay let her go," Father declared with an air of finality. His right hand waved me off, as if already bidding me good-bye. "You go." Mother looked extremely pained but did not say anything.

Behind the tolerance and magnanimity, I sensed a secret desire. Father was dying to go, himself. But his oft-expressed opposition to Communism made discretion prevail over bravado. Perhaps my going could pave the way for him. In Asia men make the women walk ahead where there likely are snakes. I knew I had won. Father had spoken. He was not about to let Mother argue about it, no, while he was savoring the Remy Martin in the snifter he cradled in his hands. It was first-class cognac of which every Hong Kong hot shot would say, "Blandy velly sexy" if asked why he preferred brandy to whisky. Mother was not going to spoil it.

The next few days Mother busied herself preparing gifts for every last relative in Hong Kong and China. Anyone fortunate enough to have made it out of China was expected to make a fortune. To go back empty handed was unthinkable, a huge loss of face. The number and quality of the gifts were to show proof my parents had not been failures. At nineteen, I was the first daughter to meet Mother's family. Mother talked about them so often everyone of them had come alive in my mind.

Hong Kong, a honky-tonk of a free port, was a riotous gateway to a glum, regimented China. The biggest Chinatown outside of China, it was a dumping-ground in the early seventies for the human flotsam and jetsam spilling out of the Mainland. Burgeoning into an emporium, it became a blister of wide-open Capitalism - and a canker of iniquity on the skin of Communist China. Here money flowed like water on the streets; traders and entrepreneurs from all over the world streamed in to get - or spend - money. Within its 400 square miles was ceaseless traffic of men and machines, skyscrapers jostling old temples, tenements bursting with people, shops spilling out onto the streets, sweating coolies loading and unloading ships and lorries, the new rich riding around Kowloon or the Island in their Rolls-Royces and Lagondas, gold and jewelry stores ablaze with neon lights at night, prostitutes in their skimpy finery prowling the alleys, rows of hotels and restaurants, sidewalk stalls with mounds of fresh produce, food hawkers selling grilled squid or steaming noodles from a wheeled cart, apothecaries offering powdered rhinoceros horn for male potency, breast pumps for nursing mothers. The Hong Kong colony was an Oriental Bazaar with western trappings, a flamboyant contrast to the austere Mainland.

I could hardly contain my excitement as I filed past the Hong Kong immigration and customs counters at Kai-Tak Airport. As soon as I was in the clear, I mumbled an excuse and hurriedly tore away from my fellow-delegates. With mounting anxiety I scanned the welcoming crowd even as I valiantly tried to steady the cart, top-heavy with bulging suitcases of gifts and extra boxes containing nearly-ripe Philippine mangoes, the best in Asia; compressed raw *cacao* cakes; roast chickens and ducks.

Why bring chickens and ducks to Hong Kong? I had the temerity to ask Mother. Wasn't it like bringing lychees to Canton? Did I not know ~ Mother retorted ~ poultry from the Philippines is famous in all China seaports for unequalled flavor, having been raised in a lush, tropical environment, free to roam, forage for food, and exercise?

Chinese always bring edible luggage when they travel: rare or auspicious culinary treats. Nobody travels light; Marco Polo saw people traversing China with incredible loads on their backs. Not clothes but food, staggering lots of it. The needs of the stomach took priority. Did the Chinese not fight a Revolution to preserve their cuisine ?

Suddenly I heard the ear-splitting scream: "MEILING! MEILING!" ~ my Chinese name. I looked. A small wisp of a woman with a long face, sharp chin, and dark, brooding eyes was waving a photograph of us five sisters. One look and I knew who she was. Her clothes were nondescript, her hair disheveled from having to battle her way through the crowd. I moved closer, scrutinizing every detail of her face, comparing image with reality. Her eyes, intense and penetrating like Mother's, dispelled any doubts, although the rest of her did not match the image. There was no trace of Mother's patrician beauty; instead, the face evinced resignation.

From Mother's stories I knew life had been hard for her sister and her mother, my grandmother. In Kowloon ~ the mainland part of Hong Kong ~ they lived in a rented room in the Hongham slum district, eking out a living doing embroidery from dawn to dusk until their eyes felt like dropping, with no relief except to sigh. They were determined not to be like other refugees who slaved as indentured labor. The area was where most recent arrivals from across the border took refuge, and it was rife with crime. Once, in a dark alley on her way home, a thief almost slashed Grandma's throat. She got away unharmed but lost her two weeks earnings which she had with her. They could not turn to police because they had no papers.

Auntie *Phang-ti* began self-study to become a pharmacist in the little spare time she had. She found a job as a courier for a small, newly set-up Chinese Communist bank in Kowloon that tapped into the savings of non-persons in the colony ~ undocumented refugees ~

who wanted to remit money back to the mainland and could not make
use of the regular banks. Her job was to collect from clients and to
deliver to the bank cash hidden in a money belt strapped around her
waist. To save on bus fare she would walk the length and breadth of
Kowloon and Hong Kong on her rounds, riding only the ferry, many
times a day, every day in the week. Though paid little, she was able to
save and in fact regularly remit small sums to her brothers and sisters
still in China. With its secret sources rapidly expanding the bank
entrusted her with larger and larger sums of money. Auntie continued
to go by bus, ferry and on foot, not losing a single Hong Kong dollar
on the way. Honest, loyal, hard working and dependable, my maternal
aunt built up a solid reputation and many friendships along the way.

Frantically I waved and rushed forward to embrace her. Gently
she pushed me away, giggling nervously. That disconcerted me until I
remembered: a public show of affection embarrassed the Chinese. It
was indecorous, somewhat shameful, and, between the sexes, indecent.

"*Wei*," she just said, smiling wanly. Then she turned and talked
animatedly to a stout, bespectacled man who had taken charge of all
my bags. She paused to address me: "This is your *E-tiong*." She spoke
in Fujian; her English was almost nil.

"Uncle," I said, bowing deferentially.

"*Meiling*, I hope you had a pleasant trip and you are not too
tired," he startled me with his quaintly formal British-accented
English.

Like Auntie, Uncle was a refugee from a neighboring village. A
matchmaker had brought them together. Self-taught, hardworking, he
climbed up in no time from clerk to insurance adjuster for a Hong
Kong shipping firm that operated all over the world. A large portion of
his now comfortable income went back as remittances to kin in Fujian
Province, where his "real" home was. Hong Kong was an alien
Cantonese world. His mother had refused to leave her village, firmly
clinging to her duty to tend her husband's grave, her lifelong
obligation. To Uncle a son's destiny was to go back sooner or later to
where his mother was. Like many Fujianese, he lived on the edge of
Hong Kong society, just as Hong Kong itself was on the edge of China,
an island-speck of incongruous affluence in a vast sea of poverty.
Someday, he knew China would claim back this haven; he feared they
were living on borrowed space, borrowed time.

It did not look like a residence. The entrance was innocuously hemmed in by storefronts on this teeming street off Nathan Road. The tiny lift took us grudgingly up to the sixth floor, where steel bars stretched across windows and accordion grates protected doors of three flats. Uncle pushed the boxes and luggage with his feet along the corridor to one of the doors. In the narrow passage sat a miniature shrine to the local *Tu-ti*, with offerings of fresh oranges and cooked food to be shared with the nature spirits.

It had three tiny bedrooms, a toilet-bath that served also as laundry room, a larger room crammed with furniture that served as a parlor and dining area as well as a passageway to a kitchen. Every inch of space was put to use, even the air space outside where a pole between two windows served as clothesline with laundry hanging to dry. One room was rented out to a Shanghai couple. A large color TV that never seemed to be turned off dominated the living room. Next to it was a glass cabinet with a small white bust of Mao Zedong.

"We own the flat. Five more years and it's fully paid for," Auntie *Phang-ti* proudly announced.

A ten-year old boy in a Batman costume sprang out of a bedroom and ran to and fro, while a round-faced twelve-year old girl in ponytails stood to one side and looked me over, smiling shyly. My eyes focused on a tiny old woman with wrinkled brows in traditional black satin pajamas and a white cotton shirt, her shiny hair, dyed black, coiled in a tight bun. She was quietly sitting on a sofa chair.

"Daughter of *Chioti*," she whispered in Fujian. I ran towards her and embraced her. An ascetic frame belied a sturdy body.

Then she held me by the arms, gently rocking me forward and back in front of her to get a better look. It was obvious she needed glasses, but it was a luxury she would never indulge in. Money saved meant money for less fortunate relatives left behind in China.

Her black, round eyes peered into mine. Although it was a chilly November, I was warm, flushed with excitement, choked with emotion. I had ached for a grandmother who would love me although I was a girl.

She squeezed my small, pudgy hands tightly, lowered her gaze, and excitedly raised my short fingers, exclaiming in Fujian, "Look how small! Good sign; good life." Inspecting me further, she purred in pleasure, "Feet like lotus blossoms. Ah, female child, you will marry a rich man."

Though my feet had never been bound, it was a stubby 4 ½ B; the short toes fanning out evenly like a lotus leaf. In my visits to China, especially in summer when I wore open sandals, my feet were constant objects of wonder and adulation.   Foot binding had long been proscribed, but my unusually small feet, albeit unbound, still made quite a fashion statement.

It was Grandmother who, when she came to live with us in Manila, initiated me into the ancient and arcane arts of palm-reading, physiognomy and phrenology, that is, reading a person's character by face, head features and body shape. It was a skill that made me popular to friends and strangers alike.

Grandmother told me they enabled one to look into the soul and predict fate, by the size, shape, convexities, bumps, and depressions of the cranium, forehead, ears, etc. People with small feet would always have wealth, it was believed. Probably the practice of footbinding in the Manchu Imperial Court spurred such a belief, or was it the belief that spurred the practice? Impoverished peasant women never had their feet bound. Likewise, those with small hands were assured a good life. People of short stature but stout frames like Napoleon or Deng Xiaoping were crafty and shrewd. A mole on the upper lip was a sure sign of garrulousness and of sensuality. A bulbous, prominent forehead promised wisdom and magnanimity, like the *primus inter pares* Immortal, *Chung-Li*, one of the Eight Immortals. A gap between the front teeth meant unending good luck, to fix it brought bad luck. Ears that protruded and came to a point at the top were evidence of exceptional intelligence and astuteness; if they were big, they predicted leadership potential. To have such ears and a prominent forehead like the inimitable Spock of Star Trek earmarked the sage, probably because "His wisdom comes from logic, not emotion, from insight that no man has ever had before."

"Granddaughter, you thin, look sick. Must eat more, means much money, plenty food. Round face and body very good, look healthy."

She pulled me closer. "*Aiya*, face so rough... not eating right." Turning to her daughter, she said softly, "Soak dried bird's nest in water. Tomorrow, I make."

I knew what she meant; I had seen Mother do it, before our exams or when we sisters were sick. She would pick out with tweezers, from a clump of softened birds' nest, the tiny hair, moss, and feathers still glued to the tangle, then boil it ever so gently for hours with crystal sugar. It was eye-straining work, but it was her way of showing affection. Turning to me, she said, "Eat when stomach empty, early morning."

"*Ama*, you must save it for yourself," I urged. This delicacy, with its supposed wonder-working properties, was rare and very expensive. Basically it was nothing more than the alkaline, gelatinous spittle of a particular species of seashore swiftlet, it uses to glue the nest together. But such nests were only found in almost inaccessible caves on Java, Borneo, Moluccas, Burma, and Thailand. Fortune-seekers had to hack their way through thick jungles and clamber up rope ladders to the caves high up cliff-faces to collect them. Some would slip and fall to their deaths, several hundred feet to the bottom of cliffs.

Auntie *Phangti* opened the bulging cartons and happily inspected the dark-chocolate blocks, trade-marked *Pueo*, molded from roasted, ground premier cacao seeds. She would boil the chocolate blocks in milk to produce an incomparably rich aromatic brew. (It was the Chinese who perfected the art of chocolate-making after the Spaniards introduced it in the Philippines.) Happily she sniffed the roast chickens, Mother's specialty, lovingly marinated for days in five-spice powder, anise seeds, cinnamon bark, garlic, soy sauce, and cane sugar.

"I give some to Second Aunt and cousins so they know you brought something for them," she said.

The children jumped about, screaming and jabbering, not minding their father's admonitions. Auntie *Phang-ti* bustled about in the kitchen, occasionally popping into the living room to busy herself with the table, clearing it, plunking chopsticks into scalding water in a bowl. She chattered loudly away, never pausing in talk or action. I watched and listened, fascinated, as she scuttled about, as if on bound but unencumbered feet. She too, had small feet, but narrower than mine. My image of her now was, one who was always running to catch a bus.

"Granddaughter, you going China. Bring watch, radio, bicycle for Uncle, brother of your mother," Grandmother said, gesturing to the items tucked into a corner. Suddenly I noticed them.

For a moment I was speechless, completely taken aback. Then I remembered Mother telling me never to disgrace her to her relations, never to forget that I had obligations to her kin. But mindful of the xenophobia of the Cultural Revolution, I muttered something about exposing Uncle to the charge of being a capitalist-roader. Besides, how could I, a member of an official delegation, tote a foreign-made bicycle with me, in my luggage? I was in a quandary.

"*Ama*, Mother has a whole suitcase of medicine and clothes for me to bring to relatives in China. Don't you think I have all I can carry?"

"Granddaughter, bicycles cost much money in China. .Not easy to get." Her smile disappeared. "Uncle..., he doctor needs bicycle to go hospital everyday. You go with foreigners. You special, no restrictions. Just pass through. Chinese, like me, stripped and searched."

This 60's Beatle-mania flower-child, ardently idealizing China's classless society, could not accept what her grandmother was saying. I thought she was just exaggerating. But I could not forget my place.

"Alright, Grandmother," I said deferentially, hoping to appease her with a concession, "I'll bring the radio and watch."

She turned away, concealing her disappointment, perplexed at the resistance I was putting up.

Auntie chimed in. "*Meiling*, we fortunate ones have to do our duty to family. You talk like a barbarian..."

"Don't you know the Chinese ideograph for individual freedom also means selfishness?" Uncle added, breaking in. "Don't be a banana barbarian, yellow outside, white inside. Like many young Hong Kong Chinese. Too much western education, too much analysis, too much self-concern ~ not good for you and your family."

Perhaps he was right. I was dishonoring my ancestors by putting myself above the collective good. But I couldn't help myself. My life experiences were so different from theirs. Unable to comprehend fully the plight of relatives, unable to apprehend the reality of their present lives, I was being unChinese. They in turn reacted in the only way they knew: exert pressure so as to make me yield to the weight of tradition pressing down on my shoulders. I felt like a ping-pong ball being batted willy-nilly between two players. Two different worlds. But my kin gave me no choice: I had to be faithful to the world *they* lived in.

A few days later, I stepped onto a strange new world. It was like beaming onto a different planet or parallel universe. Would it be a Shangri-La, or a Gulag?

The 500-meter walk or rather, stagger ~ with my heavy bags ~ from the shabby, innocuous Shumchun station on the Hong Kong side to the massive, gleaming monument at Lowu across the border brought me up sharply to a new China. British-trained, nattily uniformed immigration officers perused my exit permit with indifference, perhaps glad to be rid of me. Behind me, I left the familiar world of vendors loudly hawking Cadburys, Hersheys, Coca-Colas and grimy station wall signs that read "Beware of pickpockets" ~ a reminder that wealth had its price.

Under the watchful eyes of youthful sentries ~ looking like minority Mongol, Hui, or Chuang ~ in clean, spartan Mao military jackets, hefting rifles with bayonets affixed, I hobbled with my burdens into the station. These guards were in fact my first glimpse of the Bamboo Curtain. I finally crossed over from Hong Kong and its bourgeois trappings, its disorder, noise, and carefree lifestyle, to the classless, look-alike, austere and puritanical, well-ordered, homogeneous, "iron-bowl" China, where adulation of one leader was the norm, where Big Brother regulates every facet of life and decrees every outcome.

The size and grandeur was awe-inspiring, the uniformity unsettling. After the initial impact it turned into a bewildering kaleidoscope of strange images, sensations, concepts and ideas. White, antiseptic, starkly angular buildings of gigantic proportions rose like mausoleums along wide, tree-lined avenues. Along them, seemingly without end, torrents of people on foot and on bicycles flowed in both directions. Everybody wore gray or blue cotton jackets and baggy pants, faded after countless washings. Not a single skirt did I see; women were undistinguishable from men except for pigtails and high, shrill voices. Loudspeakers at street corners filled the air with martial music and strident, militant chants extolling the virtues of the Great Helmsman. Everywhere the *China Pictorial* magazine, in Chinese, English, and Russian editions, portrayed in brilliant glossy colors China's new heroes like Hong Kong movie stars: Mao Zedong, Kang Sheng, Chudeh, Zhou En Lai, Lin Biao, Kuo Mo Jo. Big-character posters covered fences and billboards everywhere, in factories and in the countryside. They proclaimed *liberation of China through hard work, ideological struggle and self-reliance,* extolled heroic deeds of communes, work brigades, and barefoot doctors in the villages, and played up the benefits of a merit system using workpoints.

It was a collage of striking images: oversized, lidded mugs of steaming hot water with huge tea leaves floating; bowls of gleaming white boiled rice; ubiquitous packs of cigarettes; toilets where you squat; huge tin spittoons under tables; stench of night soil, which our guides claimed produced tastier fruits and vegetables; bony old men with rope harnesses on their heads, dragging carts with impossible loads at an amazingly fast clip down the street; old women in rags, bent almost double from the effort, pulling carts that moved silently over the paved road except for an occasional creak.

Going to China was a grand pilgrimage to the hallowed sites of my ancestors, torn for centuries by imperial and feudal wars, humiliated by foreign powers, isolated for the last two decades, now undergoing another political upheaval and a radical social experiment. It made me much less ambivalent about my identity, because now to be Chinese or look Chinese was no longer embarrassing. In fact, the amount of Chinese blood coursing in one's veins was a new indicator of social standing. Pureblooded, I of course stood high.

However, the Chinese in the mainland had an aura of dignity which the typical, money-driven overseas Chinese like me did not have. What lay behind it? Could it be because, barred from amassing personal material wealth, they instead cultivated warm friendships, building up *social,* not financial, resources?

Yet, equally striking was the tirelessly repeated adulation of the group idea ~ the work-team, the army, the state. The loner, the autonomous individual, was despised. Things had to be done collectively; even art, apparently, was done by committees. The individual counted for little in building a socialist society. This was a country of disposable people and faceless persons. Groupthink, dictatorship of the proletariat, the masses, was what mattered. How could I reconcile ideology with fact, propaganda with reality?

Paradoxical also was the priority on material betterment of the group as against that of the individual. For centuries the majority of Chinese led lives of privation. Logically, an essential aim of Liberation was to rescue not only the group but also above all the individual from perpetual deprivation. However, at the moment the only concession to the individual was the boast that now no one in China starves. China's poor now owned China. Although poverty had not yet been eradicated, famine was said to be a thing of the past. The spartan way of life was held up as the ethical model; to be frugal was to be praised, as if one had a choice. Maybe this was one way to make people accept continuing hardship.

I found it disturbing that Chinese, in history so concerned with personal comfort and self-indulgence, now seemed resigned to being faceless workers in the service of an overpowering Leviathan of a state. I wondered how long they would remain so. Perhaps one day they would heed Mencius' sage counsel about the rights of the ruled. Perhaps at the end of the tunnel, when socialist society is fully achieved, self-indulgence once more becomes the norm.

In subsequent visits after 1972 ~ in 1973, in 1977 as a state guest, and in 1985 on a Unesco-China joint project in the social sciences ~ I had a chance to supplement my earlier impressions. Our Chinese hosts kept proudly repeating "China has stood up." Public parks and the Bund in Shanghai no longer carried the sign, NO DOGS OR CHINESE ALLOWED, as before.

One striking fact was the total absence of animal pets everywhere I went ~ north to the Tachai Commune and south to Simao, Kunming, and the Mekong River on the border with Laos. The only animals I saw were either for food or for work. Not a single specimen of a household pet did I see on the streets or in residences, except once in Yunnan Province in 1977, when I espied a solitary four-footed creature far off, in the fallow fields. It looked like a dog.

Dogs and cats always had mythic significance in China. Often they were portrayed in the hyperbolic guise of lions, tigers, or even dragons. Dogs, especially, were depicted as stone guardians at temple-gates, palace doors, and the portals of the Afterworld. At Yama's foot, the Lord of Death, sat a pair of faithful demon-dogs. Their mission once a year was to prowl the earth and collect souls of the departed. Family pets were often sacrificed to serve as guides to the dead in the afterlife. They were said to repel angry ghosts and trickster spirits. The dog is the eleventh animal sign in the Chinese zodiac; those born in the Year of the Dog (1946, 1958, 1970, 1982, 1994, and 2006) are said to be loyal and generous.

From ancient times Chinese were dog-fanciers. Shitzu, Chow-chow, Pekinese, Lhasa-apso guarded the imperial palaces and temples, adorned the courts and kept the concubines company. Members of the nobility doted on dogs as they did on children, and even built memorials to them. The Shar-pei was bred for sport, the Chow for herding, hunting, and food. Dogmeat ~ "dragon-meat" in menus ~ was ascribed high nutritional value as a proven source of "heat" during wintertime. Cats were given culinary status as "tiger meat" on menus.

It is said that the Southern Chinese, especially, "eat everything that flies except airplanes, everything with four legs except tables, everything that swims except submarines." What they did not eat for pleasure they took for health reasons. Gallstones of horses were to cure mental illness, rhinoceros horns for impotence, desiccated sea horses for cancer or goiter, spider molt for malarial fever, powdered elephant skin to heal wounds, monkey brains to warm the body, deer antlers to strengthen bones, dragonflies to intensify sexual pleasures. This zest for eating, this insatiable hankering for variety, the use of animal parts for medicinal purposes, had always been a major threat to the survival of many species of animals in China, particularly rare species.

The American Dream is for house, cars, wife, and children; the Chinese Dream is for personal immortality. To find and eat the peach or the fungus of immortality is the key to longevity. Food, better food, luxurious food is what gives bodily comfort and pleasure. Hedonists and epicureans long before the Greeks, the Chinese went to absurd lengths to find a recipe to prolong life. Chin Shi Huangti, the First Emperor, incessantly drank homeopathic elixirs containing mercuric compounds served up to him by the alchemist magicians Xu Fu and Lu to lengthen his life, only to cut it short. Mercury is a poison. After conquering all the neighboring kingdoms and creating a single China, the one thing he could not conquer was his own death. His quest for immortality made his reign over all of China "between the Four Seas" one of the shortest in Chinese history.

"Are dogs and cats really all gone?" I asked, avoiding looking the interpreter in the eye, a rude act connoting a lack of respect and worse, a challenging stance. I braced for a lecture; he did not disappoint.

Buddhists do not approve of killing animals, even for food. This is because they say the animal you kill could have been a human in a previous cycle. For this reason dogs and cats were plentiful in the old China.

Then he launched into a well-rehearsed spiel. "In the late 1950's (during the Great Leap Forward) when many people did not have enough to eat and household pets competed with the masses for food, Chairman Mao decided they no longer deserved a place at the table. They were consuming, not producing, food. They were parasites."

"So, no dogs in China today?" I asked, somewhat testily.

"As you know," he added as an after-thought, "we are no longer Buddhists." I felt he was evading my question. Then he continued, "Dogs have no part in building our socialist society. They are a luxury we cannot afford. Today you find them only in zoos." (I had seen no zoos at all, too.)

He quoted an editorial from the People's Daily: "Public law prohibits Chinese from owning domestic pets for the following reasons. One is that they spread rabies and threaten people's lives. Another is that they urinate and defecate everywhere, polluting the environment. A third is that they bark and yelp, scaring people and biting people."

Oh well, I thought to myself: someday when the sleeping dragon is fully awake, when there is enough to eat and a plenitude of creature comforts, I am sure the Chinese people will once more want pets, not for feeding the body but for nourishing the spirit. And when that time comes the Chinese people will find that the non-human species can truly liberate them from the shackles of their own culture.

With the thawing of the freeze between East and West, my maternal Grandmother was finally able to come to the Philippines. We had to figuratively crowbar her into the country. She was over sixty-five, beyond the age limit set by immigration.   Only a Presidential waiver could get her in. As is usual in such cases, I found someone who was a *compadre* of a Presidential Assistant and could ask favors from him. Later, Father was loud in his complaints that the amount of the bond was scandalous. Long after Grandmother had passed on and we were already in America, Mother chided me for not being filial enough to get Grandmother in free.

I came to know Grandmother well when finally she came to live with us. She was a paradox: evocative of old China, its penurious and cruel past, its exploitative feudal relationships, yet she had such an expansive spirit, a great respect for all life. In her quiet, unprepossessing way she gave living proof that the beautiful, kind and generous was what gave wonder and meaning to life. I think by it she had achieved immortality. She used to say cryptically that you are immortal while you live. I might add, when it is lived her way.

Born of earthly roots, spiritually she seemed to dwell on a higher plane. She was not religious, to be sure, for she professed no religion. But she would make the perfect Buddhist nun. She forbade me to kill even insects. One time when I saw flies crawling and buzzing around an open wound on her right arm while she sat, unconcerned, I freaked out, and ran to grab a flyswatter.

"Leave them alone," she said quietly. "Even flies are important. Maggots from their eggs can clean wounds." She went on to say she had seen badly wounded people lying in the fields for days, coming back to life if not completely healed, with their wounds cleaned. Village people said maggots had been like a living bandage, constantly sopping up the pus and scouring out dirt from the tissues in the wound.

Grandmother *Ama* came like a breath of fresh air ~ pure, fragrant, cool. She was easy and relaxed, like Sunday afternoon. I felt so close to her that I never felt inhibited to ask her anything, even about the forbidden and the private. I was then a naive young girl who imagined that pregnancy was the result of kissing! Most Chinese in public were puritanical about sex. Grandmother showed nary a trace of it, and was never judgmental. Mother used to charge all men with malicious intent. Even Catholic priests, she averred, carried on secretly with nuns.

I often wondered how prudishness stacked up with the obvious sexuality that is behind China's population growth, and the popularity of salacious literature such as *Dream of the Red Chamber*. To the Communists, libertarian attitudes toward sex were proof of the decadence and corruption of western capitalism. Yet Mao Zedong himself was sexually insatiable. He had the habit ~ and the license ~ to summon to his bed nubile peasant girls, even young female Red Guards, who no doubt thought they were serving their country in bed.

Early on, Mother decreed we marry only Chinese if we married at all. Westerners, she claimed, start hot, but passions sputter out quickly and turn cold. In America, she observed, everything has an expiration date. Even marriage. Everyone wants the latest models. Like in a supermarket, having to choose from all that variety makes you dizzy. "Chinese, we start cold," she said, "like in arranged marriages, and then it gets hot. Works better!"

"But Ama," I posed a rhetorical question to Grandmother, "where oh where are the Chinese boys?"

"Aiya, does not matter if he not Chinese," she said softly, as she curried my hair with her gnarled, but still supple, fingers. I always enjoyed lying in her small bed; from it I could see the front yard, the main gate and the driveway. It was a room with a view of all the comings and goings in our house.

"Meiling, it not only the barbarian who stinks in toilet!" Then she stopped and said with a deadpan look: "Maybe Chinese stink more because they eat better."

At first the numerous dogs in our house disconcerted Grandmother. She had never known animal pets before, or so many of them. They were a symbol of luxury to which she was a complete stranger. Until she resigned herself to our decadent lifestyle she joked that our dogs ate better than most people did in China.

"In Whei-hua," she said, "people lucky if they have rice to eat. People hang dried fish over table and imagine they eat the fish with congee."

We had ten poodles of all sizes, ages, and colors. Each one of us had one of them as her personal pet. Eldest Sister had Brigitte, an apricot miniature; Third Sister had Alfredo, a black standard; Fourth Sister had Lincoln, a silky white miniature; Fifth Sister had Camille, a beige toy; even Milagros, a maid, had her own, a grey miniature named Brandy. Mine was a gray-black miniature, Kenneth. Sarah, Susie, and Cinnamon were communally shared.

After the noonday meal, when the tropical heat reduced minds to torpor, most of us, including the maids, repaired to siesta. Except for an occasional snore and the hum of insects, the house was still. Not Grandmother and the dogs. At the spare kitchen near the back porch, she was busy chopping, slicing, dicing, and meticulously setting aside scraps for the dogs. Mother said the Manchus might have ruled China but never a kitchen with her mother in it. Grandmother reigned; her subjects were the dogs. Like courtiers, they gyrated and fawned around her feet, watching craftily to snatch the next morsel that dropped, or a handout she dangled from her fingers.

"And who is now *kao-lotsay*? I asked, with mock laughter, as I snuggled close to her in bed, cozy and warm, my legs entwined in hers, sniffing the intoxicating scent of tiger balm wafting from her leathery skin. I remembered how she used to tease and call me the dogs' maid.

Well, it wasn't long before she took a dog as her own. His name was Cinnamon, after his coloration. I could hear her sing-song voice throughout the house, calling "*Cimmamon, Cimmamon.*" The garbled name was one of the few non-Chinese words she used, in addition to "ssenkyu" [thank you] and our American names, suffixing "ya" to each.

I don't know whether it was motherly instinct, loneliness, or Buddhism, but she related to the dog as if it were a grandchild who needed her. A unique bond developed between the two. It was simple but profound: she talked, he listened; he whined, she responded; he stared at her, she scanned his mind, and did his bidding.

For Cinnamon, it did not matter that Grandmother was old, that she was a Chinese woman in a *samfu*, that she waddled and hobbled like a woman with bound feet, and that she had no money. All that mattered was the chance to be close and intimate, at peace, curled up on her lap, eyes half-shut. That for him was the be-all and end-all of existence; all else was irrelevant. He followed her everywhere, including the toilet. Whenever Grandmother was excited about something, which was rare, his long feathered ears flattened back against the head and neck, his black-button eyes peered intently into hers, seemingly asking, "Can I help, *Ama*?"

Ama started a daily ritual: powder him with baby talcum ~ the way she saw us do it ~ tie a ribbon on his head, wipe his tear glands with the hanky she kept in the folds of her tunic, clean after him, cook for him, spoonfeed him. She even let him share her bed. No morning breath, she said half-smiling. And to think at one time dogs were so alien to her.

When the family moved to America, Grandmother refused to move. Too far, too weary, she said. She returned to Hong Kong to live with Auntie *Phang-ti*. By then, I had left for Manchester, England to pursue graduate studies. Thereafter, my life took a different turn, taking me to New York and then Paris. I became fully absorbed in my own rat race to find my place in foreign climes.

One blustery, winter evening in 1986 in Paris, my two dogs Kenneth II and Camille became unusually restless. That night, a large furnace pipe in our apartment burst, causing serious water damage. The heating shut down, leaving the apartment damp and cold. For no reason my two dogs started to howl, long and mournfully. A cold breeze brushed past my cheeks. Sometime later, as I walked shivering down the corridor, something fluttered down one of the bookshelves. It was a photograph of Grandmother at play with Cinnamon. I had previously retrieved it from a scrapbook with the intention of framing it, and then promptly forgotten about it. The following day the phone rang. It was Father telling me that Grandmother had coughed up blood, and that the doctor in Hong Kong had given her medication for flu. Only, it wasn't flu, it was a heart attack. She was eighty-nine.

Although my thoughts often turned to *Ama*, I could never get in touch with her personally. You see, *Ama* could neither read nor write.

Grandmother had expressed just one wish: that if she died outside China she was to be brought back and buried in her village. To return home to China was the obligatory last act of every good Chinese. Fallen leaves return to their roots, she said.

The village people gave her a proper Chinese funeral, replete with Taoist and Buddhist priests chanting and banging cymbals to scare off malevolent spirits hanging around the procession of mourners. Gold and silver paper money went up in smoke to assure the otherworld bureaucrats that the usual bribes were on the way. Rice cakes in ceremonial dishes were laid out to feed and placate the hungry ghosts who died without family or friends to perform the last rites of passage. A Chinese coin was carefully placed on each of her eyelids to serve as travel money, her ticket to heaven.

Cinnamon had passed on before she did. She had asked that on the bier her favorite photograph with Cinnamon, which she had kept in the folds of her *samfu*, be mounted. It was placed beside the embroidered banners with Chinese characters of DoubleJoy and Happiness, under colorful ceremonial umbrellas. In her village, ancestors were properly honored and remembered, their graves tended with food offerings. She and Cinnamon would never go hungry.

I hope some day to visit my ancestral village of Whei-hua, Fujian Province. And when that day comes, I shall bring food offerings of rice cakes, chive savories and other tokens of earthly luxuries like American cars, houses and microwave ovens Grandmother never had in this life. I shall perform the obligatory kow-tow to her and all ancestors before her. Then I shall tell her about my dogs she never got to know. But I am quite sure she will say, no treasure can never ever measure up to her Cinnamon.

When, tending my herbal garden, I see the peasant crow fearlessly fling itself at the aristocratic hawk in majestic flight to drive it away from its young; when I hear songbirds give thanks in glorious melody for the seeds I set out for them, I feel the vibrancy of *Ama's* spirit in the air.

I grieve but am not sad, for Grandmother's life is happily fulfilled, and so is Cinnamon's.

5

KENNETH

He was my first dog, in fact, my first Kenneth.

I do not want to say I owned Kenneth. If I do, I must also say Kenneth owned me. Better to say "bonded." Kenneth was bonded to me as I was to him, like no other dog till then. Kenneth was the first of my bondings.

I was thirteen when Father bought Kenneth from a reputable importer of poodles from the United States. He wasn't actually bought for me, but I immediately claimed him. Each of us chose her own. By this time our house was swarming with poodles. Father always favored big dogs but poodles were now the in-thing.

Kenneth and I hit it right off; it was love at first sight. When I first held him in my arms and looked him in the eye, I was gone, smitten. He had a certain *je ne sais quoi*, a self-assurance and a snootiness that irresistibly drew me to him. His serenity was calming. Indeed, the chemistry was just right.

I didn't give him the name. It came from a great-great grandfather in his lineage as his pedigree papers showed. He was a quick study, learning more tricks than any dog I knew. I called him *Chonggo* or *Unggoy*, meaning monkey, not to disparage but to tease, to express affection. This was in accord with Chinese practice, to make him unattractive to predatory evil spirits. The name was apt, however, he did look more primate than canine.

A grayish-black miniature, his coat was shaggy. His gray eyes slanted up a bit, his nose was a little black button, his snout small and pointed, ears long and feathered, tail docked and erect. He strutted about like a jaunty Frenchman, nose in the air, insouciant, aristocratic. He would kiss up to the perfumed and well-dressed, snubbing the blue-jean crowd reeking of sweat. Like dog, like master; in no time *I* was as stuck up as Kenneth. I was proud that he was AKC-registered, consistently won best-of-breed awards, paid stud fees, and that he was mine. I never missed the chance to show him off to my classmates. When they hugged and fussed over him, I was there, proudly sharing his celebrity status. That was one way I drew extra attention to myself.

At school, the classmates I helped with a math problem would call me genius to my face. But behind my back I overheard "yellow monkey with no tail." Laughing at my short arms and legs, tiny hands, and small feet, I was sometimes held up to ridicule as "King Kong" taking off from my surname. They said I walked like a chimp. (It would have been less insulting if they said I waddled along like a penguin.) When I tried to improve my gait by mimicking American models on television, Mother stopped me in my tracks and asked if I planned to be a prostitute!

Grades, not looks, were what mattered. To be ahead of the pack, Mother made all of us sisters spend every summer hacking away at next year's books with special tutors. No parties. No holidays. Even on weekends casual reading, sports, music, hobbies were derided as a sheer waste of time. It was a uni-dimensional existence: study, study, and more study. Superior grades were the key to the coveted parental approval, the only measure of achievement. Even a handicap such as my slight reading dyslexia was considered a cop-out and was no excuse.

Inevitably my sisters and I drew a silken curtain around us. No matter how complex and hostile the outside world, our world was simple and predictable. Friends were distractions, we did not need them. Toys were frivolous, never available, so we filled our space with our own reality. We entertained ourselves, improvising our versions of the Miss America beauty pageants. Everyone got in the act: parents, maids and dogs were our willing (and unwilling) audiences, subjecting them to impromptu renditions of musical excerpts from *West Side Story or South Pacific*. We used bedsheets for curtains, flashlights for spot lighting, spoons for microphones. Some of the dogs we decked out in outlandish costumes, and made them take part. Kenneth was the most cooperative, through no choice of his. We smothered him with talcum powder so he smelled like a baby, put underwear and a baby's bonnet on him and wrapped his four paws in little booties. He was hilarious, walking funny and awkward ~ first throwing up a front leg, then a hind leg, completely uncoordinated. The entire household rolled in their seats, laughing hysterically, bent-over double.

Together we sisters were unbeatable. A unique synergy enabled us to do collectively what we could not do separately. Even our favored male cousins could not measure up to us. In informal soccer matches between families, we beat them hands down. We took every encounter seriously; winning was everything. Back of our minds we were striving to get accepted by Father's parents, who had rejected us for being girls. Along the way, we became virtually *garçons manqués*.

Nothing daunted us. Toward each other, especially toward our mother, we adopted a fiercely protective attitude vis-a-vis others. Unlike us tomboys she was utterly feminine, fragile, needing to be shielded even from Father when he was around. Father was mostly absentee. Clearly he did not like to be around, as if it was unmanly, unChinese, to be personally looking after five female juveniles.

But behind a bold front was a great deal of anxiety. Even as we frolicked, seemingly carefree, every one had an incubus on her shoulder, incessantly nagging, ever demanding. Every endeavor was a chance to prove that being a girl was not opprobrium, that we did not disgrace our parents in the eyes of kin and make them lose face. Guilt and shame made us overcompensate. We had to show we were better than anyone else. Being "devil girls" made us aim high. For now our goals were academic honors; after that, material success ~ as medical doctors making money by the ton for the family coffers. To deviate was to forfeit parental approval and the emotional pap that went with it. So each of us topped her class, or at least a close second. Eldest Sister and I graduated from high school with three gold medals: for academic excellence, religion, and loyalty.

In Chinese tradition, girls were acne on a parent's face. That was true in old China. But not here where we were growing up. Here girls were *not* devalued at all. In upwardly mobile Chinese families~inside or outside China~the birth of girls was no longer the calamity it once was. On the Chinese mainland girls now had, by law and decree, equal status as boys. The Chinese Revolution, it was said, was to liberate from inequality and discrimination. Women were one of the beneficiaries. The doors were opening wide, but not among our kin.

The monkey on our backs made us compete fiercely with one another for our parent's approbation and affections. The same compulsion to succeed in the outside world made us vie for top position on the totem pole within the family, to vie for, in Mother's words, "the biggest chair." The downside was: we got locked in a vicious spiral. A sister's triumph was another sister's defeat, leading to a frenetic redoubling of efforts by the loser to stage a comeback, thus continuing the cycle. Sororal rivalries were always at fever pitch. Remarkably, the effect was to stimulate, not deaden. It caused us to invent schemes and all types of stratagems to gain the advantage. As we grew older the competition became fiercer ~ and deadlier. Weapons became more potent and tactics more ingenuous. The winner became the biggest and cleverest rat in the race.

At the onset of my teens, I began to gradually dislike my image of myself. I hated to always be on the sidelines, teetering on the edge as it were. I desperately wanted to belong ~ securely, totally. At the time I had started to dip into Kierkegaard and the existentialists, asking myself questions like, why was I born *Nanyang* Chinese to begin with. What kind of people were they, so fecund, able to propagate from their homeland to all corners of the world, yet plagued by all sorts of doubts about their self-identity? Why could I not be certain of being fully Chinese? I did not like playing a Janus-game: a Chinese face on one side and a non-Chinese on the other. I was tired of leading a shadow existence at all times. If mine was really the superior race, as constantly dinned into my consciousness, why should I downplay my identification with it? Why should I adopt native and western ways to ensure success in a barbarian world to which my parents did not even care to belong? They were comfortable in their own skin; they had their Chinese friends and far-flung kin network. Yet if they were that secure, why did they cut us daughters off that loop?

I found myself in limbo ~ a shadowy twilight zone ~ where nothing was ever clear or certain. It was always a no-win, Catch-22 trap. Coming at me from all sides were real slam-bang clashes: modern versus traditional, individuality versus collective identity, expression versus suppression, male versus female, Chinese versus native, age versus youth. I desperately needed a way to resolve or integrate these contradictions. Each cried for a synthesis. But there was no one to help me or point the way.

I felt the sea closing in. I was in the water, thrashing about to keep from drowning. I began to lose focus on parental goals. I felt I did not have what it took to be a medical doctor. How could I do vivisection on live cats and dogs? I could not stomach that. Bleeding hearts become faint hearts. I did not have the guts, Mother concluded, I was weak. One must endure the unpleasant. No pain, no gain. Unlike the three sisters who trod the safe, high road of filial obedience (they took up medicine), I was lost in the depths, defiant and alone. Only Kenneth was with me; he was the only one who believed in me when even I did not.

Without someone to advise me, I decided on a second best choice: economics as a college major. At least it had something to do with money. Fifth Sister decided on Fine Arts. Both of us knew making "deviant" choices like these did not help rid us of demons, not even when I copped a *magna cum laude* and later, earned two graduate degrees in the social sciences. I knew at bottom Mother was disappointed. I had not scaled the heights. I was just doing Second-best things, and did not deserve "the biggest chair."

Those who went to medical school received the best of everything. Food was literally taken out of the mouths of the unfavored and put into those of the favored. The technique was to punish and to motivate, goading the unfavored to do more and better.

When we were young, Eldest Sister and I developed a *contra-mundum* mindset, us against all. Sharing of fates drew us closer to each other. As I grew older, I became increasingly jealous of her. We were both poppies in the field, standing tall and proud. To let her stay lush and full, she needed to be fertilized ~ I did not. She was a sophomore Pre-Med., and I a freshman BA when our parents gave her a car. I was expected to hitch a ride with her, walk, use public transport, or ride with others. Eldest Sister was on track toward a medical degree. She needed all the nurturing, for she would be the first to achieve our parents' ambitions.

One day I saw her bright-red *Beetle* parked in the garage. On an angry impulse I sneaked it out. Wanting to show off, I picked up a few of my classmates and drove around, stopping at a convenience store. As I waited in the car, two pot-bellied ruffians, menacing and foul-breathed, appeared out of nowhere. One took the driver's side, and the other the opposite side. The one on my side stuck a gun into my face and pulled me out. Then they drove off, leaving me on the curb. I groped my way home and collapsed. My head was spinning, my palms sweaty.

Manila and suburbs at that time were virtual free-fire zones. Lawlessness and crime was rife: muggings, hold-ups, burglaries, murders, kidnappings were daily affairs. The gun was the law; almost everyone, openly or not, carried a gun. Shoot-outs settled political and personal feuds. Manila was awash with blood.

That evening a telephone call came, demanding money. Naively, I persuaded Father to go instead to the police. They demanded a stiff price. Like a good Chinese, Father paid. Since insuring cars was not common in the country, our cars were not insured. We never recovered the car; I never recovered.

Mother never allowed me to forget. She said, because of my headstrong attitudes I took what was not mine, and *caused* the carnapping. To Mother I *intended* it to happen.

"Silence! You are without shame! Trouble with you, your head is as hard as *pili* nut."

"I did not mean... " I started to say...

"A devil girl with a willful mind is evil. Brings nothing but bad luck to her family," Mother exclaimed, squelching my feeble attempts to explain. Then she went on to lay the blame on me for a recent burglary in our house.

The carnapping incident eroded my sanity like a deadly virus. Believing I was the source of all the turmoil in the family, I became hypersensitive and paranoid, all tied up in knots. Fully internalizing a deep sense of shame, I left home. I walked and walked, going nowhere and everywhere. I woke up to strange voices and acrid smell of antiseptic, unable to move. I had been sedated. I felt suffocated, nauseated. Tests, electro-encephalograms, brain scans, drugs, more drugs ~ I ran the gauntlet.

What the medics injected into my system altered my biochemistry and mind. Acne grew in profusion on my face and back. Eating became compulsive. I was stuffing an angry heart. Mindlessly, I lost valuable things, like the 24-carat gold chain necklace with a crucifix Mother gave me for my birthday. Everyone grew angrier and angrier with me. And I grew angrier and angrier with everyone.

In China, I was told, a person like me faced brain surgery, confinement in an institution, or a long-term regimen of compulsory hard labor. If tagged a sociopath I would be resocialized by less than subtle means. Emotional disorder of any type was a capitalist reactionary disease, a frivolous luxury of the idle. Harsh social sanctions for deviants were the norm in China, in today's China as well as old China.

Why did not any of my other sisters have such "imaginary" problems? Why only I? In the first place, I had no business being depressed in a land of plenty. I had all the creature comforts. To anguish was to indulge in unproductive, idle activity. Soul-searching was a sheer waste of time; it did not produce food on the table or cash in the pocket. It was a luxury one could ill afford.

In the second place, to go to a stranger like a psychiatrist or therapist to discuss personal, family matters was an act of disloyalty that betrayed the family honor. Better for me to fall sick and die than for the family to lose face. Sociologists, psychologists, psychiatrists, family counselors, therapists, social workers ~ all would starve in China or put on trial for subversion. Dung must not be stirred; the stink only gets worst.

In the third place, why not follow *wu-wei* ~ by doing nothing you do something. By not talking about a problem, by not thinking about it, it will go away. No action was the best action. Silence, stillness, lest lurking devils get ideas to stir up more mischief.

I never understood this way of thinking until much later. Doing Asian studies, trying to penetrate the "Chinese mind," I found myself leaving the bright lands of Newton and Aristotle and groping my way into the murky abodes of wicked demons and snake spirits. It was a universe not of natural, physical forces set in motion by a wise and all-knowing Prime Mover. Rather, it was a swirling, roiling mass of contending spirits, a Manichaean world ~ a never-ending guerrilla war between malevolent and benevolent shades. The two "worlds" often intermingled, humans becoming victims ~ or participants ~ in the melee.

Chinese thinking and imagery is always concrete. For example, "good" as an abstract moral judgment is expressed by combining the character for "mother" with that for "child;" obviously mother-cum-child is the essence of goodness. Again, "sun" together with "moon" produces the concept of "bright." Maybe this explains why the Chinese usually personalize. A live person, or one that is putatively alive ~ such as a ghost (an ancestor), a demon or spirit ~ causes things to happen. An impersonal, neutral cause? Never. Whatever happens cannot but be the result of an intention ~ benign or malign. Only humans, gods, and demons can have intentions. There is no such thing as an accident caused by impersonal forces; someone must always be causing the event.

Thus I ~ second daughter ~ was the cause of mishaps in the family. I ~ a young devil girl ~ was willfully bringing them about. I was the black pig of the family. An uncontrollable force deflected me toward strange, aberrant behaviors. I became totally non-compliant, negative, chronically belligerent, verbally aggressive. When there was no one to aggress against, I turned on myself. It was a wild ride from one disordered state to another. I was hitting out blindly, irrationally, becoming more and more marginal to a family that itself was marginal to clan, to race, to community.

Kenneth never agonized with me in my psychic turmoil, my angst. Neither was he bothered by problems of self-esteem, self-doubt, self-pity, and self-destructiveness. Furthest from his mind were dark suicidal thoughts such as I had. In his unconcern, he succored me. He became my anchor, my pillar of strength. If any of my human friends ~

well meaning though they might be ~ had come to me and offered support, I would have immediately suspected them of ulterior motives. I did not want to be patronized. I did not care to be understood. None could have, anyway. What I needed were reassuring signs, *n'importe quoi*, of genuine, unaffected sincerity. The way Kenneth treated me. No put-ons, no questions, no commentaries, no criticisms, no recriminations, no guilt, no punishment. Just devotion, a wagging tail, a wet tongue. Even when I turned ill-tempered and ugly, insufferable and impossible to live with, Kenneth was there for me, unconditionally, unambiguously. And he asked nothing in return.

By giving me no feedback, he was my ultimate therapist. But at the time I was not fully aware of all the things Kenneth meant to me, least of all that this pet was really my therapist.

And so it was *wu wei* that led to a resolution. Kenneth was my avenue of escape, easing me out of an imposed reality into the beginnings of a world of my own making. I simply repressed my agonies. And turned to alternatives: earn higher degrees, hoping to gain the approval I craved. I won a scholarship to pursue graduate studies at *Todai*. Mother promptly said that because I had become more filial, less headstrong, I had turned bad luck into good luck.

Going to Japan was a break. Japan had become an Asian economic model of growth. An island nation with a population whose greatest asset was an unswerving political will and loyalty to Emperor and nation, Japan rose from the ashes of war to become second only to the United States, surpassing Europe and the Soviet Union. Going there to study promised to reverse my misfortune.

Perhaps now I could begin deserving the biggest chair in the family. Little did I know that Japanese students bore fiercer demons on their backs. If they did not live up to expectations, often they had no other recourse but to commit *hara-kiri* (known to the Japanese as *seppuku*). Dedication like this, plus a tightly-knit polity, made for an economic and industrial leviathan known to scholars as Japan, Inc.

Then one day I realized fanaticism was not my cup of tea. In an overseas call to Father, I blurted out a desire to come home. If he read that as an admission of failure, Father was careful to sidetrack the issue, by talking about Kenneth instead. He said that Kenneth was getting fat, too fat. I asked about Kenneth's pal, Pierre. Wasn't he playing with and exercising Kenneth? When Father abruptly changed the subject I became suspicious. This time, I insisted on a reply. There was a long silent pause, a nervous hesitation. Finally the truth came.

A delivery van had come in through the gates, and left. Nobody noticed that Pierre was missing. What dog-owners in the Philippines dreaded had happened: Pierre had been dognapped. Dogs, especially breed dogs and household pets, were targets for dognapping. Their flesh were claimed to be more tender and tastier. Dogmeat aficionados paid big money for them.

I shook with anger. Why weren't the maids more careful? Who was to blame? The trusting, quiet, good-natured Pierre, who we thought was mute because he never barked until he got to be much older, was gone.

Pierre's fate brought vividly back the memory of a dog, its legs tied together and stuffed into a burlap sack. I was walking to school that day when, on a sidestreet I heard a dog yelping and screaming. Then I saw this half-naked man beating the sack with a heavy stick as the dog thrashed about. With both hands, the man flailed harder and faster, as the panicked cries rose to a high pitch, until they began to die down. It was like a human scream. Unlike Pythagoras, I had no way of stopping him. I cupped my hands over my ears and shut my eyes. I could not bear it. Heart racing, knees shaking, I moved closer. The sack was motionless by this time, though I could hear a faint moan. I pleaded with the brute in his native tongue to put an end to the suffering, not to let it drag on. Turning, pole in hand, grinning idiotically like a madman, he shuffled towards me. His sweat smelled of wet dog ~ those who eat dogs smell like a wet dog. Pointing the stick at me, he snarled, mockingly:

"Tonight, come for the *azucena*. (*Aso* is Tagalog for dog; *cena* is dinner. *Azucena* is a native flower) Slow death, taste better."

I scented danger. This character cannot be trifled with. Trembling, not out of fear but from a sense of helplessness, I fled.

My thoughts came back to Pierre. Dear God, I prayed, if he had to go, I hope he went quickly.

Shortly after, I left Japan and came home with a bag-full of rationalizations: the playing field was not level, I was *gaijin* with not enough proficiency in *Nippongo*, a woman, and too young. The imponderable seniority rule meant waiting in line until the more senior candidate, the one ahead of me, had completed all requirements. *Hara-kiri* was furthest from my mind; *wu-wei* was far better.

Japan unleashed me to new possibilities. Returning to my parent's house, the choke collar was quickly slipped back around my neck, this time even more tightly. I made a bold decision: to leave home and rent my own apartment. Thoroughly displeased, my parents never set foot in the apartment. Good unmarried Chinese girls stayed home with their parents.

With Kenneth at my side, I buckled down to earning a Masters degree. With this degree under my belt, I went on a scholarship to England to further my graduate studies. I still had my eyes on "the biggest chair."

Eldest Sister had become a research doctor at the St. Thomas Hospital in London, after earning an MSc. from the London School of Hygiene and Tropical Diseases. I suspected Mother was happy about my going to England because she hoped I could persuade Eldest Sister to snap out of a fantasy mode that included winning a Nobel Prize. Mother wanted Eldest Sister to enter clinical practice in some American hospital, instead of writing non-lucrative academic articles on immunology in the British *Lancet*.

I looked forward to seeing Eldest Sister again.

The entire family, including Kenneth, saw me off at the airport. Looking unconcerned, he ambled about, tail erect, proudly displaying his lion-clip. Strangers stopped, fawning over him, but he wasn't impressed. When it came time, I lifted him up to kiss him goodbye. His mane, which I had carefully brushed back and garnished with a blue ribbon, still smelled of the talcum powder I had generously sprinkled on it after his bath. His eyes shone and seemed to say, "Don't take too long, old girl. We still have lots of things to do together." As I walked towards Gate 11, his scent lingered on.

That was the last I saw of Kenneth. My parents took him in again. I had no choice. British law required a six-month quarantine to protect against animal diseases of the Continent.

Some years later, Kenneth slipped quietly away in his sleep. He was sixteen. Towards the end, Father wrote, Kenneth had become almost blind from cataracts and started bumping into furniture. I'm sure if eyeglasses were made for dogs, my parents would have gotten him one. He hung on as long as he could, waiting for me to come back for him.

I never was able to say a final goodbye, to tell him how much I missed him, how incomplete my life was without him, to ask for his forgiveness. The month that Kenneth passed on was the month my husband and I arrived in Paris. Immediately I arranged for him to join us. It was too late.

We never really parted. In one incarnation after another, he always managed to slip back into my life. The first time was in the unlikely guise of a French mutt in Paris, my introduction to the privileged canines of Europe. There, I became leashed to a dog, not the other way around, and I didn't mind it one bit. And when the second Kenneth passed on, he came back once more in the guise of an ailing Jack Russell terrier in America.

Today, whenever I tuck ET a.k.a Kenneth 3rd to sleep in his well-cushioned bed, and smother him with kisses, the air is redolent with the scent of baby powder.

6

TURFA SHEEHAN SULAIKA

S he halted abruptly, lifting up her narrow head and long
sharp snout, slant eyes transfixed at a Piper Cub cutting
across the sky. Without warning, she launched herself after the plane
with the blazing speed of a cheetah, outrunning cars on the road. She
moved effortlessly, rippling forward with sheer elegance and
smoothness. It was a breathtaking display of kinetic beauty. Her sinewy
body undulated under a silky paprika-brown coat; long ears flapped
loose and free. Feathery fringes on ears and long legs, and feathered
tip of her tail quivering in the wind, she bounded over the terrain like
a regatta-boat in full sail, pennants all a-flutter.

Suddenly a car came bearing down. Oh My God! I stood
paralyzed. If she crossed the vehicle's path, she would instantly be hit!
Fortunately, her momentum carried her past the present danger and

onto a spacious grassy island. After some distance on it she stopped, winded. She had mistaken the airplane for a falcon.

"The royal dog of Egypt" ~ depicted in the hieroglyphs of the ancient Egyptians and said to be the model for the sphinx ~ reputedly went back 10,000 years as a breed. Persian poets described the Saluki "as old as time, swift as a split second." Because of its phenomenal speed on desert sand, Egyptians and later the Arabs used it for hunting gazelles, the fastest of antelopes. Pharaohs rode to the chase with falcons on their leather-clad wrists and saluki running alongside untethered. Today it is used the same way but only for sport, most of the time in tandem with a trained falcon. While in flight, the bird points out the prey to the dog by some signal, launching it into unerring pursuit.

In the old days, the saluki was not permitted to be sold. It could only be acquired as a gift, or as a donation for important occasions. Generally, Moslems consider dogs *haram*, forbidden because they are supposed to be unclean. However, the saluki is the exception; it is the only breed freely allowed in the tents of sheiks. Moslems believe Allah sent the saluki to them. Among the Pharaonic Egyptians, the saluki favorites were often mummified along with them.

Belonging to the greyhound family, the saluki is capable of pursuing its prey at fifty miles an hour in short bursts. It runs down the gazelle and breaks its back, or simply holds it down until the hunter catches up on a camel or horse to take over. In short sprints, it is faster than the greyhound and superior in strength. Fortunately for the breed, its headstrong, willful nature has kept it out of the racetrack.

Our saluki was a wedding gift to us.

I was the first to marry. Still a graduate student, on my way to a career, getting married was another unfilial act. Marrying a non-Chinese was another act of deviancy.

To Mother it didn't matter that he was a distinguished scholar, a Harvard MA and Ph.D.; or that he was a Dean, an Academic Vice-President, a Chancellor at the prestigious State University. Unfortunately he was *huan-na* (barbarian), almost twice my age, divorced, and well, not stinking rich. It dismayed her.

Not until after we had all moved out of Asia to America did Mother begin to be reconciled to my marriage. Now it is she who reminds me that marriage is a lifetime commitment that needs to be constantly affirmed, no matter how difficult it gets. The *li* of social order should be observed under all circumstances. No marriage is made in heaven, she would say.

My being Chinese stirred up misgivings among his kin. My being second wife made me a mere courtesan in their eyes. From the beginning, the cards were stacked against me. However, Kenneth and Sulaika were there to provide the unreserved love I needed at this point, without asking anything in return. They kept my cup full.

He was my graduate school professor. Popular with students, his lectures were never regurgitated stuff, and best of all, he gave high grades. When I received my degree the following year, I invited the Professor to a party a close friend ~ a paraplegic Jewish-American journalist ~ threw to celebrate. He came with his violin and took my breath away.

Named after the Nicaraguan Liberation poet, Ruben Dario, his was a turbulent, event-filled childhood: the Great Depression, Japanese occupation, Liberation by the Americans, and Philippine Independence. I never got to know his parents. They were long gone when I stepped into his life. He recalled a kindly mother whom he loved marketing with, toting her shopping bags; and a stern, autocratic father. His mother, ten years younger than his father, was a student-nurse when his father was staff-surgeon in the General Hospital and professor in the University's College of Medicine. After five children, a progressive illness confined her to a wheel chair. She never got well.

His father was something of a revolutionary, a rebel and freethinker in the medieval and rigidly Catholic society under Spanish colonial rule. As the American civil government took over from the Spanish, he won a scholarship to study in the United States. Graduating with a medical degree from the University of Illinois, he returned to the Philippines to pioneer in public health service. He became a personal physician to a rising political leader, who went on to become the first President of the Philippines. At the peak of his career, he left the capital to become a Director of a Provincial Hospital.

His father's younger brother, also a graduate of medicine from an American university, returned to become the first reconstructive surgeon in the Philippines. He had become a U.S. citizen. Settling down in Davao on the southern island of Mindanao, he set up his own hospital. In the last days of the Pacific War, as the American Liberation Forces stormed back island by island, an Imperial Japanese Army unit massacred the entire family ~ down to the last child and maid ~ in a paroxysm of murder, looting, rapine before retreating into the jungle. Ironically, many of his patients were Japanese civilians from a nearby colony that had existed since the 16th Century.

Schooled by the Jesuits, my husband majored in English Literature and Philosophy and at age 22, was appointed Instructor in Logic and Philosophy. After Harvard, he turned down a teaching job at Smith College to return to serve his country. For the next twenty years he taught sociology. Among his philosophy students was the political leader Ninoy Aquino, whose assassination led to the toppling of the Marcos dictatorship.

He helped a Jewish-American student from New Jersey get admitted into the veterinary school of the University. While in a kibbutz in Israel, the Goldmans had fallen in love with the saluki breed and brought back a pair to the United States, the same pair they brought with them to the Philippines.

I grew exceedingly fond of Charley, their male, all-black saluki. Walking him on a leash made me feel so puny next to his bulk. He ambled along like a zombie, turning his head occasionally as if to stare at me, but from a sightless glass eye. Behind an impassive mien was passionate loyalty. The Goldmans told me about Charley's heroic deed that saved them in a skiing accident. Charley's mate produced a litter of four. The Goldmans gave us a female puppy to bless our marriage. We were probably the first in the country to own a saluki.

An Arab hound should have a royal Arab name. Casting about for an appropriate name, I turned to my husband's colleague who had professed Islam at Cornell and upon returning to the Philippines become the leading Muslim scholar in the country. His father, a Syrian officer in the Turkish Army, had come to the Philippines when the Ottoman Empire fell, to seek his fortune in the Philippines, and had married a native girl.

He suggested Turfa Sheehan Sulaika, Arabic for "luxurious star saluki." I nicknamed her "Laika."

Luxurious she certainly was. Without a by-your-leave, she appropriated our brand-new wicker sofa in the living room and converted it into her siesta bed. On it she slept for hours, often on her back, long lanky hind legs spread-eagled, front-legs sticking up in the air. Whenever she voluptuously stretched her fawn torso on the cushions, almond eyes demurely eyeing us, I thought she fancied herself a princess from Arabia.

A star she certainly was. A star of a thief, as cunning in evading detection as Ali Baba's forty thieves. With her wide peripheral vision, and height ~ 26 inches high at the shoulder ~ no meat on kitchen counter or dining table was safe. One afternoon I saw her surreptitiously sniff her way across the kitchen floor to the counter, and then, *toute-de-suite* in one fell swoop snatch a piece of roast meat, quickly heading towards a get-away. Gotcha! Watching from behind a door, I emerged to confront her. Caught red-handed, stolen goods between jaws, she acted with nary a flinch, feigning innocence. Feathered ears pulled back, she looked askance at Kenneth, as though he was the real culprit. Kenneth? Ha! Too aristocratic to do such a thing, he always had to be coaxed and cajoled into eating. He was too haughty to stoop to such a low-life crime. Scheming was an art Sulaika kept practicing. Practice makes perfect.

I am a believer in the old saw about dogs being sociable, unlike cats who are solitary. Sulaika belied the conventional wisdom that all dogs are hung up on human company. Even as a puppy, she preferred to be by herself. At the roofed back stoop of the modest cottage we rented at the outskirts of Manila, she spent long, pensive moments in solitude, gazing eastward far to the distant hills of the Sierra Madre range. If she espied circling eagles high above us, she sat unmoving, her eyes intently following their soaring glides and aerial gyrations until they disappeared. At dusk when all around was already dark but the sky was still a shimmering azure, and winged creatures could still be espied aloft, Sulaika sat sphinx-like, alert to the slightest swaying of tree branches or the faintest whisper of breeze. Was she trying to fathom the strange world of the lush tropics, so different from the empty, featureless desserts of her ancestral villages ?

Like Sulaika, we soon found ourselves uprooted, through no choice of our own. These were the years of the Marcos conjugal dictatorship, when that infamous couple systematically despoiled and morally devastated the entire country. Whatever they touched they corrupted. Since their object was to incessantly amass personal wealth, far beyond what they could possibly use in their lifetimes, they needed total power and control of all resources. These included the intellectual resources represented by the leading lights of the country. To exploit their talents and lend the Marcos era an aura of legitimacy they had to be co-opted. This was done by corrupting them whenever possible. Those they could not corrupt had no place in the country.

It was not easy to resist the Marcos blandishments. Few, even among the most morally upright, could. To resist was to become targets of vicious and vindictive attacks.

At an academic conference in Singapore, my husband pointed out glaring contradictions in Marcos' "New Society" such as a rise in the Philippine agricultural production side-by-side a marked deterioration in nutritional levels for the majority of the population. It drew the attention of Marcos' hatchetmen. When, ominously, he was "invited" to a midnight debriefing by the notorious head of military intelligence, the message was clear. Foreign Minister Carlos P. Romulo, a close friend, quickly arranged for his departure from the country. Not a moment too soon, for already his name had appeared on a list, drawn up by Marcos' intelligence goons, of persons to whom exit permits were to be denied.

He went on sabbatical leave and joined me in England. There we lived on my small scholarship stipend. It was, at first I believed, a temporary pause in our lives. I entrusted Kenneth and Sulaika to my parents. I had no other recourse. In the U.K., the six-month quarantine of animals made it impossible to bring them along. Little did I realize I was moving into a new chapter of my life. We had left for good.

Soon I was immersed in graduate study at the University of Manchester. However, out there was a country, storied and splendid, beckoning us to explore. Seduced by the idea, I took stock of our thin resources and persuaded ourselves to buy a car.

Paying cash for what Mancunian mechanics would later call "British rubbish," we became proud new owners of an old, battered, maroon Avenger, sweet-talked into buying it by a statistics instructor. It was all we could afford. It had 95,000 miles on it and appeared to be barely clinging to life. Body parts were beginning to rust and corrode under the paint, engine components to fail. Incredibly, it proved to be an over-achiever, as if driven by a demon all its own. On motorways it quickly sprinted to 80 mph and stayed there, the gas pedal nestling into a well-worn groove. Defying speeding lorries for space and thundering past newer, flashier vehicles, it promised to be a dependable transport in heavy rain, pea-soup fog, or blinding sleet.

Until finally, one day, just before dusk, it coughed to a stop on a lonely winding road at Exmoor. Glowering beauty and contoured grace line upon unrelieved line of dark horizons with misshapen oak trees, thorn coppices, and beech hedges enveloped us like a shroud. Soon the blackness was Stygian. I was grateful it was not raining, just the normal English gray overcast.

I remembered seeing through the haze a small thatch-roofed cottage with ivy clinging to its walls, under a lonely row of trees a mile back. We hurried to it on foot and timidly knocked on the door. After a long wait, sensing eyes peering out from behind window drapes, a gaunt man, bent almost double, opened the door. He had dark half-circles under his sunken eyes and a hook nose, looking for all the world like Charles Dickens' Fagin, or "the old woman who lived in a shoe," or the witch in Hansel and Gretel. Our imaginations conjured up characters evoked by the foreboding setting. He did not betray any emotion, not even surprise, to see us at his door. Listening attentively to our plight, he said "Just a moment, please" and then disappeared into the house. Minutes passed; my heart started sinking. Here we were, stranded, in the middle of a wild English moor at night, facing the prospect of sleeping in our immobile car surrounded by all that blackness. It was beginning to be nippy; the cold fingers of autumn were probing through my thin jacket.

Finally, a rickety car came rattling out the back of the house. Waving his hand, he signaled us to jump in. It was a long and winding road to the village, seven miles away. When he learned I was Chinese, he turned to look at me, his eyes lighting up. Pure-blooded?

"Of course, sir, I am Han, a pedigreed Chinese," I said, stepping on imaginary brakes as the road took a sudden turn.

It turned out he and his wife were once missionaries in China. He asked for, and we gave him, our names and address. We never met his wife; at first I thought he was single or a widower.

The tiny village was humble; its main street a handful of small shops selling the basics. He drove us to a little farmhouse on a narrow street just outside the village. As we waited in his car, our Good

Samaritan talked to a middle-aged man working on a lorry. In a little while, a young man hopped into a tow vehicle and headed out for our stalled Avenger. As there were no hotels or other lodging facilities arrangements were made for us to stay overnight at the farmhouse. Then our Good Samaritan bade us good night.

Soon, people of the village started dropping in. A retired schoolteacher invited us all, including the farm mechanic's family, to "share a meal" of steak and kidney pie at her house. Our contribution of a fifths of scotch, purchased at the tax-free airport, which I always carried on long trips to help me sleep, sparked a lively exchange, ranging from British politics to what made scotch superior to any other whisky. It reminded me of the hospitality and friendliness of village people in Asia. How universally alike they all are.

"Me missus needs us at the barn. But don't believe 'em working class elites of the North," our farmer-mechanic friend said, squelching the opinions I parroted from the Mancunian scholars about how Margaret Thatcher would ruin the British suprastructure, etc.

I walked behind, trying to match his giant steps. At the barn, nature wove her magic before my eyes. For the first time, I saw a lambkin being born. And as if to preserve this moment for me, I saw a troop of lean hounds standing by, reminding me of Sulaika.

"Aye, luv, whippets are snapdogs. Go see 'em race in the mining towns of the Northeast, near Manchester. Right popular with the betting young 'uns, and good sport for 'em that hunt," the bearded man said, smelling of sweet malts and bitter hops.

The following morning, I woke to the aroma of bangers and eggs sizzling in lard. Our Good Samaritan returned, announcing that our Avenger was ready. Thirty-five Pounds Sterling for everything ~ towing, parts, labor and even board and lodging! Thanking him profusely, I asked his name.

"It's secret," he said tersely, his deep-set eyes looking intently into mine. I thought he whispered the words. I assumed, then, that he did not wish to reveal his identity. I did not press the matter.

Three months later in our Manchester apartment we received a package through the mail containing three pocketbooks by C.S. Lewis. On a scrap of a paper torn from a notebook page were the words "With apologies for the cover design. Collins (the publisher) must be crazy."

There was a handwritten letter written in typical English script on lined notebook paper with three holes on the left-hand side, a quarter of the paper neatly torn out. The note read (I reproduce it exactly as it was worded):

> Ison Cottage
> Wheddon Cross
> Minehead, Somerset
> 6/5/79
>
> Dear Friends:
>
> I remember our short time together with pleasure and thankfulness. My wife and I felt it a reall privelage to give that little help and beleive that our meeting was of the Lord 'designed of the Lord.' Our fellowship is with the Father & with the Son Jesus Christ. How good when this extends to visitors from the antipodes.
>
> Would you accept as a gift, a small gift, these books by way of remembrance. You are doubtless very busy so please do not spend your precious time to reply.
>
> If you find them helpful we are rewarded. I long to communicate & count it a privelage to have this oportunity with you, and do pray that the Lord will be with you both.
>
> Yours Sincerely
>
> Lewis Secrett

So that was the secret!

It was not until fifteen years later, after a beloved Borzoi was murdered in a hate crime, did I unravel the secret and meaning of this chance encounter. The gift of C.S. Lewis was to teach me to be at peace with myself as well as with those who caused me pain. After all these years, Lewis Secrett once more became my good samaritan, reaching out across time and space to comfort me.

Upon completion of my studies, we left for New York City, and shortly after, Paris. All this while I felt keenly the absence of Kenneth and Sulaika. Now in Paris, with my husband's appointment at Unesco, I could at last arrange for Kenneth to join us. But it was too late. He had passed on.

As for Sulaika, she was aircargoed to O'Hare Airport, to live with Third Sister's family in suburban Chicago. Fifth Sister, still unmarried, lived with them. We all agreed that Sulaika would be far happier in a house with a yard than in a cramped Paris apartment with no view.

I visited Sulaika often in Chicago. Always it was a bittersweet reunion. The first time, she stood still, her black-rimmed eyes looking intently into mine, apparently reaching into her memories. I waited. A tinge of remorse stabbed through me. She looked dispirited and somewhat disoriented. Ignoring me, she walked past me to the basement, to join Lincoln, Fourth Sister's white poodle flown in from Manila to keep Sulaika company. I felt her rebuffing me for deserting her.

I guess she never really adjusted to her new life: from the warm, humid tropics to the bone-chilling cold of the windy city. Life in the First World was bland and monotonous. She preferred the free wheeling and anarchic lifestyle of the Third World, free of animal control rules, leash laws, dog pounds, dogcatchers, and liability suits. Leftover scraps were better tasting than dry, factory-made dog food and mass-produced canned mush masquerading as meat.

Two years passed. Fifth Sister married. Despite Third Sister's protest, Fifth Sister took Sulaika to live with her in another suburb of Chicago. This act ~ and many others involving pets and other "possessions" ~ developed into a real donnybrook in the family. A gate lifted and released a flood of passions, threatening to drown us in endless bickering.

One afternoon in Paris a year later my telephone rang. It was Fifth Sister, incoherent, crying hysterically. After a few seconds, I gathered something terrible had happened to Sulaika. In the closed confines of their house, her menstruation odor had made things unpleasant. They brought her to the vet to be spayed. On the operating table she died. She was only five years old.

The autopsy showed that too much anesthesia was injected. The veterinarian failed to exercise the necessary caution with a breed that had too little body fat to withstand the chemical shock. Was he just incompetent? Or was he negligent and careless because my family were obviously immigrants?

The veterinarian finally agreed to settle, by paying Sulaika's market price. But no amount of monetary compensation could ever make up for her loss. For me she was irreplaceable.

Sulaika was the first pet I lost in America. Was her death an omen, so early in the family's sojourn in this new land?

Fifth Sister had Sulaika's remains cremated. Today her ashes are in a Chinese urn, on a coffee table in the family room of our house at the foothills of the Appalachians. It stands beside framed photographs of the family, where everyone is smiling in harmony and joy.

PHASE TWO: PARIS & EUROPE
(1978–1988)

7

KENNETH II & CAMILLE

The *guardien* stood awkwardly on the landing, head bent down low to something he was cradling in his arms. I was used to his unshaven presence and that of his buxom wife. They were always hovering about whenever I came down from our second-floor apartment to sally forth to the wonders and perils of the streets of Paris. This morning I was up earlier than usual, to go to the open-air market at the Marché de l'Avenue President Wilson at the Place d'Alma a few blocks away. I wanted to get my pick of the best *canard de barbarie* and the freshest *lotte*.

The two usually ignored my goings and comings, except for an occasional "*Bon jour Madame! ça va bien?*" More than that would be a bit too intrusive for the residents of this *quartier*. This time I felt he was out to intercept me. Stealing a sly glance at me, he chuckled and grinned, exposing wine-stained teeth.

"*Regardez le petit chien!*" he said in a friendly but gruff voice.

It was a cute puppy, cordovan brown but nondescript. I stopped to pet it, thinking he just wanted to show it to me. "*Quel mignon!*" I cooed. He held it out to me.

"*Tenez,*" he urged, exhaling alcohol (at eight in the morning!). I stood dumbfounded, at first unable to react. Still struggling with my kindergarten French, just a month in Paris, my husband and I were still settling in. We were expecting Camille at Charles de Gaulle airport the following month, flown 10,000 miles across the Asian continent. Camille, a sister's miniature Poodle, was a swap for our saluki that was flown to Chicago, where Third and Fifth Sisters lived.

In my confusion, I hesitated. That was my mistake. I was hooked. The *guardien* had caught me at a vulnerable moment. Grinning like a Cheshire cat, he put the furry thing in my hands. Sensing my uncertainty, he immediately said ~ and suddenly I understood every word ~ that if I did not take it he would have to turn it over to the dog pound. It did not take much to sway my decision. Still I was torn by doubt.

Here was this *guardien*, whose job was to shoo away strange presences, urging me to adopt the intruder he found that morning snuggling contentedly on a pair of soft slippers on the landing. Somebody had left it there. The couple could not keep it in their tiny closet of an apartment on the ground floor. They thought of me, the newcomer in the building.

I said *Non merci, Monsieur!* No, no, no. Why should I bother with a foundling from the street?

"*Alors, le petit chien sera mis a mort,*" he declared matter-of-factly.

"Be put to sleep? A healthy puppy! Why?" I turned to my husband who had joined me.

My mind flashed back to Central Park, New York, a year ago. It was a sunny autumn afternoon. We had been jogging. On our way back to our apartment-hotel at Southgate Towers, across from Madison

Square Garden, I noticed a big black dog following us. At first, I did not make much of it. Then out of the corner of my eye, I noticed the dog stop at the corner, watching us cross to the other side of the street. He continued trudging in the same direction on the opposite sidewalk. We quickened our strides and then pulled up. He too stopped, watching us. At that point, the suspicion dawned that this Manhattan denizen had singled us out from the motley crowd in this machine-cum-human jungle. Black dog, bad omen, I thought to myself. In the blooming, buzzing confusion of midtown Manhattan, with drivers and russian-rouletting pedestrians I worried he might get hit or run over. However, he expertly threaded his way through the horridly tricky traffic, crossing streets only on the "Walk" signal.

When we finally arrived at our apartment-hotel and turned to go in, he stationed himself at the entrance. I looked him over closely ~ he was a Labrador-mix. Patting his head, I stroked his deep chest and muscular neck. How much I missed my dogs. He lowered his head, somewhat apprehensively. Then his brows crinkled, his ears folded back. Hunkering down so I could search into his eyes, I read a plea. I quickly sent my husband up to get food and make some telephone calls. A few minutes later he came back with a defeated look; none of our suburban friends were home. We had no one to give him temporary shelter or adopt him. It was getting dark. Well maybe, I could sneak him past the front desk. And sweet-talk the hotel clerk into bending the rules. Negative. A firm No, sorry ma'am. When I went out again the dog was gone. I felt a pang of guilt and frustration. Here I was, helpless to act. The Chinese believe a dog that comes to your door is the bearer of good fortune.

Here in Paris another dog was knocking at my door. My karma ~ or good fortune? ~ was catching up with me. Just for a moment, my husband and I stood irresolute. Then, without saying a word to each other we turned back into our apartment, the puppy in my arms.

That was the beginning of the second phase of my life with dogs. I named him Kenneth, convinced he was Kenneth re-born and come back into my life.

Unlike the first, this Kenneth did not look like much. But after a while I discerned a mind working in ways I never thought possible in a a dog. Like a Russian doll, his was a layered personality with more mood-swings, preferences, aversions, prejudices, and quirks than any dog I had ever known. I began to care less about how he looked and more about what lurked behind that plain, ordinary exterior. Where the old Kenneth was a manikin, this one was a riddle wrapped inside an enigma ~ with complex workings that had many a puckish streak in them. Where the old Kenneth was a prissy aristocrat, this one was a raunchy peasant ~ given to occasional outbursts of ill temper. Be that as it may, this cunning rascal of a foundling never took a back seat; he always demanded, or was given, star billing. Very French, very Parisian. Irrepressible, irresistible.

It was amazing how he overleapt his sheer plainness. When Camille, an annato wisp of a *petite caniche*, joined us in Paris, Kenneth continued to hog the show. He never failed to provoke laughter or cries of *petit cochon!* with his corkscrew of a tail. As he gorged on the delicacies conned from neighborhood *bouchers*, *fromagers*, and *boulangers*, he began to bloat like a pot-bellied porker. Or like a termite queen. No one knew what breed he was, or what hybrid. Nor did I care. I had completely fallen under his spell.

So it was in Paris ~ of all places ~ that I got into the world of strays and mongrels, the underworld of dogdom. Kenneth was living proof that randomly-bred dogs have a unique intelligence absent in most pure-breeds. Is it perhaps that they come from a larger, more diversified gene pool? Or have more complex brains like those of animals in the wild?

Here in Paris I became tightly leashed to a dog, and I did not mind it one bit. His persona engaged me, totally. He took center-stage, pulling me along to his level of sagacity or into situations I never imagined I would ever be. He opened doors, unlocked gates. He conspired to bring both of us into the secret recesses of Paris society. His presence let me get to know more about French ways. He was a whiz at dissolving the antipathy of Parisians toward strangers and evoking friendly reactions, even affection, from most everyone. He became my entrée into Paris life. I was not just another foreigner, another barbarian. To Parisians, I was as human, as civilized as they were, because I came with a dog. Kenneth completed me.

He managed to insinuate himself into practically every one of my activities, even when I did not intend it. How could I not let him? If I ignored him, he would go into his "gi '-me-five" act: squat on his haunches, raise his front paws and claw the air until I took notice. He learned by mimicry: watching me teasingly wave both my hands at him, as though to say goodbye, urging him to do the same. Soon afterwards, whenever he craved attention or wanted to go for a walk, he would go into this act.

I brought him along everywhere: on forays into Galeries Lafayette, Faubourg St. Honoré, picnics at Fontainebleau, jogs at Bois de Boulogne, trail walks at Barbizon, sun-tanning on the *naturiste* beaches of Les Landes, Bateaux Mouche canal-rides down to the Samaritaine, *calvados*-tasting at Honfleur, *degustations* in the country, bargain-hunting at Pigalle, sitting down to a *croque-monsieur* at a *brasserie* or to a *cafe crème* at a favorite bistro. In fancy restaurants, the waitstaff welcomed him with a bowl of water garnished with a sprig of mint. In hotels, staff brought out extra linen for him. At the Chateau du Pré in Amboise, while we breakfasted on croissant, *confiture*, and coffee, Kenneth feasted on *paté* and *jambon*!

His constantly being with me was never much of a problem. Pets are allowed almost everywhere except in supermarkets, churches, museums, and boucheries. Often they enjoy equal ~ if not higher ~ status than children. The average French couple prefers pets to children. (No wonder the population growth rate by natural increase is almost zero.)

This became clear to me while apartment hunting. I did not have Kenneth yet. The realtor asked if I had children. Most proprietors, she said, were negative about children. I said we had none, and then debated with myself about Camille I finally decided to take the bull by the horns and pulled out photographs of my family pets, identifying Camille as the one we were waiting for, who would share the apartment with us. Instantly her sternness dissolved. With a "Pouf!" and a wave of her hand, she dismissed my anxiety with a "*Vous n'avez pas d'problème.*" Landlords, she said, do not object to dogs. Her surly, supercilious manner softened. She no longer saw me as just another uncivilized foreigner; despite my bad accent, I was now French. She even took the trouble of steering me toward another apartment, this one of standing and *caractère*. It was here in this apartment where a lowly mutt wormed his way into my life, thereafter assuming dominion over my stay in Europe.

I remember the time a neighbor and I went for a stroll at the nearby Champs de Mars with Kenneth on a leash. The young Dutch girl, married to a Frenchman from Lille, was pushing her blond, blue-eyed ten-month old baby girl on a stroller. As we waited to cross Pont d'Iéna to get to the Eiffel Tower, an elderly woman peering out of her royal-blue chapeau looked sourly at Kenneth. He was straining on his leash; forepaws splayed out like a duck, impatient to get to the park where he knew he would be unleashed.

The light turned green; Kenneth abruptly dashed forward. The leash looped around my legs and almost sent me sprawling. Unleashed, he ran like a maniac this way and that way, around and through the bushes and flowerbeds. This was like the game of tag he played with young roller-skaters at the Palais du Chaillot, on its broad expanses of concrete and marble. It was where I myself often went roller-skating with Kenneth pulling me along, all twenty pounds of him, helter-skelter. Unleashed, he would take off and join the roller-skaters in games of tag.

"*Délicieux, ta copain. Quelle race est-il?*" she murmured, faintly smiling. She spoke Parisienne. I was mute, unable right off to put my thoughts in correct French. She scrutinized my dog, only a foot high but already full-grown, noting his Dachshund legs, his dainty Poodle paws, his Beauceron muzzle, and his curled up tail. *Peut-être*, a small Swiss mountain dog?

"*Mais la tête, c'est incroyable,*" she exclaimed in wonder. I was not sure what she meant. I was already aware of Kenneth's unusually large head. Perhaps, I thought, she was talking about brain-to-body ratio, about Kenneth's data-processing potential. Indeed his intelligence was awesome, at times frightening, a blend of brilliance and drive ~ more than that of any other dog I had known.

Though she spoke practically no English, and my French was still so-so, Madame Poindron became a good friend. I became a regular guest at tea parties with her bridge partners ~ all elderly ~ at her elegant Avenue de Montaigne apartment. When my parents came to Paris, she invited all of us, including of course, *le petit garçon*, to her place. Kenneth was at his wriggly best, swaying his behind from side to side as if it was part of the piggly-wiggly tail he was trying to wag. His brash manner dissolved any hesitance, and quickly put everyone at ease. In his excitement the ludicrous knot of a tail became a spike giddily pointing upward.

Whenever at these parties I started helping myself to Le Nôtre bonbons and Hèdiard *paté de fruits*, he would go into his clawing-the-air act. Getting no response from me, he then launched his dying-dog act until I caved in and slipped him a tidbit. However, with him around I could never segue into a gourmand mode. His antics kept everyone's attention glued to us. In polite society this could be a problem.

This *bâtard* did what cats do best: seduce humans, climb social ladders. But he was also an incorrigible brat. He would sidle up to a well-dressed woman sitting with legs crossed, slip his termite body under a leg, and then jerk his body ~ and the leg ~ up and down. I did not know whether to laugh or to apologize. Usually I would do both and try to shoo Kenneth away. There was no stopping him. In his own way he was cutting down humans to size, if not humiliating them. As he matured, he did with finesse what he used to do crudely: solicit attention. He would slip his snout into the palm of a receptive hand, and if that brought results ~ a pat, a scratch, or a bit of food ~ he left, contented.

Our first Paris houseguest was my husband's younger sister, a soprano graduate of Curtis Institute, and an opera diva. Emerging unclothed from the shower on her first day, she was startled to see Kenneth quietly squatting, ears cocked, lecherous eyes on her. Kenneth had managed to push open two doors, slip into the bedroom, and then sat in wait, unnoticed. I was used to his audacity, but not my sister-in-law. Red-faced, she grabbed a towel and wrapped it quickly around herself.

"Hey! There's a Frenchman's soul inside that dog!" she sang out in a high coloratura, that evening at dinner. "I could have sworn he was inspecting me with those eyes!" She laughed in mock indignation.

Other houseguests took their turns falling victims to Kenneth's voyeurism. We could do nothing but joke about our Peeping Tom.

That was just an instance of his prankishness. Together with his strong likes or aversions, they added up to a pixiness unusual even for a playful dog. His dislikes were pronounced, even scandalous. He was only ten months old when, walking with me down a street, he noticed a handsome gendarme with a *kepi* striding in our direction. Kenneth suddenly pulled up, back-pedaled ~ his screwdriver tail between his hind legs ~ and began furiously barking. I apologized. Unruffled, the uniformed officer extended his hand with a lighted *Gitane* between his fingers, saying "*Hallo petit chien!*" Kenneth could not be pacified; he was aversive to smoke, too.

I concluded that mine was a dog with an attitude. It turned out he had four *bête noires*: men or women in uniform (including service workers); those who limp, use crutches, or walk with a cane; *clochards* or street bums; gamins or street urchins; dark-visaged persons. Where did he get such prejudices? Certainly not from me. I thought dogs were color-blind, classless, democratic, and more or less adept at adjusting to different personality types. He had not met many people before. Collective unconscious? Genetic make-up or the way his brain was hard-wired? Memories of past lives? Who knows!

That was not all. He was sensitive to social class. Despite his plebeian, probably rustic origins, class markers mattered just as it did to the first Kenneth. He was inordinately fond of well-dressed women in long, flowing skirts. When one came along he would snuggle close and try to ingratiate himself. But unlike the old Kenneth this one was an anarchist, a breaker of rules. To law officers he showed a disdain that reached scandalous and, I feared, dangerous proportions.

Around the corner from our apartment was a small hole-in-the-wall police station. When he was still a puppy, I noticed that his favorite spot was the sidewalk right smack in front of the station. He would pull me there and do his thing quickly. My scolding fell on deaf ears. When he started to walk the block without a leash, he made straight for the spot, did it, and then dashed away in his herky-jerky, silly way, I bet laughing all the way home. I began to steer clear of that street for fear of police retribution, particularly after espying shiny police shoes brush against dog poop. Kenneth always managed to escape the guillotine.

I think he was just being French. Most Parisians are resigned to having sidewalks become obstacle courses. Except a wizened, crotchety octogenarian who berated Kenneth ~ and me ~ for making his walks a torture. Kenneth and I pretended we did not understand French.

Actually, Kenneth did understand. French or English. Shortly after we adopted him, on my way out to the fromagerie, I reminded my husband to take the dog out. I did not use Kenneth's name nor even looked in his direction. No sooner did I say it than his ears flicked and he was jumping up and down, panting in excitement. Not only that, but his vocabulary expanded to include "let's go," "shall we," "on y va." In fact, he had quite an extensive vocabulary. He responded to "dog" as he would to "Kenneth." Did he know "Kenneth" to be a particular instance of the universal "dog," or did he take "dog" to be another name? I had never called him "dog" to his face. Or was he simply responding to the word "out?"

On our guard, we started spelling out words that might refer to him. He always had an ear cocked to whatever we were saying. We had a spy in our chambers. One time, while wondering aloud how pedestrians like us could cross sidestreets, where cars parked literally bumper to bumper, not one inch of space between them, Kenneth suddenly shot cater-cornering across the street. He recognized the word "cross" and thought we had ordered him to cross! Fortunately, there was little traffic that day.

This was during the six-week summer hiatus when Paris was a ghost city and we had it all to ourselves. In August, an annual, almost sacrosanct ritual ~ a mass exodus to the coasts or to the mountains ~ empties the city. Labor law requires all French workers to be given a six-week paid holiday in summer. Overnight Paris transforms into a village of non-Parisians, mostly tourists.

A hundred yards from our apartment were three restaurants. One was the four-star, nouvelle cuisine Jamin, run by celebrity chef Joël Robuchon (whom I got to know). Across was the upscale Vietnamese-Chinese *Vifoc*. Nearer our apartment was the Lebanese *Fakhr El-Din*, which never seemed to be without a gaggle of Rolls-Royces and Bentleys parked nearby. Their earthy names brought a wicked smile to naughty English-speakers. Jamin had international standing ~ the place to dine in Paris. Reservations had to be booked three months in advance, despite the incredible price. Time enough to save up money for such divine gastronomy! In France, top chefs are cult figures, with a status equal to American movie stars, commanding prestige and stratospheric incomes.

Thus, there was a constant flow of celebrities and tourists to our street. One day Kenneth broke away from me and rushed toward a group of teenagers, obviously Americans, boisterously goofing off. Yipping loudly, his rump wagging, he demanded attention, as usual.

They ignored him. Circling the group, he persisted. Annoyed, they shooed him away. That did not dampen his enthusiasm one bit. I had to finally pull him away, muttering excuses.

To Kenneth their twang was familiar, sounding like an American neighbor who was exceptionally indulgent to him. Anyone who talked that way must surely be kind, like her. He did not respond with the same enthusiasm to French English, Chinese English, or any other kind of English.

His aptitude for languages was phenomenal. Just after adopting him, I spoke to him in English laced with Fujian terms. Cocking his head sideways and intently staring into my eyes, he seemed to say "That's not French." Several years later in the United States I met a Québecois. I had not spoken French for a long while, and had forgotten the exactitudes of Paris French. But the looseness of street argot came back naturally. All of a sudden, Kenneth was bounding up and down ~ his trademark ~ as if to say "that's my native tongue!" My fractured French and her archaic French did not faze this nose-in-the-air Parisian.

Thus it was in Paris that an abandoned mongrel wormed his way into my life and became a true companion. Our moods melded together in total sync. We catered to each other's emotional needs and momentary whims. Even Camille, who was formerly just a breeding machine (Cinnamon was her son) became a true companion as well. This pedigreed Poodle from Asia ~ fluffy continental clip adorning her neck up to her waist, and bracelet curls around her legs ~ began to demand equal time.

Now she required to be tucked into bed at night. One evening I cajoled my husband into doing this for me. As soon as he left our bedroom, Princess (as I called her) started yapping. I had learned to "read" her barks, whines, yelps and yaps. I asked my husband: "Did you cover her with the electric pad?" No, so he stood up and went back in. Comfortably ensconced once more in his easy chair, we heard her yap again. "What is it this time?" he asked impatiently. I listened for a minute, then asked: "Did you switch it on?" Without saying anything he again went back in. After that we had a quiet evening.

Princess was coquette to Kenneth's machismo, the yin to his yang. She was reserved and shy where he was loud and pushy. She was frail where he was tough. She was uncomplicated where he always had an agenda up his paws. I often wondered if their close contact with humans shaped their differing personalities, or was it just a matter of genetics? Unlike Poodles in France, Camille was wary of strangers. Was she afraid she might end up on someone's dinner plate, like some pets in Asia? Kenneth on the other hand was obstreperous, forcing himself on everyone, as if it was *comme il faut*. Did he know that the French preferred pets to people? Similarly, Camille and Kenneth had divergent food preferences. Growing up in Asia where leftovers went to the dogs, Camille never acquired a taste for processed dog food. She preferred food with Chinese flavors and turned up her nose at the *Pont L'Evêque* which Kenneth loved, or any other kind of cheese.

A little bit of Kenneth's *joie de vivre* rubbed off on Camille. From a habitual lethargy she became more alive, revealing an aptitude for singing. Picking up the cue from my fractured rendition of *Alouette* on the soprano Recorder, she would raise her snout, purse her lips, and ululate in varying pitches while rhythmically nodding and lifting her snout. It was a diva act that took equal billing to Kenneth's showmanship.

Here in Europe, Camille lived out her senior years in style ~ Paris, good food, and a macho French lover. It was during a holiday trip in Barcelona when I realized I had a lecher on my hands. Camille was then in estrus. Flaunting her rump high in his face and twitching her pom-pom tail provocatively sent Kenneth's testosterone breathing fire. To prevent accidents, I separated them and detained Kenneth in the hotel bathroom. He acted demented, furiously scratching at the door non-stop and banging his body against it. No amount of scolding or attempts to divert him worked. He kept us awake all night.

This was only the beginning of his displays of lewdness.

Sitting in a sidewalk cafe, dawdling over an espresso while gawking at the madding crowd swirling by, was the Parisian way to make The Love Connection. Some use dogs as go-between or as an opening gambit. Socializing with each other under tables, dogs were ideal for breaking the ice. With its magnificent view of Tour Eiffel, Place Trocadéro boasted two always-crowded brasserie-cafes, a couple of hundred strides from our apartment. On one of these anthropological field trips, I sat next to this *très chic* but a bit jaded woman, probably in her forties. Fondling a *kir royale* between manicured fingers, she tried to catch the attention of a middle-aged man at the next table. As she archly sipped her drink, he stood up, *pastis* in hand, to join her. *"Mais oui!"* she cooed with exaggerated delight. Animated conversation followed. Aha, love.

After a few minutes, to my surprise she sprang to her feet and swung her Louis Vitton bag, giving him a glancing blow on his balding pate, screaming *"Salou!"* plus some other choice expletives. He said something to placate her. Instead, she spat on him. *Ooh-la-la!* Some casually turned to look, then looked away. It was nobody's business, just a private altercation between lovers. Nothing is more common in Paris. A while later, after whispered caresses, both walked out arm in arm, pets following with leashes entwined. I could never quite plumb the zigs and zags of the Latin temperament, nor could I appreciate Cartesian dialectic expressed this way.

Then I noticed amused looks directed at me. I had not noticed a torrid foreplay going on under my table. My jaw literally dropped. It seemed my satyr of a pet was struggling to impose himself on a boxer bitch. Panting, drooling, he was giving it the good old college try. But he was too low in the ground to do it. Attempting to press her down and get on top, he kept thrusting but vainly into thin air, his rear legs humping. This French gallant could not make it. Nothing is as devastating as failed love, unrequited lust. However, the Latin in Kenneth was not going to let him give up just yet. Mortified, I picked him up growling. People stared at me reproachfully. I beat a retreat from the scene of Kenneth's humiliation with all the dignity I could muster. As I exited with Camille in my arms and Kenneth on a leash, I heard a man call out "Kiss me," and with the typical French shrug, he pointed to his dog, saying in French his dog's name was Kissme.

Kenneth's sexual proclivities reached scandalous heights at an important dinner we gave to a clutch of Asian diplomats. The occasion was my rite of passage into diplomatic life. I went to great lengths to make sure every detail, every protocol was observed, even hiring a *serveuse* for the evening. After the first few courses, I noticed the Thai Ambassador shifting positions and moving his chair. He did not like the *rôti d'agneau,* or was it perhaps the *Pomerol?* I was afraid to ask. He seemed relieved when we moved to the living room. Then I noticed Kenneth sitting innocently at the foot of the Thai Ambassador's wife, who had on a long Thai-silk gown.

Suddenly, without warning, he grabbed one of her legs between his forepaws and began humping on it. She giggled nervously, covering her mouth with her hands, pushing him away politely. Undaunted, Kenneth persisted. Quickly, I picked Kenneth up and grounded him ~ in the bedroom. I realized then what was bothering the Ambassador. It was too late, the damage was done.

Do you think that being persona non grata stopped Kenneth? I must admit though I was quite impressed by his single-minded lechery, the way he picked out and targeted a specific couple. Because he got his way with the man, he assumed he could, too, with the woman. Was this just a random choice? How did he know who was the most compliant couple in the group? Did he know that Buddhists would not harm him? It was simply beyond my ken.

It was the last straw. I had on my hands a shamelessly oversexed satyr of a French dog. A decision had to be made: castration or ostracism. Kenneth was simply out of control, liable to make a shambles of our social life. But at that time, I was not an enlightened animal lover. I had been brought up to look at neutering as mutilation, animal abuse, and a sadistic act of vivisection.

Casually I mentioned my decision to a friend in the Division of Human Rights, who knew Kenneth. In mock outrage he drafted a *"J'accuse!"* denouncing us of depriving Kenneth, in the prime of his youth, his fundamental, inalienable rights to the untrammeled expression of his sexual instincts; to sow his wild (French) oats and perpetuate his own kind. It implored us ~ tongue in cheek ~ to cease and desist on pain of being denounced before a United Nations Tribunal.

Not surprisingly the fiery document drew an avalanche of amused signers ~ Kenneth was a frequent visitor at Unesco headquarters where he made himself popular as a clown. With page after page of signatures, it was presented to us with all ceremony. Unfazed, we decided to risk the wrath of the righteous; we could not risk Camille getting pregnant. Quietly, *sans furore*, we had Kenneth neutered. The operation changed not one bit of his sex drives or his prankishness. The clamor quietly died down.

Several months later, Camille was again in heat. Kenneth tried once more. Not much luck or so I thought. Shortly thereafter, I noticed Camille's swollen abdomen and rather enlarged nipples. She began neurotically to scratch herself. I was at my wits' end. Indignantly I took her to the vet who had sterilized Kenneth. After examining Camille, he said it was *grossis nerveuse*. I understood it to be false pregnancy, aggravated by hormonal changes at her advanced age. As for Kenneth, he said if he had had a normal sex life before being neutered, he would never forget how to do it. Cute, I thought: French canine psychoanalysis no less. I asked that Camille be immediately spayed. It probably extended her life.

With Kenneth and Camille always at my side, things took a sunshiny turn toward new dimensions. Kenneth had a knack for making friends, unlocking hearts and bringing kindred souls together.

Perhaps it was that which brought Angela and me together. But it seemed to be purely by chance. She lived at the top floor of our apartment building, where she had a charming view of the rooftops of Kleber and Longchamp. I was coming down the stairs from our second floor apartment with Camille in my arms and an unleashed Kenneth padding along for a daily stroll. At the gate of the rickety lift a tall lady, her right foot jammed against the lift door to keep it from shutting, was muttering something in English under her breath as she strained to muscle out an overladen cart of groceries. Before I knew it, Kenneth dashed into the lift, greeting her with his trademark rump-wiggle. Kenneth thought that if she spoke English, she must be a friend.

Angela and Kenneth turned out to have much in common, including an irreverent and puckish attitude. Although her husband was allergic to animals, Angela allowed Kenneth into her apartment. She became quite fond of him and soon there was little she would not do for Kenneth.

In no time, Angela and I discovered a common passion for gastronomy and the culinary arts. We started to comb Paris together, Kenneth and Camille on the backseat of the car, on the look-out for the marvelous and edible. I was her transport, she did not drive. We were always in a tizzy discussing what next to explore, what next to sample: Auvèrgne *saucisson* or Ardéche *saucisse*; *quenelle* or *boudin blanc*; *paté de campagne* or *terrine du porc*.

We hit it off well, being both alike and unlike enough to complement ~ and foil ~ each other. I was water to Angela's fire. She had the straightback self-assurance and dry wit of the British and the sunny flippancy of the Italian, the blood of both hotly coursing in her

veins. I had the inscrutability of a Taoist and the practical mind of a
huachiao. She towered above me both in height and age: she was forty
something, I was thirty something; she was six feet tall, I five-one. I was
straight woman to her goofiness. I think each brought out the best in
the other: the brash egging on the shy, one claquing for the other.
Daring each other to thumb a nose at the stuffiness of protocol,
constraints of class, and tyranny of bureaucracy, we shed inhibitions
and let latent talents loose. Synergy steered us safely through many a
potentially disastrous adventure, collusion hurdled impasses and
surmounted frustrations. Co-conspirator Kenneth was indispensable --
as our point dog.

Both of us grew up in a tightly knit family of girls. We had a strict
Catholic upbringing. No children. While each had an independent
career of her own, in Paris we opted to backstop our husbands' careers.
Tight-fisted, calculatingly stingy, we were one in our buying priorities --
what merited spending our carefully hoarded money. Our values
converged.

In temperament, we were poles apart. She brought a carefree,
waggish attitude towards life, never hesitating to give the finger or a
shove-it gesture to the obnoxious. I was more restrained, a slave to
ritual and *de rigueur*. Moreover, I suffered from bouts of depression.
Circumstances often had an overwhelming effect on me. Where
Angela was always on top of things, I was always under; I would
toboggan down to sullen, self-deprecating depths, and pull down the
curtain for days on myself. At other times I would revert to a Type A
personality, switch to overdrive, and go tearing myself to pieces
thinking of goals still to achieve. A degree at the Sorbonne, computer
programming at the American University, oenology at l' Académie du
Vin perhaps? I could not quite make up my mind. Feverishly I would
swing into action mode, but toward what, I hadn't the slightest clue.

Angela would have none of that nonsense. She was not driven at
all. She just wanted a kick. With Kenneth as a pretext, she provided
the diversion and the hard-nosed sense of reality I needed and secretly
welcomed. She could snap me out of my depressed moods and never
take No for an answer. Sometimes I chided her for distracting me. Did
that stop her? Not at all. Still, it was good she blustered and cajoled,
for nothing else could snap me out of my funk.

After a while I managed to match her manic, carefree moods. We drew up a list of tourist traps we simply had to check out. One of these was the glitzy Hotel Crillon on Place Concorde, right next to the American Embassy. But a measly espresso at twenty French Francs, *service non-compris?* No, sir, that was a bit too much to swallow. Instead, we treated ourselves to unlimited coffee at my apartment. We ground and ground the Colombian Supremo beans, fastidiously chosen at Fauchon, until they became a fine powder. Then I made great amounts of espresso in my manual press-down coffeemaker. With our pinkies properly curled up, we sat back in style sipping the exquisite brew out of Herend demitasses, after stirring in bits of rock sugar.

That afternoon Angela noticed Kenneth looking glum and listless. He is starting to look like you, she teased. Kenneth had noticed my slipping on high-heeled shoes and read what it portended. He could always tell from the type of shoes. High heels meant, "Mama is going to have fun without me;" walking shoes meant "I'm gonna have fun with Mama." He lay in a corner, looking dolefully at me. He knew that he and Camille were to be left behind, home alone. Angela winked at Kenneth, meaningfully screwing up her face. "Oh, let the poor bugger come. I'll be a good sport and mind him, she said, her robust mezzo resounding through the corridor. In an instant, Kenneth was bounding up and down.

As we entered the Crillon, Kenneth tagging at our heels and Camille in my arms, Angela mounted a barrage of whispered commands: walk nonchalantly past the reception, avoid eye contact with anyone, and for heaven's sake Keep Cool! Act like one of those filthy-rich hotel habitués prowling the corridors or slouching on chaise longues in the lobby. She scowled and asked: you know why they call them filthy-rich? Uh-oh, I saw a gag coming. Taking pre-emptive action I quickly retorted: "because they gorge on putrid game and rich pastries that ferment in their stomachs and make for beaucoup deadly farts." Angela's eyes widened. Hand over mouth, she feigned suppressing her infamous guffaw. But finally a choking sound escaped her mouth and she let go with a roar.

Next, she joshed me about the handsome doorman's effusive *"Bonjour Mesdames."* He had his eyes on you, she hissed. Don't give me any of that, I shot back. It was like this always, with her the banter never ceased. Irrepressible, she needed an outlet. I was conveniently around.

We meandered deeper into this grandiose monument of a hotel, making like a couple of bored, eccentric millionaires traveling with a nondescript mutt. Haute-coutured Lady Camille gave us a touch of class. Swaggering into a cavernous, regal salon, we feigned ennui as our gaze swept languidly over the ornate ceilings, elaborately detailed friezes, decorative panels and pillars, and lingered over the tapestries, art pieces, and period furniture.

Angela signaled me to walk faster as she sniffed her way like an English bloodhound on the hunt to the powder room. The Northern Italian on her mother's side and English on her father's side were quite an amalgam. A kinetic Englishwoman no less. I tried to match her giant strides, but how does a petite Chinese girl walk elegantly in figure-hugging Balenciaga and Charles Jourdan stiletto heels, trying to keep up with two dogs in tow? Always sartorially utilitarian, Angela had on a Jaeger tweed and Clarks chukka boots. Thank heavens she was not wearing her atrocious Sherlock Holmes headgear. Her ash-blond curls were neatly coiffed to a high bouffant ~ a weekly treat she gave herself, part of her feel-good program. When we stepped into the powder room her blue-gray eyes quickly fastened on the faience porcelain, Hermes cologne flagon, monogrammed linen towels, perfumed cameo soaps, satin-cushioned divan. Hah! So this is how the *toilette* of the idle rich looks ~ and smells!

Curiosity satisfied, we started back to where we were parked, beside the Espace P. Cardin. Kenneth whined, fretfully. It was now his turn, we had had ours. We unleashed him in the *jardin*, where he lost no time gyrating his way around in his usual clownish way, insisting on greeting every *bien habille* woman. Camille just watched.

"Drop your mail quick, Kenneth," Angela commanded. "Got to go home to prepare din-din for the husbands!"

When he heard the word "home," he looked expectantly at us, waiting for the signal to start for the exit. Angela winked at him. Dutifully he raised his leg against some shrubbery, turned around, and lifted the other leg to achieve closure. Nonchalantly he kicked up dirt with his hind legs, scattering debris about, and then took off after us. Kicking dirt put a period on his message to other dogs.

A squirt of a Citroën had forcibly appropriated the small remaining space in front of my Hatchback, and a Peugeot behind had jammed against my rear bumper. In Manhattan, my yellow Datsun was often hailed as a taxi, or else derided as "half-a-car." Here in Paris it was resented, and subjected to car-bashing because it occupied a quarter more parking space than the local vest-pocket tin lizzies.

Squeezed in, I acted exactly as any Parisienne. Early on, I watched in disbelief as drivers deliberately carved out space for their vehicles by rocking them back and forth, pushing the rear bumper of the car in front, and then banging into the front bumper of the car behind, whether their brakes were on or not. All drivers do the same to get out of impossibly tight spaces. I was a quick study: when in Rome...

After executing this maneuver and finally getting my poor battered *voiture* on track, we turned into the storied Arc de Triomphe, a mistake if ever there was one. I took the Champs Elysées route to get back to our *quartier* and so could not avoid the Etoile. Getting caught in the inner lanes of that intricate roundabout with its eleven intersections was a miserable error. We had to go on, forever, past Grande Armee, MacMahon, Wagram, Hoche, Friedland, Champs Elysée, Marceau, d'Ièna, Klebér, Hugo, Foch ~ arms radiating out of the circle as in a starfish or spiral galaxy. Only heroic measures could get us out. The trick, I knew, was not to be elbowed into an inner lane. If this happened get to the outer lanes fast to escape the endless circling and then turn off at the correct arm quickly, before a car from behind cuts you off. Easier said than done. Round and round we went, working our way in mounting desperation to the outer lanes. As soon as we succeeded to get there we now had to keep an eye to the right, because a crazy driver could suddenly shoot out one of those arms and into your path, all the time claiming his or her *priorité a droite*, and inviting a collision in which I would be at fault.

Extricating ourselves from that deadly circle was so enervating the adrenalin rush made it hard to shift into a more leisurely mode. Besides, Angela wanted us to lollygag and rubberneck instead of rush. She had no deadlines to meet.

Anyway, here we were driving home slowly, when this car came tearing down from the left at an intersection, intent on crossing it before I did. Instead of claiming my *priorité*, I jammed on the brakes and gave him the right of way. My stopping surprised him ~ no Paris driver would do that, he would have kept on going. As he passed in front of us he turned around in his seat, made a face, and thumbed his nose at us. Well, I gave him the finger. Angela shook her fist after him and shouted an Italian obscenity as he disappeared to our right. Kenneth's floppy ears were up, his eyes alert. He did not want to miss the excitement.

Paris drivers are maniacs by neurosis or natural inclination. They do not take prisoners. They follow three kamikaze rules: *one*, when in doubt, accelerate; *two*, seize any space that's open; *three*, seize it even if it is not open because two cars can occupy the same space at the same time.

Having survived the Etoile, I breathed a deep sigh of relief. In a matter of minutes, we would be at our apartments enjoying mango tea. Just as we turned into our street, traffic ground to a halt. When it started again my engine went dead. The car behind honked, rudely and insistently. Its driver, a supercilious dude in a fancy Gùy Laroche raised both hands with typical Paris impatience ~ very Gallic, very ungallant. On my rear-view mirror, I saw him gesturing, giving me the arm ~ an extremely insulting hand-and-arm movement ~ and then a finger pointing to his temple. Then he put his car in gear and tried vainly to push my car forward. Seated in front with Kenneth partly on her lap, Angela started snorting fire.

How many times did these fiends behind a wheel humiliate me! Angela avoided trauma by refusing to drive. The most gracious and ingratiating Frenchman or woman is an ogre behind a wheel. It is useless to complain to police, for their noses will be up in the air as if one was speaking gibberish.

A Waterloo-Compiègne complex must be behind an overwhelming urge to compensate. A car with its power is a chance to get the upper hand. But I had a wild card up my sleeves: diplomatic immunity, blatantly advertised in orange and green on my car plates. I had the chance that few others had ~ to get even. With these plates, I could park anywhere, anytime. And never get a ticket. I was provoked to use this immunity just to get even. Angela, my praetorian guard, sat menacingly by my side, our point dog safely behind.

Nonchalantly I got out of the car, put Kenneth on a leash, and tucked Camille into my arms. Angela grinned knowingly.

"You silly tit. Where'd you get all that chutzpah!?" she guffawed as we sashayed up our street. Over her shoulder, she waved "Ta ta!" to Mr. Gùy Laroche.

Sensing the nearness of home, Kenneth pulled harder, straining at his leash, his forepaws splaying out like a duck. A stiletto heel, caught in a crack on the rough-bricked sidewalk, sent me unshod hopping precipitously after him. Hobbling back to retrieve the shoe, I could see Mr. Gùy Laroche huffing and puffing in his car. Traffic was piling up behind him as he tried vainly to get out from behind my car now serenely parked with its diplomatic plates in the middle of Rue de Longchamps.

Home at last, Angela gleefully recalled the feisty middle-aged English teacher who was quite proud of her French. One day she found herself caught in that fiendish trap, completely disoriented. Stopping right in the middle of that maelstrom, she waited for succor. A gendarme descended on her and imperiously signaled her to keep moving. She lost her temper, leaned out, and shouted *Couchon!* She meant to say *cochon* or pig. Instead, she had invited him to sleep with her. Somewhat startled but unruffled, he bowed, saluted, and said with no little enthusiasm: "*Avec plaisir, mademoiselle.*"

Laughing until tears came, we recalled our first diplomatic function, a reception at the South Korean Embassy. Our French was still raw. To a query put to her by a French diplomat: how did she find the climate? she replied "*Mon chevaux sont toujours très sec.*" (My *horse* is always too dry.) She meant to say *cheveux*, that is, her hair was always too dry. He looked at her and nodded with a puzzled smile. Meanwhile at my corner, I was committing my own gaffes. I had translated "I am cold" to "*Je suis froid*" with the appropriate shudder, to emphasize my distress at the inadequacies of the heating system. What I got was a far more condescending look than Angela got. Only later did I realize I should have said "*J'ai froid*" instead of grandly announcing how frigid I am.

It was one *faux pas* after another. Like during a cocktail party we co-hosted as volunteer work for UN field experts visiting Paris. A Maltese guest unfamiliar with the *siopao* we served asked if the paper square holding the roast-pork steamed bun could be eaten. With Kenneth at her feet, Angela assured everyone that rice paper was not only nutritious but also low-calorie. Hey ~ I whispered - it's just ordinary bond paper! Rolling her eyes, she laughed, long and hard. She had wolfed down with relish her share of bond paper and all.

Like Kenneth, nothing pleased Angela more than stealing a scene with her goofiness. For example, every month together we organized international cooking classes where we featured chefs from various embassies demonstrating their native specialties. On one occasion we managed to corral the renowned Robuchon of Jamin to share his secret *rôti d'agneau aux herbs en croute de sel* recipe.   On that eventful day, Angela ~ who could easily pass for a Julia Child clone ~ was her normal puckish self. She sampled everything, showing her appreciation each time by grabbing the chef and bussing him on the forehead. Carried away, she pulled a handsome assistant chef to her and pressed his head on her bosom, rolling her eyeballs artfully and exclaiming "*magnifique!*" How I envied her audacity, her getting away with it by acting silly a' la Jerry Lewis. Now I know why she and her husband did not have a television set in their apartment. She was enough.

When it was our turn to demonstrate our *chef'oeuvre*, Angela was literally all over me while I cooked up a storm. Like in a quiz show, she badgered me with question after question, for example, why add water to eggs to brush on piecrusts,   discombobulating me no end. However, when my recipe went pfft! she saved the day, clowning, kissing me on the forehead, and absolving us both. One time she noticed how rattled I was when the delicate meringue with rum custard filling ~ a Spanish-inspired dessert called *Brazo de Mercedes* ~ would not fold like a jelly roll as it should. She quickly diverted everyone's attention by trotting out her recipe for Better Than Sex cake. I thought she was making it up, along the way, only to find out later that indeed such a recipe existed. And when things got dull and monotonous, she gave irrelevant asides, for example, add baking soda to hot water to relieve tired feet.

At the end of the day, no matter how tired we were, she never forgot to collect food for Kenneth and Camille. The moment she plunked down the brown bag on the car floor, Kenneth was at work, prying it open with his snout, rummaging, sorting things out, and then selecting what he wanted. To him a filled paperbag in the car was fair game.

Our two families became part of a coterie of a dozen elderly people, mostly retired.   We were a multi-cultural group: besides

French, there were Italians, a Dane, a Belgian, Argentineans, a Breton, Asians, and Americans. Together we went on *degustations* to seek out a Medoc or Fronsac for our respective caves, to food festivals, haute couture media shows. Most memorable were the round-robin dinners we organized in each other's Paris apartments. In spring, when the vine roses were in full bloom at their private garden and the heady scent permeated the air, the Rands hosted musical soirees at their Place Theodore Rousseau apartment. Guido at his baby grand and my husband with his Italian violin from Cremona rendered sonatas by Mozart or concertos by Vivaldi. Never mind if they played Veracini's Largo or Beethoven's Rondino execrably. Being able to play together, reasonably in sync, gave them infinite delight. Salle Pleyel could not have offered more.

On such occasions, Kenneth and Camille stayed home alone. Did they suffer from separation anxiety? Well, yes and no. Once I had to go back quickly to get a mantilla I forgot. *Voila!* They had taken over the silk upholstered Louis XIV, my most expensive chaise, lounging in blissful contentment. They did not choose the more comfortable, soft velour Castro convertible brought over from New York. I guess forbidden fruit taste better. Caught red-handed, they slunk down with guilty looks. On later occasions they did not even bother to get off, daring me to do my worst.

Home alone, Kenneth's first act of protest as a puppy was to shred shoes and vandalize my sewing kit. He identified the sewing kit with me because when we had just adopted him, I spent entire afternoons sewing drapes for the apartment. I finally figured that perhaps, if he had a part of me, or a sensory trace when I was away, he would not feel abandoned. I started putting clothing I had just worn on his bed. It worked. The concierge's teenage daughter who babysat for him when we went on long trips reported that Kenneth dragged it around the apartment like a security blanket.

As often as we could we took Kenneth and Camille along on our many trips all over Europe. They became seasoned travelers, contentedly sleeping away long hours until we stopped. At rest stops: hotels, restaurants, they knew exactly what to do. They even knew how to behave riding a cable-car ski lift going up the Matterhorn, where we had to pay children's fares for them.

It was a novel experience for Camille. In Asia, pets must stay domestic. To be allowed inside the house is exceptional. Pets are never welcome at shops, restaurants, hotels, and public buildings. In contrast, all over Western Europe, pets are treated as part of the entourage. Countries differ in shades of acceptance, with France being the most accommodating. When checking into an *auberge*, linen and *petit dejeuner* is provided our pet companions.

Traversing Germany, late in the day we saw the unmistakable sign "*Zimmer.*" The bed-and-breakfast was somewhat strange; they were refusing our occupancy. At first, we thought they were discriminating against us. After some sign language, we discovered to our chagrin ~ and amusement ~ it was a special hotel for dogs, not for their human companions! It was a dog motel!

As Camille got older and frailer, we took her along even to places where dogs were *interdit*. She learned to be completely unobtrusive in her fake Burberry pet-taxi, seldom making a sound or movement. Kenneth, who never could be discreet, had to sit it out in the car. In ventures behind the Iron Curtain ~ Eastern Europe, and the Balkans ~ to bring lawless, anarchic Kenneth along was too much of a hazard. We had to entrust him to a Chinese refugee family from Laos.

At the Alcazar, a 14th century palace built by Pedro the Cruel, where sultans of Granada received the annual tribute of 100 virgins, I almost got exposed. Camille was lying quietly inside her pet taxi, which I toted as if it was a large duffel bag. A little boy peered intently into its transparent plastic window. He excitedly turned to his mother and blurted out: "*Mira, mira Mama, un perrito,*" pointing at Camille. To escape being embarrassed I quickly turned around and exited.

In Prague, Camille went to an opera at the National Theater ~ the gorgeous Narodni Divadlo (where Milos Forman's Amadeus was filmed). We were quaffing Pale Pilsens first at U Fleiku and then at U Pinkasi, pubs just a stone's throw down the street from Mozart's Till Theater, when a student offered tickets for Prokofiev's *Bethrothal in the Monastery* at an astonishing two U.S. dollars apiece. It was a serendipity offer we could not let pass. So we tucked Camille into her pet-taxi, where she slept quietly throughout the opera, while we laved in the awesome ambience of the Baroque hall and the splendor of the opera unfolding before our eyes.

From Prague we went on to Berlin through Dresden, one of the most devastated cities of Germany, with its empty, desolate but spanking-clean streets. We took a quick tour of a famous museum. Close to midnight, cold and exhausted after a labyrinthine drive into West Berlin, we arrived at what we thought was Checkpoint Bravo. Because we had diplomatic plates, I expected perfunctory border formalities. After a five-minute wait, we saw round disk mirrors on long poles being slid under our spanking-new Benz. Did the *Vopos* really suspect that someone was clinging to the undercarriage? Then two jack-booted specimens came out, curtly asked for our papers, and then peered inside. Two items caught their eye, openly lying beside Camille on the backseat. They were two rare finds we came upon at the Mala Strasse in our serendipity shopping just before leaving Prague. One was a 19th Century German violin, the other a leather-bound *Complete Works of William Shakespeare,* an 1854 English edition published in Leipzig, Germany and printed by Giesecke & Devrient for Baumgärtner. I had not bothered to put them in the trunk. The younger police took the book; leafed through it, asked where it came from, and demanded a receipt. As I nervously scrounged around for the receipt from the Prague bookstore, the older guard pulled the black violin case out of the car and opened it. Satisfied that it was only a violin, he put it back, laying it beside Camille. Camille gave him a coquettish look and he patted her on the head. I could not locate the receipt. Looking at me suspiciously, the younger guard turned to the title page pointing to Leipzig as the place of publication. He said curtly that such museum items were not permitted to be taken out of DRG. (We were never in Leipzig.) Taking the book with him, he disappeared into a room. After an interminable wait, he returned, ordering us out of the car. It was bitingly cold; snow was on the ground. I slipped Camille inside my well-padded coat as we stood in the glare of klieg lights. The two jack-boots stripped the back seat and went through the trunk. It was a full-scale inspection. Naturally, they found nothing. I demanded a receipt if the book was to be confiscated. It was a tense situation. Fortunately, after what seemed endless minutes, a guard came back and handed back the book, without a word. The gates lifted. We could go. After crossing into West Berlin, my husband turned to me and said, "Did you know that was Checkpoint Charlie?"

Kenneth and Camille transformed my life into one high adventure after another, ushering me into many a magical corner of Paris and Europe. Life as a diplomat's wife presented too many stimulating events for me to stagnate in the same familiar grooves. When my parents visited and stayed with us, there was no longer any thought of a parental leash; the Confucian pressures no longer bore down on me as before. With Kenneth and Camille now at the other end, the leash became a magician's wand, expunging any neurosis left in me.

Nevertheless, I was not immune to panic reactions to unexpected events. One bitingly cold autumn evening, I had to rush my husband to the hospital for an emergency gall bladder operation. I returned to a miserably damp and cold apartment. It had been raining continuously for four days. The indoor temperature dropped to 55° F yet the concierge adamantly refused to turn on the *chauffage*, asserting it was four days ahead of the official heating days (7 October to the 1 May). I was livid with anger, distraught and desperately alone.

Kenneth was lying quietly on his side beside me. Suddenly he started opening and shutting his jaws, yelping not loudly but in a thin, whiny, high-pitched way. A hind leg spasmodically jerked with each yelp, while his front paws rhythmically clawed the air. Oh my God! I panicked, he is convulsing, maybe going into epileptic seizure! What was I to do? After a while, he stopped.

Then, it hit me. He was not in dire straits, neither was he in agony at all. He was simply trying to clown me out of my depression, just acting silly. With a queen-termite body and a piggly-wiggly tail, his acting was indeed outlandish. Afterwards, whenever he felt I should be distracted out of my funk, or sensed a comic relief was needed, he would stage a "fit." Many a time I had to explain to friends that we were not having a dying dog on our hands. He was just goofing off. The vet had assured me there was nothing wrong with him.

All this gives a clue why Parisians love their dogs the way they do. Perhaps they see in dogs something that is lacking in themselves and in others: uncomplicated relationships and existential happiness. The French worldview is angst-suffused. Like their city with its multiple modules, the Parisian has a multi-layered personality. Without inner conflict, life is bland and mediocre. Complexity and contradiction add intensity to living. Without a neurosis, one has little character. Indeed, to be happy one must be more than happy; one must be insanely, passionately manic. With dogs, they can be completely themselves ~ deliriously, uninhibitedly happy, even silly ~ and not have anybody judging them.

When Fifth Sister married a medical doctor named Kenneth, I renamed my Kenneth ET. The movie ET was then the rage in Paris. Kenneth looked very much like Yoda but I thought "extra-terrible" was a more apt appellation. When they visited us in Paris, whenever Fifth Sister called her husband "Ken" or "Kenny," ET came forward with his trademark rump-tail wiggle and boisterous high jumps.

After Paris, we moved back to the United States to be beside my kin. ET and Camille made the transatlantic flight with us, Camille in her Burberry pet taxi carry-on. ET had to languish, tranquilized, in the baggage hold. I had to choose between leaving him behind or putting him in cargo. He did not pass the 20-lb. limit for carry-on dogs despite my putting him on a stringent diet.

The elderly American who sat next to me gasped with relief when he saw Camille emerge from the duffel bag under my legs. He was visibly shaken by the squirming in the bag. He told me he thought it was a snake, or that he had drunk too much champagne. Camille luxuriated in every perk only Air France flight attendants could give.

When we arrived at Fifth Sister's house in suburban Chicago, a graduation party was under way for her husband Kenneth. My parents, who remembered ET as "Kenneth," excitedly called out: "Kenneth, Kenneth! Come!" Still tranquilized, unsteady on his feet, eyes squinting, ET staggered from his container. I never knew for certain if he was putting on an act. Joy, a six-year-old niece, instantly took charge of him, proudly calling him her French cousin.

We settled down in the American South. As a city dog from Europe, ET adjusted easily to life in the country, better than I did. He quickly drew neighborhood dogs to our property and soon became the alpha-dog. I'm not sure if it was territoriality, the French mystique, or that he smelled "different," but the pack members deferred to him. Often, after butt-sniffing rituals and despite being neutered, ET would try to mount this or that dog regardless of its sex.

But he was not going to be alpha-dog for long. From having star billing as my *copain* in Paris, ET relegated himself to playing second-fiddle to the freckled hillbilly who sprang out of the woods to become his *copain*. In this our neck of the woods, the country dog soon took over ET's life, transporting him to high adventures in woods and grassy meadows. Every time the beagle-mix went bounding into the deep woods to pursue a hare or squirrel, ET followed in hot pursuit. He tried hopping like the agile beagle but usually failed to make it over dead tree-trunks and other jungle booby-traps. Sometimes, a low branch would give him a whack, making him yelp in surprise. Notwithstanding, he did not give up trying, doggedly tackling obstacles in a futile attempt to keep pace with the new love of his life.

A year and half later, while we went about building our new house, Camille unexpectedly contracted pneumonia. She had become extremely frail. One veterinarian told me her condition was terminal; an undetected uterine cancer had metastasized to other organs. I would not let go. I consulted many other veterinarians, desperate for a miracle cure to prolong her life. In retrospect, my efforts only prolonged her suffering.

I had a special maternal feeling for Camille. She was the only dog who traversed three different regions of the world with me: Asia, Europe, and the United States. For some reason, she needed more nurturing than ET. Born in Asia and raised by my parents, she lived better than most Asian dogs. Yet strange sounds panicked her, sending her scrambling under the bed, shivering. When she came and lived with us in Paris, her life became fuller, her world more varied. When we retired to the American South to live beside my parents and sisters, Camille was to live out her old age among those she loved and who loved her. She had come full circle. Unlike the supercilious and demanding ET, she never took anything for granted, she never asked for much. She was always grateful for all the things we did for her.

That morning in early autumn she wailed continuously and piteously. I knew it had become unbearable. The double dose of Demerol did not alleviate her pain. I tried to comfort her in every way but she continued crying. I will never forget the look in her eyes. It still tears me apart when I think of it. She was assuring me it was all right; it was time for her to go. And not to worry because there are no tears in heaven. Lump in my throat and going limp all over, I wrapped her fragile body in a woolen blanket and drove her to the vet's clinic. The vet looked her over and said gently, "It is time." As he carried her in,

Camille turned and gave me a last look ~ comforting, full of dignity, peaceful.

For the last time I caressed her still-warm body, still redolent with the scent of talcum powder, and bade her farewell. We laid her to rest in a plot of tulips and daylilies, with a marble tombstone "To our Princess." She was sixteen.

I was distraught for weeks, unable to get out of bed to face another day. I felt I let her down, that it was euthanasia that had ended her life. It was not until much later that I accepted it was the disease that took away her life.

ET moved on; I moved on. To be sure, he never lost his princely privileges as my copain. But he never realized that in this new environment he did not enjoy princely status. He thought he was still in the company of friends like Angela who doted on him. He had no reason to believe that anyone who spoke English like Angela would ever be unfriendly or less indulgent, least of all, hurt him. It was a mistake. Paris had made him too trusting.

One afternoon, he came up the driveway, whimpering. Gasping, his legs gave way. Losing his balance, he lay on the ground, trembling. I thought he was putting on one of his expiring acts. But his eyes started to glaze over; he was breathing with difficulty. Oh God, he is having a real seizure! I screamed. Then I noticed a small puncture wound on his underbelly. He had been shot.

I had seen ET and Lucky at a neighbor's house a thousand yards below my sister's house. There was no doubt in my mind they had something to do with this. A teenage boy lived there with his moneyed parents. On this road leading to my sister's house there was only one other house occupied by an elderly widow living alone. I immediately telephoned the boy's mother and then talked to the young man. He owned up to the shooting. He was just playing with his BB gun, he said. Being new in the neighborhood, I did not make a legal issue out of it. That proved to be another mistake, I would find out later.

X-ray pictures showed an air gun pellet had penetrated four inches into his abdomen, missing his stomach. ET made it. Despite this traumatic experience, irrepressible ET never, for one moment, lost his affinity for humans.

Three years later, in the autumn of 1991, ET suffered a real epileptic seizure. He lay motionless, in a coma. I rushed him to the veterinarian but it was too late. I never knew for sure what caused it.

We prepared a grave for him at the edge of the woods under the oak and sweet-gum trees where he used to romp with Camille, Chornley, Lucky, Baby Girl, and all his other canine buddies. Third Sister's family held hands with us and prayed. Little Joy sprinkled his body all over with talcum powder and kissed him goodbye. He was thirteen years old; she was nine. From the time they met, she and ET had a unique and extraordinary empathy for each other.

Hares and squirrels come visiting the little cairn behind a hedge of red azaleas that mark ET's grave. But ET had never really gotten to know their kind in Paris.

His life straddled two continents, giving him the best of both: the excitement and color of city life in his prime, and the adventure and daring of country living as he grew older. Both worlds were replete with people and other canines who loved him exceedingly well.

When, on a starry night, my gaze turns toward the celestial realms, I sense irrepressible ET (a.k.a. Kenneth) there, disguised as the Blue Dragon in the Eastern sphere, clowning with the White Tiger in the West, clawing the air in a vain attempt to catch the Vermilion Bird in the South, and "gi'-me-fiving" with the Sable Warrior from the North.

PHASE THREE: THE AMERICAN SOUTH
(1988-   )

8

CHORNLEY

Bereft over Sulaika's unexpected death, Fifth Sister bought a Russian Wolfhound puppy to replace her. Bred from the *Laika*, Russian for Collie, it was sheer coincidence that this puppy took the place of "Laika," our nickname for Sulaika.

The breed name, Borzoi, comes from the Russian *borzyi* meaning swift. A coursing hound, it was developed by the Russian aristocracy in the 17th Century to hunt wolves, deer and other game. Working in tandem they run down the prey from each side, wresting it to the ground for the huntsmen.

He was named Charnley after a British orthopedic surgeon. Somehow, Charnley became Chornley. It was not until long after his death that I found out. However, I remember him as Chornley and I shall always remember him by that name. Sulaika's father was Charley, another strange coincidence.

I first met Chornley on one of my annual leaves, visiting Fifth Sister and her brand-new family in suburban Chicago. Fifth Sister and I were particularly close to each other, she being the youngest and to me the sister who most needed my help. In Manila when I had just gotten married and she was a collegiate arts student, she moved out of our parents' house to live with us.

Chornley was then just a leggy, gangly puppy. By next visit, he was almost as tall as a Shetland pony. He had mushroomed up to his full height, three feet tall at the withers, a hundred pounds or so. When he stood on his hind legs, placing his front legs on my shoulders, and I hugged him, his head towered over mine.

Strikingly handsome, waves of sandy silk enrobed a torso splotched with islands of brown over back and haunches. His nose was aquiline; his lips, pincer-like. Hazel eyes stared intensely from Chinese-like slits; his ears were small, fine and feathered at the edges. His head was long and narrow, forehead slightly domed. I loved running my fingers over broad shoulders that sloped down to a narrow, deep chest. His gait was quick but slightly stiff, an unmistakable Borzoi arch to his back as he pranced on spindly legs feathered at their trailing edges. His long saber tail, also feathered, described an upward, reverse arch behind him. Everywhere he went his stately bearing made heads turn.

Belying a somewhat intimidating look, Chornley was at heart kind and gentle, especially around Fifth Sister's infant daughter Katie, who was then just starting to walk. Once I saw her trip on Chornley's huge bulk as he lay prone, startling him. But all he did was whimper, almost inaudibly. He did not even get up. It was as if he knew a sudden move could cause Katie to stumble and fall.

Each year I looked forward to being with him again. I watched him win ribbons at dog shows. "Big boy," as I called him, enjoyed taking walks on a leash with me. The first time, he started pulling me with all his might past five houses to where his friend Susie, a sassy ball of a West Highland terrier, lived with her owner, a retired postwoman. The impudent squirt came charging at him, whereupon Chornley whimpered as if to say "Please, I'm just visiting. Don't be scared." Every March, Susie and her human companion celebrated Chornley's birthday with a fancily decorated "cake" of raw, freshly-ground sirloin steak layered with cheddar cheese on top, complete with candles.

Three years passed. Fifth Sister's family moved to the foothills of the Blue Ridge Mountains. The twenty-two-acre wooded estate seemed the perfect place where Chornley could roam and romp. But alas, there was a fly in the ointment. Unlike in Chicago here he was an exotic breed unfamiliar to the locals. Not to take a chance, the family kept him chained to a long cable stretching thirty feet apart between a hickory nut and sweet-gum tree, his doghouse under one of them. He could slide his tether from one tree to the other, but unfortunately, often it got caught on an azalea bush, rendering him immobile, sometimes for hours. He would sit sullenly, barking rhythmically to catch someone's attention. Other times he would whirl round and round in place, maniacally, as if chasing his tail.

Oceans of allergens made him scratch himself non-stop, sending him into fits of coughing, his eyes watering. Nature was unforgiving. It would begin in March with tree pollen, then grass pollen in May, and ragweed in August. Bored at the end of his chain, he occupied himself by constantly nibbling at his legs, ankle, and belly, causing sore spots to develop. Very likely, it was an atopic hypersensitive reaction to elements in the soil or to insect bites. He became extremely irritable and difficult.

Chornley in the Carolinas was no longer the Chornley I knew in Chicago. At first, he was unleashed late at night so he could get some exercise. However, the risk was ever present. Most everyone around had a gun. Frequently, staccato discharges of high-powered guns ~ probably target shooting ~ would crash through the trees. There was no choice. Chornley had to stay on a leash. It made him restless at first, then uncontrollable. Hoping it would help to calm him down, they decided to neuter him.

I felt for Chornley. I knew he desperately wanted to be free and roam the woods. He was a child of nature. Nevertheless, I recognized the risk ~ with regret, not knowing the community and how it would react to this wolf-like dog ~ and agreed it was prudent to keep him tethered. Still, my heart ached for him.

In Asia, city houses have high walls. In America, despite the absence of fences, people surround themselves with invisible walls that none, including neighbors' pets, can breach save at their own peril. A living creature is less important than material property. Property rights, oftentimes embracing public streets along one's frontage, are jealously enforced. In America, the word "sue" is more often a verb than a name.

Chained, Chornley took to howling at night, long and mournfully, like a forlorn wolf in search of its kind. His plaintive wails were distressing to hear. My mind immediately conjured up Jack London's White Fang.

In my heart, I felt Chornley was still the kind and gentle dog I knew. My aging Poodle and French mutt knew it, too. The diminutive Camille would leap up and snap in his face whenever he bristled and barked at the mail carrier. Chornley would hunker down, whimpering like a child being scolded. Other times, when ET (a.k.a. Kenneth II) came within reach, he would try goading him to play by nudging him with his snout. Not always inclined to be chummy, cantankerous ET would snap at him. Ah, yes, but when the mood seized him ET would playfully nip at Chornley's heels and before Chornley could react, dash madly away. Doubling back, he taunted him again. He knew Chornley's long chain kept him from hitting back.

Flicker knew it too. From the start a strange chemistry developed between them. Nose to nose, nose to butt, the two hit it off well. From a distance, they looked deceptively alike. Flicker was an aged Shetland pony who had been retired from her job of giving rides to children. Fifth Sister acquired her before she was put out to pasture. Freely wandering across the estate but always stopping short of property lines, she earned her keep as a non-stop lawn mower.

There was something about Chornley that drew Flicker to him. Earlier on, she had taken to sleeping at night in the deep woods rather than in the stable. But now she began sleeping near Chornley's doghouse, in the open when it did not rain. In the daytime, the two often took naps side by side. Flicker could be seen taunting Chornley, flaunting her hind parts in his face, flirting as only female ponies with long bushy tails can.

A tit-for-tat feeding arrangement took place. Bored with his dry dogfood, Chornley often upended his dish, scattering bits of dogfood on the ground. Flicker took this as a cue to go chomp at the rejected food. On the other hand, whenever he had the chance Chornley would head straight for the stable and help himself to Flicker's sweetfeed, relishing its molasses content.

Not chained, Flicker had an edge over Chornley. Each morning she displayed herself, blatantly, on the lawn right in front of the breakfast windows. This way she managed to weasel her favorite morning handout ~ slices of white bread with chunky peanut butter ~ from the amused children. From a distance, Chornley jealously barked.

And when a children's party was in progress, Flicker would emerge from her secret hideaway to demand her share. Chornley, who had become less predictable, was seldom allowed to participate. The sunroom doors being usually wide open, Flicker would shamelessly invite herself in. Once, she even attempted to enter the kitchen after successfully sneaking past the Florida sunroom undetected. Carrots were the only way to assure her she too belonged ~ outside, not inside the house. If she saw the saddle and bridle being brought out for the children, unless physically restrained she took off, galloping back into the woods. After all, it was from such a chore she had been liberated when she retired. She had had enough of human exploitation. Party over, Flicker would sashay her way back toward the sunroom from her sylvan hideaway. On the brick pavement outside she would stomp sharply with her hooves ~ for her share of scraps. This was Flicker. But she is another story.

The place seems like a Norman Rockwell type of community in which to raise a family. On its main street older residents lounge in a soda fountain for homemade chicken salad. In spring and early summer the greens and blooms of reviving life drape the hills. Bouquets of azalea, rhododendron, dogwood, crocus, daffodil, and yellow Chinese forsythia splash the landscape with the pastel shades of an impressionist palette. In late summer the palette turns vivid with daylilies, phlox, poppies, peonies, marigolds, bonfire salvia, forget-me-nots; the air becomes redolent with the fragrance of honeysuckle. On the untended, open countryside wild blackberries, huckleberries and honeysuckle compete with the smothering kudzu. Cows graze alongside horses in pastures on the hillsides. Elderly country folk sit idly on rocking chairs in verandas, dogs at their feet, waving to cars passing by. Doll-like houses with crimson or pink geraniums in hanging baskets at the foot of mountain ranges evoke images of Swiss Alps villages. The mountain air is sweet and pure, spiced with many delicious scents. A few miles away lie the town of Ferguson, the setting for the tragic Tom Dooley and Laura Foster story. A little further looms the Blue Ridge Mountains, gateway to the Appalachians.

We built our house beside Fifth Sister's. All the while we were under scrutiny. We found an unsigned, unstamped letter in our mailbox complaining that our lights were on late into the night! It seemed that bothered someone. The nearest neighbor was down the hill, 550 yards away, screened from view by tall trees.

Ignoring such incidents, we went about making this our home, our last stop. We began inviting people over and tried to become part of the community.

It was clear the old stereotypes about Asians persisted: laundry, restaurant, grocery business, mail-order brides, military service wives. We were not active in any of the local congregations. That made us really different and isolated. For, the only way to belong to the community, I learned later, was to belong to a local church.

"Y'all 'tawk differeint. Y'all 'ave an acceint. Wheir 'ya from?"

"We live here."

"But y'all ain't from here originally, ar 'ya?"

"No. How about you?"

"Yay, we're Murkins."

"Are you native Americans then?"

"Lordy. Naw, course not."

Unlike the overseas Chinese in Southeast Asia, the Chinese who came to America in the 19th century were mostly contract workers, coolies of peasant origin. They were "imported" as guest workers in the mad race to span the continent from West to East and from East to West with railroad lines at the height of the gold-rush fever. They came mostly from the southern province of Guangdong, adjacent to Hong Kong.

Because of its proximity to China, the region of Southeast Asia (Nanyang) was the favorite destination of Chinese who were traders and seekers of commercial opportunities. They were usually not of peasant origin but from mercantile or artisan classes, mostly from the coastal province of Fujian, but some from Guangdong and other southern provinces. Those from Fujian Province made up the Hokkien of Taiwan, the Philippines, and Indonesia. Teochiu and Hakka made up the majority of those who sojourned in Malaysia and Singapore, Thailand, Vietnam, Laos, and Cambodia.

The economic success of the Nanyang Chinese as a whole gave them higher social status in their host societies in contrast to their compatriots in America. It provided them the leverage to assert their own identity unlike the Chinese in America. Here in America the majority white culture was so dominant that any minority group that tried to participate was subject to tremendous pressures to conform. However, the Chinese by law and for racial and cultural reasons were at that time barred from participating; society was not yet disposed to accept multiculturalism. In Southeast Asia, host cultures were less dominant and not too different from that of the Chinese. The Nanyang Chinese felt they were dealing with native cultures on even, if not superior terms. Therefore, they felt little need to conform and assimilate, unless required or forced to do so by law.

In the 1970's, Chinese who had already been naturalized in Southeast Asian countries began pulling up stakes and remigrating to America. The causes were multiple, but foremost was the liberalization of U.S. immigration laws in 1965 that permitted a sudden influx of Asians. There were other push-and-pull factors. Political upheavals in Southeast Asian countries caused a resurgence of scapegoating aimed at the resident Chinese. As before, those who were successful in the business and professional sectors were targeted for blame in the wake of growing difficulties in those countries. Pressures to emigrate became stronger; at the same time these modernized Chinese were now well equipped to make their way in American and European settings. Business was steadily becoming global in character and reach; professional and technical skills made these Chinese well suited to carving out new careers for themselves in the industrial societies of the West.

Such new immigrant waves were a far cry from earlier ones. A new term was needed for them. Wang Gungwu, a noted Nanyang Chinese historian, began to refer to them as the **hua-i.** *They were products of Western-style schools and had the training and abilities other new immigrant Asians had. All came to America better equipped to fit into American society   than their predecessors. America by this time had become better disposed to accept them as potential contributors to the scientific, technological, educational, cultural, artistic and commercial progress of America. They joined the ranks of the descendants of pioneer immigrants, who themselves had moved up and were now making their way in mainstream America with notable success.*

Every new upheaval in Asia - the Korean and Vietnam Wars, Pol Pot, Tien An Men, the turnover of Hong Kong to Beijing, the overthrow of dictators Marcos and Suharto - spewed up fresh waves of eager immigrants, transferring considerable wealth to their adoptive country. The majority - with the exception of refugees from Vietnam and Cambodia - came with adequate financial resources and education. Such was the nature of the Hua-i. The character of the Chinese Diaspora had undergone a major change.

After two years, Fifth Sister's family pulled up stakes and moved south to a city near Charlotte. They left Chornley to me. Camille had in the meantime passed on. By now, a country yokel we named Lucky had become a member of the pack. Lucky and ET took turns briefing Chornley about our house rules.

In effect, Chornley had to be resocialized by all of us working together. As he became more secure and assured of his place in the family, he became more expressive about his needs, desires, and feelings. It was gratifying to watch his personality open up, disclosing layer after layer of formerly suppressed facets.

One summer afternoon the pack of three was with me as I was washing my car on the concrete driveway overlooking a neighboring subdivision. All three sat idly surveying their domain. Suddenly Chornley started howling. He threw his head back, raised his snout to the sky, and in a long, sustained falsetto, let loose a melodious

WHOOOO! Moments after ET and Lucky followed suit with their own little WHOOs! at a different pitch but with the same intensity. All three had their heads upraised, howling in unison, taking their cue from Chornley, who clearly was the star diva in this performance. The a cappella harmonies resonated down the hillside. Playfully I took the cue and ululated along, raising my head heaven-ward and emitting my pitiful version of WHOO! The frequency and duration of their howls took on an assertive tone, attaining higher decibel levels. I was now one with the pack. Chornley was our shaman, linking us all to the sky spirits.

Surprisingly, ET maintained his top dog ranking in the pack. How could that be? In the wild, size and strength was certain to give Chornley dominance and ascendancy. But here he was at the lowest rung. Was it ET's seniority? Perhaps his Paris origin? His insolent persona? Alternatively, was it human fiat that decreed for fairness' sake that the one associated longest with humans had to have the highest rank?

Indeed, ET stayed at the top, especially at the feeding trough. In the wild, wolf morality required the older ones eat last, usually getting just the leavings. ET, being the most senior, had to eat last. Instead, ET opted for Chinese values, which decreed the primacy of age. The wily Lucky, though five years Chornley's junior, ate next. Lucky developed the anti-social habit of sorting out, pushing aside the rice and potatoes with his snout, and then gobbling up the meat. Salivating as he waited in the background, Chornley would plead with his eyes and turn to me, and if he caught my eye he would look back to the rapidly disappearing food as if to say, what about me? He would do this, alternately shifting his gaze until I got the message and forcibly instituted democratic reforms.

Chornley's dilemma made me think about parallels between animal and human cultures as far as priorities at the feeding trough were concerned. In Asia, dining means universally sharing from a common pile or collective dish on the table. Giving way or eating last is seen as an act of deference or courtesy, taking precedence is a matter of higher status and privilege. In America, people eat from individual platters. One takes what one needs or wants. The rule is first-come first-served. However, when a dish is rare or in short supply, timidity can be a sign of weakness, admitting lower status. Sadly, in my own extended family where differing cultures are commingled, the question of precedence at the feeding trough all too often was misperceived, causing much tension.

As I got to know Chornley and he me, just a look into his eyes and I knew instantly what he wanted. Sometimes he wanted a car ride. Chornley thought of the car as his chariot to new vistas, sounds, scents. Because quality of life mattered even to dogs, I felt obliged to daily drive him and the pack somewhere, even if it was only 500 yards downhill to pick up mail.

Dogs too, get bored from just sitting around the house all day. Car rides and its close substitute, going for a walk (for vehicle-challenged city dogs), give the opportunity to be in touch with dogdom in the world out there. And of course a chance to leave messages behind for the next nosy canine.

The car was a gray Cavalier station wagon generously wrapped around with windows. The rear seat folded down, allowing "Big Boy" to squeeze in by stooping a bit as he clambered in. If he stayed upright his back scraped the car ceiling. With the car in motion he usually sat like the sphinx. Lucky sat beside him, sad beagle eyes staring back at people "in dull surprise." With his squad of Pfc.'s at the back, Master-Sergeant ET rode herd from the front passenger seat. At traffic stops, other drivers, usually stone-faced, broke into wide grins the moment they caught sight of the trio of small, medium, and (very) large comedians. I got a lot of honking and thumbs-up signs on the road.

Among the three, there was constant jockeying for the best seat. Once, returning to the car loaded down with two heavy grocery bags, I panicked when I saw no dogs! Maybe I had not bothered to lock up. Running around the car, I saw Chornley's humongous bulk contorted to fit into the front passenger seat, long legs dangling to the floor. Triumph was etched all over his face. Big Boy had decided to be Number One this time. But ET would have none of that. He simply moved up a rung ~ that is, occupy *my* seat. After all, he was the Alpha dog. Lucky, who fancied himself Heir Apparent, took the floor beneath the driver's seat. Canine social stratification?

This question of hierarchy brought back vivid images of a 1978 trip to China. Landing at Kunming, Yunnan ~ a Southwest province bordered by Tibet and Burma on the west, Laos and Vietnam to the south ~ the team leader, my husband, was ushered into the lead limousine, a black *Hongqi* (Red Flag) sporting the numeral 1 on its plate. The rest of us piled into three *Shanghai*, numbered accordingly. However, Chinese protocol decreed a car precede the motorcade to clear the way. Since the lead car was number 1, the point car had to be 0. Imperiously, it led the way, honking incessantly through the unbelievably dense bicycle traffic. Chinese sense of order?

In no time, Chornley was a full-fledged member of the family. He learned to solicit perks such as a body massage by slipping his ponderous body under my hands. Whenever I brought out their grooming kit, toothbrushes and all, he was first in line. He especially liked the feeling of baby powder raining on his coat. However, he avoided nail clippers as if they were instruments of torture.

Chornley brought my nurturing instincts into full play. He responded like a child I never had. Our mutual bonding grew by the day. My husband reported that whenever I left him behind, Chornley turned catatonic. He would lie in his bed refusing to eat, emerging only, again becoming alive, when he heard the garage door opening.

It was not until a year later that I became confident Chornley would not hurt anyone ~ humans or dogs ~ entering his space. We had driven 280 miles to celebrate the tenth birthday of Joy. A neighborhood boy, not more than two-and-a-half feet tall, suddenly came running toward Chornley. Children sometimes mistook Chornley for a pony. Chornley was idling under a sweetgum tree, watching me rake autumn leaves and debris on Third Sister's front yard. Sitting on his haunches Chornley was taller than the boy. As the boy got closer, Chornley scrunched down and bowed his head low. Then he lay down on his side, emitting his usual tiny whinnies. He was inviting the boy to pet him!

I was not surprised when Joy said she wanted Chornley to feel really special in her house. She remembered Sulaika in Chicago and instantly connected with Chornley. A sensitive child who, early on, had adopted a stray kitten she named Susie, Joy talked about being a veterinarian someday so she can save orphan animals. Even when she was still young, she was always for the underclass. Joy sensed Chornley's insecurities. She bought him treats with her allowance, gave him her favorite toys, and at night, sneaked him into her bed (he is not allowed in mine). Both slept back-to-back, Chornley often spread-eagled, jaws agape in utter bliss.

Guileless acts of kindness from the pure at heart restore and heal. Chornley immediately showed their magical effect: he began to look revivified. No longer did he have a hangdog, tail-between-legs, crestfallen look. His demeanor became calmer, more self-confident, even presumptuous.

One evening, lounging on a leather couch and watching Star Wars, Joy called out "Chewbacca" to Chornley on the floor. Without so much as a by-your-leave he stepped up with alacrity onto the couch and plumped down beside her, resting his snout on her lap. Playfully she stood up and straddled him as she would a horse, in the style of an equestrienne that she was. She then wrapped her arms and gangly legs tightly around his body, bussing him all over his face. That was Joy. Even when she was little, her heart was capacious.

Chornley came to my life at my most vulnerable. I identified with him because we were both lowly omegas. The precariousness of our situation aggravated my insecurities. My husband had retired on a minuscule pension; we faced a drastically reduced lifestyle. For a year we literally lived like gypsies, shuttling between three separate households: my parents', Third Sister's, and Fifth Sister's. Around us boobytraps and sleazy schemes littered the landscape, and we could not escape making a few financial missteps. It was an America so unlike the Europe we had just left. Minority groups were, as they always had been, marginal. The playing field was not level.

I felt I was a failure. In a society where material success was the be-all and end-all of life, not to succeed in this sense was inexcusable. Instinctively I turned to my kin. But this was like steering my ship into the teeth of a storm. The family's feverish climb up Gold Mountain had whipped up a storm. Culture clashes arising from interracial marriages had done grievous damage to the family. Contradictions from this source threatened to wreak endless havoc on family relations.

Back came old psychic pains. It was then I realized I had not really broken loose from the Confucian leash. Like an unweaned puppy, I found myself again jockeying with the other pups for the choicest teats. I had not quite cut the emotional umbilical cord. I found myself at a disadvantage in the games people played. Once more it was a game of clawing our way up the totem pole, all at once, trying desperately to avoid being forced back down. Not only was I a failure in this society, I was also failing in the competition closer at hand ~ within my own family. Chinese demons slithering out of my past and Western barbarians clamoring at the gate were there once more.

It was in this bleak situation of infantile dependence that Chornley came to me and instantly became a source of solace and strength. Mutualism took seed; Chornley himself needed rescuing. Needing help, he gave me help. He had absolute faith that I could respond to his mute pleas. Though I was crippled inside he knew I could be his guardian angel. His trust, in turn, empowered me.

Chornley's presence made me conscious that I had to succeed in something of value to me: succoring another living being even as I myself needed succoring. Mired in self-doubt, I had to have confidence if I were to help him. I knew if I failed, he was not going to complain, criticize, or accuse. And that would give me more anguish than if he were to question my failure.

He was unfailingly loyal where humans could be deceitful; gracious and magnanimous where humans could be abysmally petty; generous when they were inordinately greedy; simple when they were complicated. He comforted me when I was depressed.

This giant put himself completely in my hands. He showed it in many ways. Stepping up gently onto the sofa, he would try to squeeze his hundred-pound bulk into my lap, or, failing that, he would just plunk his large head with its long sharp snout on my lap. His attempts at being a lap dog made me laugh. When he started to ape my habits, down to my sleeping late mornings, I said well, imitation is the highest form of flattery. He even took to eating grapes and vegetables, not the usual fare of carnivores. Our bonding grew bright, never to grow dim.

Thus, Chornley filled a great void. When he curled up beside me, it was as if to reassure me it did not matter how successful or not I was, how much or how little money I earned, how well ~ or how dowdily ~ I dressed and looked. What mattered was what kind of a person I was.

I had been looking for love and acceptance in all the wrong places. This animal was bringing home to me the true meaning of bonding between humans and other animals. He was aware of my inner turmoil and despair. I knew he felt my pain as I felt his. He was a kindred soul; both he and I had simultaneously broken through the interspecies barrier. Of infinite satisfaction was my knowing what his life was like before, and what it was now. His successful makeover was above all *my* success story. By my uncovering hidden talents that otherwise remained suppressed, he liberated my own suppressed capabilities and sensibilities.

When late one hot, summery morning in 1993 Chornley had not returned from his early morning frolic, a small fear, not yet a premonition, took root and slowly grew into one. It was not like him to stay away for more than half an hour. Then a frantic scraping on the front door made my heart jump. With a mixture of anxiety and relief, I rushed to open it. It was Lucky, unusually agitated, eyes fear-stricken. The new ET, a Jack Russell, was trembling all over. Not one sign of him. No Chornley.

It was around 6:30 that Saturday morning when all three ~ Chornley, Lucky, and ET ~ woke me up by their restless movements in our bedroom where they all slept. Still half-asleep, I opened the front door to let them out one by one, but the three bolted out together. Their canine friends had come calling, for a romp through the woods. I was sleeping later than usual after a three-week car trip to Santa Clara, California, where my husband had a family reunion.

It was our first long trip after Europe. I did not want to take the trip because it meant leaving the dogs behind. My husband's relatives were allergic to dogs. With much reluctance, I finally conceded. I decided to bring Lucky along, for he was the most flexible. ET would have to stay behind and keep Chornley company.

I arranged with a working student, who had a small dog of her own, to stay at our house and look after them. Every day I telephoned, without fail, to check how the "boys" were getting along. I was worried that Chornley could not handle my absence. He did not. Upon returning home, I realized how much he missed me. He had a confused, bedraggled look. The student told me he started to frequent Fifth Sister's estate next door, which by this time was sold but still unoccupied. Existential ET, always just living for the moment like the frisky Jack Russell that he was, did not appear to have missed me at all.

I lost no time looking for Chornley. Normally he responded immediately to my whistling and calling his name. I began making inquiries with neighbors. By this time Chornley was known, and I believed admired, by everyone. He gave style and elegance to the community. Surely, someone should have seen him that day. Someone did.

The blind owner of a convenience store nearby, who himself had a seeing eye dog named Iris, told me what the delivery lady of a local newspaper saw that early Saturday morning. She had seen a big white dog lying, with blood on its side, apparently dead, on the road leading to my sister's former house. I myself had passed the street early that morning when I began my search. I did not see anything there.

At first, I did not get the import of what my blind friend was telling me. Perhaps I was not prepared to accept what he was saying. In my confusion, I telephoned the woman who lived in the house near where Chormley was seen lying. Naively I confided to her what the blind man said. I knew the family; my husband even occasionally played the violin for their church. I thought we were friends.

I asked if her son saw Chornley that morning. She replied, matter-of-factly and without a trace of emotion that she would ask him and he would call me back. He never did. Even before the day was over and there was not a sign of Chornley, I began to have a sinking feeling in the pit of my stomach.

For nine days and nights I combed the neighborhood, every nook and cranny of it ~ yards, gardens and woods ~ in an ever-widening circle. I asked everyone, followed every lead, panic and despair welling up inside and driving me on. I let nothing deter me, neither the enervating heat nor a threat of tornadoes. Each morning I hurried to the front door upon the slightest noise, hoping it would be Chornley sitting there. I dreamt he was calling me, begging me to come and save him. I imagined every possible scenario. Kidnapped and sold to some laboratory for experiments? Hit and injured by a passing car? Caught in a trap in the woods? Lying prostrate somewhere, suffering extreme dehydration?

I searched, much as a desperate mother would for a missing child. I went to radio stations, veterinary clinics, humane societies, animal shelters of four neighboring counties, city and county sanitation services, and the department of transportation. The local newspaper ran the story with my substantial cash offer for his recovery or for information, with a recent photograph of Chornley. I distributed flyers and posted lost-pet signs at supermarkets, gas stations, telephone poles, churches, and trees around the neighborhood. I stuffed every mailbox in sight with flyers.

Spurred by a cash reward offer of $1000, no questions asked, people reported "sightings" not only in our county but in neighboring ones as well. I left no stone unturned. When rumors came that a dog answering to the description was being put up at a livestock weekend-auction, I went. When another report came that some local hunters intended to sell a hunting dog, in Virginia, I went to befriend the men. I followed every lead. Every one led to a dead end.

In the course of my search I uncovered the extent of dog trading going on, something I thought was true only of Third World countries. I heard about dognapping syndicates covering several states, that specialized in snatching pets from backyards for organized dogfights, a favorite sport in neighboring Tennessee. Specially desired were feisty little breeds like poodles and chihuahuas to be pitted against the bigger breeds such as rotweilers and pitbulls. Dognapping by backyard breeders was common. So was target shooting of animals; family pets were easy moving targets for testing firearms of every conceivable type ~ hand-made or store-bought.

When the local sheriff solicitously advised me it was dangerous to name a specific dollar figure in the reward offer ~ to him, an unusually large amount ~ I began to understand why people get paranoid in America. I could not sleep, or eat. My husband worried about how this was affecting me, gnawing on my mind, shriveling my spirit, and ruining my health.

On the fourth day, in response to my flyer, the newspaper delivery woman who had seen Chornley's body telephoned me. She was surprised to learn I was still searching for Chornley. Did the blind man not tell me what she saw that Saturday morning? she asked.

My heart beat fast as I breathlessly plied her with questions. It was a hot muggy afternoon but I broke into a cold sweat as she repeated her account. It was about seven in the morning as she went about delivering papers on the Dead End street, when she saw a big white dog on the edge of the road, almost on the road shoulder, lying in a pool of blood. She noted a gaping wound on his belly. Twice she drove by, to check if the dog was still alive. He had on a fancy red collar, just like what Chornley was wearing that morning. He was so clean, she said. Someone must have loved and cared for this dog very much, she thought. She wondered who could have done such a heinous thing to someone so beautiful.

My mind in a whirl, I returned to the place where Chornley's body was last seen. It could not have been any other dog except Chornley; there were no others like him around. When I looked closely at the paving where he was supposed to have lain, close to the road shoulder, I saw what looked like large bloodstains, now dry.

What happened to his body? With this question hanging over me, I desperately cast about for clues. Three elderly persons were leisurely walking on the same street. I recognized the man as the father of the teenage boy. I approached the man, he met me with a cold stare. I told him what the eyewitness said she saw. He did not say anything. The elderly woman whom I did not recognize finally spoke up, saying she had heard gunshots from over there (pointing to the Archie Bunker section nearby). That was all she said. Then they all walked away. No sympathy, no commiseration. I did not know then that she was the aunt of the young man. I did not know that they were residents of the two recently built houses on this same street. I did not know they were all kin to each other and that this kin group had "appropriated" this street to be their "family street," this Dead End street where dogs could *end dead*.

On the ninth day, at about eleven in the evening of a Sunday another eyewitness came forward. I did not know him personally. Neither did he know the other witness, the delivery woman. They were an elderly couple from Philadelphia who had come to live here to be near their grandchildren. He worked as a security guard in a big furniture plant. They had just returned from an out-of-town trip and had found my "missing dog" flyer in their mailbox.

I might as well end my search, he told me over the telephone. A neighbor's son had shot and killed my dog. His house was right next to the perpetrator's house, their driveways were adjacent to each other.

This witness was getting into his car to go to work that Saturday when he heard two deafening gunshots from the direction of the carport of his neighbor, thirty yards away. Startled, and not knowing who was being shot at, he ducked. The blasts were so loud his wife who was inside their house quickly came out to see if her husband was all right. They heard what were unmistakably the sounds a stricken dog makes ~ a thud followed by a yelp and then a loud gasp, at the instant it is hit. Not wanting to be late for work, he did not tarry to investigate. As he drove off, he slowed for a moment at the Dead End corner, and looked down the road toward the cul-de-sac. He saw a big white dog lying on the roadside. It was 6:45 a.m.

My stomach heaved. It was the same youth who, five years earlier had shot my Paris ET with a BB gun! That time, when confronted, he owned up to it. On that occasion, I did not make much of it. A teen prank I thought. I believed he would never hurt my pets again. His whole family knew how much I loved them. There was no reason at all why anyone should harbor ill will toward Chornley. It was my mistake to have taught Chornley to be so trusting of humans. Otherwise, he would have steered clear of them.

I needed to know what happened and why? I phoned the mother immediately to discuss the matter. She said she would talk to her husband after which she would get back to me. When I did not hear from her, I telephoned her again. In a matter of minutes, she switched her stance, unexpectedly, to a rude "I don't know what you're talking about." No regrets, no apologies. Just hostile silence.

"All I want is closure," I pleaded. "Give me back his body, so I can give him a proper burial." Burying a loved one and laying him to rest is an essential, and valuable, part of the grieving process.

When it became obvious she was stonewalling, I had no choice but to turn to the law. After obtaining preliminary testimony from the eyewitnesses, the detective who handled the case called in the suspect, who did not come in for questioning until four days later. In the meantime, the eyewitnesses told me the suspect's mother had queried them on what they saw. When the suspect finally showed up, he refused a lie detector test, and said all questions should be directed to his uncle, a prominent local lawyer. This lawyer was an old acquaintance of mine ~ we had used his services in the past. I went to see him. He admitted he had gotten a call from the father that Saturday morning about a dog they identified as belonging to me. The lawyer agreed with me that the decent thing for them to do was to give me back Chornley's body. He promised to call back. He never did.

In the course of my inquiries, I learned for the first time about the perpetrator's record of juvenile delinquencies. Except that by now, he had turned twenty-one. I realized his family knew too well their way around the criminal justice system. The perpetrator was never going to be brought to justice and reap the consequences of his acts. They kept saying the law required "evidence beyond reasonable doubt." I did not even know this phrase then. They knew that without the body, the case would not prosper in the local courts, especially since I was not one of the good ol' boys. Because the *corpus delicti* was made to disappear and could not be used as evidence of crime, they knew the evidence would be circumstantial despite the eyewitness account of two reliable persons.

I had thought in simplistic terms: a crime is a crime; criminals must be punished. I thought the law protects the victim, not the guilty. Despite all good intentions and protestations to the contrary, the law enforcement system seemed to be biased and pusillanimous. It became clear that in my case, justice would not be served. Justice was not blind at all.

Those who previously had similar frustrations with the law took me aside and said: around here it's an eye for an eye, a tooth for a tooth. Clearly they were telling me what I could do.

The upshot was: I became a victim twice over. Once, by the killer; twice, by the system that failed me. In this system of laws, and in this scale of values, there is a world of difference between shooting a neighbor's dog and slashing his car's tires. Shooting a dog is just a misdemeanor; slashing a tire is a felony if malice is proven. A living creature, no matter how priceless to its human companion, is less valuable than automobile tires. Material property is more valuable than a life. What does this say about a society and its sense of values?

In our courts, abuse of a spouse, child, or the elderly is often no more than a misdemeanor. Spouses, children, and household pets are one's chattel; "property" to be treated as one pleases. What one does to them is nobody else's business. Life as property has lower status than material property. (Nevertheless, abuse of life as "property" could have dire consequences as in the O.J. Simpson case.)

At first, I thought Chornley was a victim of a random act of violence, as common as DUI. Was he just another statistic in America's sorry record on violence? Has the mean-spiritedness of the '90s become as American as apple pie? Cynics say mindless violence, like the flu, is here to stay. So, live with it. Or die with it.

Disbelieving, challenged, I immersed myself in the current literature on violence. Violent acts, I read, are seldom random. Often they are part of a syndrome, a coherent pattern, that reveals a growing propensity toward violence. Unless stopped ~ either by law or by therapy ~ the violent person is likely to commit progressively more serious acts, culminating in murder. For example, animal cruelty at an early age, usually dismissed as a childish prank or sport, could very well jumpstart the syndrome. At a later stage, other types of abuse such as child or spousal abuse may crop up on the police blotter. Such a proclivity may not discriminate as to victim, but always one who is weak and defenseless.

The message whistle-blowers send comes to mind. Animal abusers become people abusers, and it goes the other way too. If a person is cruel to animals, is it perhaps because he or she is a victim of abuse? An abused child in turn becomes violent to others weaker than itself, including helpless animals. In addition, he or she in turn could become an abusive parent producing violent children, repeating a fatal cycle. Did Chornley just get in the way of a vicious cycle?

A growing body of research backs up this correlation. While it may not be perfect, is it not prudent to heed early signs, in the same way that we take body temperatures, or watch economic indicators? Should not acts of animal cruelty be recognized as early-warning signs of a rage that could escalate beyond control unless addressed early?

It is of record that many convicted murderers started by committing acts of animal cruelty that were ignored. There was Henry Lucas, who when young killed animals and had sex with the carcasses. Later he killed many women and did the same thing. Another, Jeffrey Dahmer, the white serial killer who butchered and even cannibalized his innumerable victims who were mostly African and Asian-Americans started torturing animals at an early age. Davis, Polly Klass's kidnapper-killer, confessed to abusing animals. New York's "Son of Sam" launched his career of thirteen murders by shooting a neighbor's Labrador Retriever. Fourteen-year old Eric Smith who killed 4-year old Robie in Savona, New York said in a recent network interview, that when he was eight and felt rage he strangled a puppy.

However, there was something even more insidious about Chornley's killing. As I was putting the pieces together and conducting my desperate search, I befriended a man, "Six-pack Jack," at a poolroom in a working-class corner of the neighborhood. Every week, after collecting his welfare check, Jack would repair to this bar-poolroom-grocery honky-tonk joint, a favorite hideaway in a dry county. Commenting on my "reward for information" flyer posted at the poolroom door, he said "Don't jew me girl, dat's raht smaat lotsa money foar a dawg. 'Ya shore luv'm, don'cha?"

Then he said something that troubled me.

"Ya knaw, girl, ef a neigger waulked up da hill wid his dawg, we cain't kill him, but we shore cud kill his dawg," he chuckled and grinned, showing a gap-toothed mouth, the remaining teeth tobacco-stained. He looked very much older than his fifty years.

I wondered if he was joking or in dead earnest but the message implicit in his words kept echoing in my mind. Was there a connection with Chornley's killing?

I began to get it: my pets and I were fair game! Chornley had been singled out; he was a symbol. It dawned on me Chornley's murder was not senseless after all, not a random act of violence, not a juvenile act. Indeed, it contained a message, a subtle "Down-Boy" message directed at us. It was like a shotgun blast in the night, a midnight rap on our door. The dirty little secret was out.

No one who has never been in such a situation can ever imagine how cutting such a message can be, how much it assaults the human spirit, how difficult it is to handle, and how helpless it makes you feel.

I read the clues. First, there was a conspiracy of silence in the community. This indicated a closing of ranks, a battening down of hatches against people who were "different" ~ their term, not mine. It seemed that having a rare, classy dog like Chornley only served to play up that difference. Being different was not making a difference; it meant coming under pressure to be the "same." The perpetrator of Chornley's murder was a weapon forged by such attitudes. He expressed hate in another culturally accepted way.

"Why get upset? It's just an animal!"

This bald statement, ricocheting across meticulously manicured lawns and backyard barbecues, disturbed me as much. We were right smack in the middle of the Bible belt. However, God was not in this picture at all. The message implied that since animals do not have a "rational" faculty, they have no mind, no soul, no self-consciousness, no intelligence, no emotions or feelings. They just have instincts and reflexes. Because they are "different," their right to life does not exist as ours does.

Devaluing what is different justifies prejudices, debasing it excuses violence in all its forms.

When total strangers started leaving dogs and puppies at my door, it must have been a sincere gesture to comfort me. But in my grief and anger I thought it a subtle way of telling me to get on with my life, because, after all, it is just an animal, and it can be replaced.

Five days into my search, a bright red pick-up zoomed up my steep driveway with a light-colored miniature collie in the open back. Before I could say anything, a young, blond woman pulled a rope-leashed dog out and tied him to a stump by our driveway.

"Cost 'ya nothing for that dawg yonder. We seen yore dawg's picture in the papers. Looks like this 'un," an older woman, in a colorful cotton-knit shirt, drawstring polyester pants and Reeboks, called out from the pick-up, sounding like a salesman hard-selling me a second life-insurance policy.

How could anybody say a Sheltie looks like a Borzoi? A herding sheepdog for a coursing hound? This dog was only about fourteen inches tall, barely half Chornley's size, and probably weighed not more than twenty pounds. Then I noted the facial resemblance. Except that this one had dull, listless eyes. He stared with a fixed, colorless expression.

"This is not my dog," I said, with a sinking feeling again. No one could ever replace Chornley. Do they know something I do not, I wondered? I wanted Chornley back. I did not need a new problem on my hands. I could not handle it.

"Weill, I guess 'e goes to the pound," she said testily.

Hastily I took a second look at the dog. He had a choke collar on and was panting heavily; his thick coat all tangled and knotted. The summer heat was topping 95^0 F in the shade. His eyes were watery, a foul odor, the smell of pus, permeated his body. Gnats swarmed around red, raw scaly patches, oozing with body fluids, on his thighs and belly. He was frantically scratching the raw spots with his hind legs and then biting the exposed skin with his teeth. As gently as I could manage, I reached out to pet him. He shifted his weight to his rear legs, and without warning, neither a growl nor a bark, clamped down on my right wrist with his teeth. I felt a stinging pain.

I was angry not because he bit me, but because of this unwanted interruption in my search for Chornley. However, I was fearful of rabies. I knew that rabies hits the central nervous system, as the Ebola virus devours every organ of the body. I had heard in the news of isolated outbreaks of rabies in King's Mountain, seventy miles away. I asked if the dog had had his rabies shots. She did not answer. Instead, she diverted my attention to the dog's AKC papers, that someone else was interested in breeding him. Then she went to say that a schoolteacher had bought him as a Christmas gift for her four rambunctious boys. When he allegedly bit a neighbor's son and the father threatened to sue, the teacher passed Laddie (the name she gave him) to a fellow-teacher, who in turn passed him on to another. All in all Laddie had had five owners in two years. All kept him outdoors on a chain, because he always runs away. I thought, if I was tied to a chain all the time I would also run away.

I could not say no, of course. They left, leaving Laddie. Wasting no time, I brought Laddie to my vet for a complete medical work-up, the usual shots, and neutering. The vet said not to worry about the bite because there had been no local outbreaks.

Laddie proved to be an extremely difficult charge. He suffered from a split personality, engaging and friendly one moment and hostile the next minute. At first he just hid under chairs, his back to the wall, watching the goings on. Sociable ET tried his energetic best to connect with Laddie by enticing him with his squeaky toy, yipping as he did so. Laddie just stared stonily and suspiciously. After a while, the sight of a relaxed Lucky, lying on the Castro convertible, paws in air, spread-eagled, and oblivious to everything assured Laddie that he was in a non-threatening situation. Much calmer, he came out from hiding. Barking shrilly, he began responding to ET's taunts. Now it was my turn to built Laddie's trust. What has more power than a food offering? Good food has universal appeal. Laddie accepted my overtures. Despite his bad teeth which made chewing difficult, Laddie showed his gratitude by looking up at me whenever he tasted something he liked.

One night, confident I had won his trust, I stooped to hug Laddie who was sleeping on Chornley's blanket. I failed to notice the muscles of his face tensing up and his lips drawing back, baring his teeth. Without warning, he turned on me in a flash. The shock and pain shot up my head, and I felt faint. The bite was deep and broke the skin. I rushed to rinse the wound with soap and warm water, squeezing out the blood. Then I poured iodine and hydrogen peroxide on it. Suddenly, I was extremely afraid of this dog.

After much thought and with great reluctance, I decided he was too much for me to handle. I did not know what else to do. Driving to the local animal shelter, past traffic signs that bore bullet holes from trigger-happy rednecks, I kept thinking: What made Laddie snap? I was convinced that he was inflicted pain and associated it with humans. Remembering the pain, he anticipated it by protecting himself in the only way he knew. He was merely defending his space.

What I saw, heard, and smelled at the animal shelter quickly resolved a lingering doubt that was there even before I left the house. This was the fate of disposable pets. Death hung like a physical presence in the air. The stench was overpowering. I saw dogs, some purebred and healthy, in cages, drained of spirit. Some cowered in corners, legs trembling, tails between their legs. Eight dogs were crowded tightly in a cage, bigger dogs mixed in with smaller ones. I had the feeling that in such cases only the stronger left the cage alive. Then fewer needed to be gassed. That morning, there were fifty on death row. I saw dogs, whose turn had come to die, one after another stuffed into a small metal box that had known better days. Cheap, low-grade carbon monoxide (to save money), and a make-shift attempt to seal leaks in the "gas chamber" with duct tape, unnecessarily prolonged the execution process. If a dog was too big, a control officer sat on the lid to keep it shut. I saw and heard many, panic-stricken, struggle to get out, then the anguished screams of pain that gradually died down into moans and whimpers until I could hear no more. Others cowered in fear, as if aware their turn would soon come.

I raged silently at this example of a killing field. It was debasing to my humanity. I was told that their screams and cries, "mere animal vocalizations," did not mean the same thing as those of humans, because animal pain is not the same as human pain. Animals don't have a complex nervous system like those of humans.

That was what they used to say of Chinese coolies from Fujian and Guandong, stripped naked and branded like calves, beaten and hung up by their thumbs, chained and kept in bamboo cages, in ships bound for America to build the great railroads. Many Chinamen died in transit, or were burned alive when ships caught fire. Some who could no longer bear the pain simply jumped overboard.

What made it worse for me, this was about the time I learned that Chornley had been brutally murdered, that he would never come back to me. Here I was, unable to express my grief; too weak to be strong; too drained of energy to keep morale high. I felt like one of those caged dogs, a puissant, irresistible force poised over me, trapped and helpless to get out from under. The crying images never went away. Till this day, when I close my eyes to sleep, I can hear the silent screams.

I wanted to bring home with me every dog in that shelter. But Laddie was the only one I could manage at that time. Chornley would have wanted me to minister to Laddie's needs and not give up too quickly. Laddie taught me that giving him respect, not the use of the choke collar, was the way to connect with him. The moment I gained this insight and acted accordingly, he began to respond in ways I never imagined. Soft, tender eyes replaced a vacant, confused stare. I was suddenly aware of a potential in me: to give another being a new lease on life, releasing his own potential, so that he in return can bestow meaning and love to human lives. It was a good feeling, a very good feeling.

Laddie now lives happily with Johnny and Lori Mikeal, a young couple who loves him like a son. They have no children. They say he has added quality to their marriage. With a transformed Laddie in tow, the couple occasionally come visiting. They thank me for making Laddie a part of their life. And I thank them for making me a part of their life. Lori tells me wonderful stories about Laddie: how he dashes off to chase the sound of thunder; how he puts off eating until he is certain nothing better was to follow; how he has grown fat on pasta; how he jumps into their pick-up every Wednesday to remind Johnny it was their day together for running errands; how he ignores Lori when Johnny is around; how he quickly endears himself to people, even strangers; how he manifests his gratitude to the couple for sharing God's blessings with him. Laddie even teaches their two new Dalmatians the meaning of the words "settle down!"

My experience in the animal shelter, and what I learned from research, pulled me out of my cocoon of innocence. The data was mind-boggling! Seventeen million domestic pets are gassed, lethally injected, or dispatched by guns every year in the United States. Then they are thrown as refuse into landfills and dumpyards, at a yearly cost of $1.4 billion of taxpayers' money.

Why we should continue a vicious circle like this, taking life to make room for life, life that is mindlessly created by pet breeders entirely for profit, is beyond my comprehension. What does it say about a society that makes the callous disposing of an unwanted pet no different from throwing away a broken toy? Is such a wooden inability to empathize not a symptom of mean-spiritedness, or the actual, primal root of violence? *What does it say about anyone who regards living creatures as worthless and fair game for exploitation?*

I resolved to do something in redemption of Chornley's sacrifice. The brutality of his death and the gentleness of his life were a stark contradiction. It made me confront blatant oxymorons such as animal "shelters." Pets belonged in homes and with people the moment humans domesticated the wolf 11,000 years ago. However, if pets have to be done away with for one reason or another, their suffering does not have to precede their extinction.

Appalled at the abominable conditions that obtained in the local dogpound, I launched a reform agenda and did not stop agitating from that moment. After a bruising period, my persistence paid off. The day came when a sympathetic county manager convinced the county commissioners to institute much-needed changes. In January 1996, the county inaugurated a spacious, modern facility with a more caring staff, better adoption policies, spaying-and-neutering programs, and a more humane way of putting unwanted pets down. But someday, I hope, even such facilities shall no longer be needed. Nowadays, when animal control officers in my county investigate animal abuse cases, they recognize such abuses as red flags signaling the probable existence of other forms of abuse against spouse, child, elderly, and disabled.

Remembering a deceased companion in a way brings him back to life. Sadly, it also revives the traumatic events of his sudden death. Because I never recovered Chornley's body, there was no closure, no resolution, no final healing. The grief never seemed to go away. Someone very dear and important had been taken away from me in a hateful manner.

I tried to place Chornley's death in the perspective of Tao, drawing solace from our little collection of books. Light comes with darkness, the good comes with the bad, crassness with the sublime. Contradictions finally come together in a harmonious whole.

Meditating on these thoughts, my eyes drifted to a small pile of paperbacks by C.S. Lewis as if guided to them. *Problem with Pain, Surprised by Joy,* and *Mere Christianity* were the books our Good Samaritan in Somerset, England mailed us shortly after our happy meeting fifteen years ago. He had given us a helping hand when our car broke down one chilly evening on a desolate moor in southern England. I had dismissed them as typical inspirational Christian tracts and thought I had consigned them to a garage sale, only to discover I still had them.

I retrieved one, *Problem with Pain,* and began to peruse its pages. An insert slipped out and fell on the sofa beside me. It was an old newspaper clipping about the conversion to Christianity of a Confucian in the year 1873 in Cheng-hsien, China. Mr. Nying questioned the missionary Mr. Stevenson about God's will. "If God stands for good, why does he allow the helpless to suffer such pain? Is the Supreme Being far too great and distant to take notice of our little affairs?"

At that moment I could not fathom its meaning. Is suffering a necessary part of happiness ? The question transported me back to when Lewis Secrett opened the Shadowlands of C.S. Lewis to me. Was this diffident Englishman again reaching out across the gulfs of time and space to give me once again of his generous spirit, secretly to comfort me? He was gifting me once more.

Was God opening a window after closing a door? Was this yet another coincidence, a synchronicity?

I still hear the soft thuds of Chornley's huge paws on the oaken floors of our house, smell his talcum scent as I enveloped his body with my arms and locked him in a tight embrace with nary a sound of protest from him. I remember the warmth of his belly as he lay prone and I snuggled my head on it. I will never again witness the power and majesty of his galloping strides, his muscles rippling and his feathered tail and mane floating rampant like pennants across a field. Nor shall I ever forget the sheer joy and exultation in his face as he plowed, belly-deep, through the snow. I shall never again be able to laugh at his mimicry of a wolf, and to ululate along with him. I miss his silly little whine whenever a smaller dog bullied him.

I cherish the memory of our last night together, as he sprawled on the floor of our family room, his long, lanky front legs demurely crossed before him. He had been looking on as Lucky and ET squabbled over "chews," completely at peace. Our eyes met, and suddenly I had the impression he was thanking me for making him a part of my family, of my life.

I never did get to say good-bye to Chornley, to thank him for sharing with me four glorious years of his nine years on earth.

I know he is now in heaven, dutifully bringing up the rear behind Cinnamon, Yama, Rikki, Hamlet, Winchester, the two Kenneths, Camille, Sulaika, and all the other dogs that have shared their lives with me. I know he has met Grandmother and sits adoringly at her feet. Let me wish that once in a while he gets away from the crowd and peers down at me. I am afraid, though, the others keep him too busy playing.

Where he is, no one is on a leash.

9

BiG BOSS

Blank stares vanished, eyes lighted up and stony faces cracked into smiles. Residents sitting listlessly and unmoving in the lounge stirred to life. As their four-legged visitors trooped in and circled the room, checking out each resident, some reached out to pet them. Even the staff eagerly pressed forward.

The sudden appearance of Lucky and ET at the retirement home for the elderly turned on a switch. The effect was immediate. Reactions were of genuine, spontaneous delight. As I looked on, more than ever I thanked God for putting animals in the Ark.

At the activities room, where residents usually sat around bored, Lucky's famous tailwag and wet tongue flicked on switch after switch. With each loving pat he became friskier and livelier. I could sense him warming up. Usually I could not get him to put on a show except with a great deal of reluctance and no little amount of persuasion. It was beneath his dignity to be forced to do anything that was not his idea. This time he did not need urging.

Stopping before a resident, first he stretched out a left paw, then the right. The audience chorused "Howdy! Gimme five!" Pointing my index finger at him, I barked, "Bang, Bang! You're dead!" At this Lucky did his "Don't shoot, I give up" routine, collapsing and rolling-over, then lifting up a paw as if to plead for mercy. When asked, "are you nothing but a hound dog?" he bayed like a hound on the scent. It was obvious he relished every moment of his superstardom.

His doleful, basset eyes shone proudly as the seniors applauded each of his award-winning performances. Flaunting a red cowboy kerchief around his mane, he arched his rump high and fanned the air with grand sweeps of his bushy tail. Strutting from one enthused resident to another, he collected his fee ~ a pat here, a caress there. As he made the rounds, he came up to a stern-looking gentleman glued to a wheelchair behind which a nurse-therapist stood at the controls. Pushing his freckled snout into the man's immobile hands, he waited for the pat. With a mighty effort the man tried ~ the nurse making encouraging prompts ~ to lift a palsied hand to pat Lucky. It was in vain. It was obvious at that moment Lucky was succeeding in triggering the man's will.

"Since he lost control of some muscles the old man's been cranky and doesn't talk much," she said to me, sottovoce.

As if he recognized the problem, Lucky licked the man's hands. The man began to speak, haltingly and in a low, rasping voice: "He's freckled as a guinea egg . . . like the dawg I had ..." Nostalgically and in a halting voice he talked about his own dog of happier days. Afterwards, as we moved on to others, he looked fondly after Lucky and managed to say in a loud voice, "Y'all come back, d'ya hear?" It was also addressed to me.

It was remarkable that, though this was the first time they met, the two had bonded quickly, comfortable in each other's mute presences. The species barrier virtually had ceased to exist.

At the other end of the chamber, ET busily did his thing: roll frenziedly on the floor like a log. This was how he usually called attention to himself. Like the first ET, he was an unabashed show-off. He drew from a rich bag of tricks that he created from the games we played at home.

When a speech-impaired woman tossed a tennis ball in the air for ET to catch, he leaped high, twisting his body in midair, catching the ball with his mouth as only short-haired Jack Russells can do. After another resident dropped a toy into a pail of water, without hesitating ET dunked his head underwater to retrieve it. Then he did his cliffhanging, "look, what strong teeth I have" act. While lunging at the knotted rope I was whirling about, like a gymnast ET pirouetted and twisted in mid-air. Getting hold of the rope with his teeth, he hung on for dear life, wiggling his buttocks while suspended in air. A wave of applause swept through his audience; they began to chant, "E-T, E-T!" With Lucky and ET in the room I felt a rising of spirits.

Dressing him in a shocking-pink belly-dancer top and a lace bikini, ET's burlesque brought the house down. The nurse suggested I prop ET up on a sofa beside an old man suffering from dementia. Pleased with the attention, the man mumbled "Wha' kahn of a dawg is that, et's so praity, cute as a bug's ear."

Lucky moved on to a well-dressed woman in the audience, and proceeded to lick her perfumed hands. "He loves me, he loves me," she sobbed softly to the nurse aide standing behind her. The nurse whispered to me that every day this gentle lady waited for her only son to take her home, not knowing that he had sold her house. The son rarely came to visit.

During that brief visit my dogs managed to open sealed lips and floodgates of the mind. A retired schoolteacher pulled my hands to hers and reminisced about the Poodle she once had. She spoke of the sadness she felt having to give him up before coming to the nursing home.

All this was a eureka experience for me. I realized it was the gift of love that brought these kindred spirits together, my dogs and residents, and mended the broken ones among them. The sense of aloneness and alienation that made each person languish in private despair metamorphosed into a single, all-embracing and comforting rapture. It led to catharsis and release for everyone. It was a bonding of separate minds and souls, a synergy of disparate therapies.

When we came home, Lucky's eyes were shining as never before. "I've found a mission," they seemed to proclaim. In mid-life, launching a new career as pet therapist was therapeutic for him as well. He needed to get over the loss of Chornley as I did. Like me, he had a page in life to turn.

Lucky had witnessed Chornley's violent end and it affected him deeply. Listless at times, at other times he seemed to lapse into melancholy. Outdoors he would sit and gaze pensively down the hill, toward where Chornley was shot, and whine softly to himself. He shared my unspeakable sorrow too.

Up to this point I was preoccupied almost exclusively with my surviving pet companions ~ what they meant to me and I to them. One day, idly leafing through some reading material, I came across stories of animal-assisted therapy programs in various human situations. The idea resonated with me. Animals can heal humans as well as be healed by humans. Just as my dogs healed me, they can heal other distressed humans. My mind, now activated, flashed back to what I had previously read about the *Gaia* act of sharing among different creatures spanning species barriers.

I pondered two possibilities. Lucky's serene persona suited the needs of retirees in nursing and retirement homes. ET's Type A personality complemented the needs of hyperactive children. He could match their hyperkinetic tendencies, keep up with them and show them how to keep excess energies under control.

I thought of Chornley and what a marvelous therapist he could have been. With all that attention directed at him, he would have been at his regal, well-mannered best; he would have given the elderly residents the treat of their lives.

While I never believed in making any of my pets earn their keep (making them virtual slaves), my pets genuinely enjoyed the human-animal interaction. Perhaps we are all together on earth precisely for this reason ~ to enrich each other's lives. Convergence of lifelines may have been intended to enhance an individual's karma.

To what else could I attribute the way Lucky and ET came to me? And how they helped lift the bamboo gate, letting me into the secret garden? Lucky was a *coup de bonheur*, literally bounding out of the bucolic landscape.

Pleading for succor from under the sun-drenched bushes of wild blackberries, near stands of oak and maple, beech and sweet gum, black and white pine, this scruffy ball of fluff, alive with a hundred fleas, came crawling into my life. At the time, I still had the Paris ET, Camille, and Chornley. I was not ready for another one. But again, it was one of those synchronicities. I did not have to be reminded of the Chinese belief that to turn one's back on a dog that comes to you is to turn away luck.

Lucky is a "pretty" dog, if that properly describes a male, albeit neutered dog. To me it is the only word to describe him. Picture a sporty Beagle head, a graceful Springer Spaniel body with black curls springing here and there from a wavy silk coat, and soulful Basset eyes. His gait is like that of a wind-up mechanical toy. In spring and summer, when I trim him down almost to the skin, he looks more like a Beagle and is often mistaken for one, except when he flaunts that unmistakable tail, one that no Beagle could ever dream of owning.

Locals call him a "Sooner"~ sooner this than that ~ but what a mix! A white elongated triangle points down his gently sloping head to his nose, brown dots freckle his face and legs. His nose is slightly upturned, like a Cavalier King Charles Spaniel; long floppy Beagle ears have the black, silky-soft fringes of a spaniel, random curls springing up here and there. His paws are thick and large, heavily padded for treading on the underbrush like those of a coonhound; his legs are feather-fringed. But the tail is his crowning glory. It is like a Pointer's tail but adorned with a magnificent plume, like that of an Irish setter, and tipped with white. Whenever he hops, skips and jumps through the underbrush that white tip marks his progress, waving high above the brambles, weeds and rushes, as a ship's crows-nest rides high above the waves of a roiling sea.

He was not born with a silver spoon in his mouth, but he sure picked one up along the way. Not the luck of the Irish, of course, but the charmed life of a lowly mutt. Lucky was to prove that one's fate lies not in the stars but in one's character. He was a survivor, and as it proved, the most plucky. He certainly knew how to take care of himself.

As he emerged from puppyhood it was clear he was destined to be an overlord, bossing all around him. Inevitably, we dubbed him "Big Boss." In a quiet but no-nonsense way, he imposed his will on anyone around, never brooking opposition. He ruled with an iron paw. If displeased, all he had to do was to grimace and frown, his lips twisting in scorn, squelching all further disputation. Soon everyone ~ dogs and humans alike ~ was kissing up to him, even my parents. Lucky was the Emperor; he had the mandate of heaven. Of all my dogs, he had first claim to the title, *Tuatauke*, which in Fujian means "tycoon."

Father was completely unaware we had given Lucky this honorific title. I was at Father's house one day. Hurrying to post a letter, I impatiently shooed Lucky into my car. As usual, he was dawdling.

"Let's go, Tuatauke, quick," I said. I had not seen Father come out the back door, trash bag in hand.

"I'm not going with you," Father hastily replied, waving a hand and shaking his head.

Lucky came running, his bushy, fringed tail held high. I got out to open the door for Tuatauke and he quickly jumped in. Looking out the front passenger window with his nose pressed against the glass, lips curled in a secret smile, Lucky peered out at Father outside. For a moment Father glared fiercely out of beetling eyebrows. Then realization grew. He smiled from ear to ear, his eyes disappeared, and then he chortled. That he had lost his monopoly on top-dog status in the family to a dog vastly amused him.

Lucky had this irresistible appeal. People were always enamored of his looks, and impulsively felt they had to own him. Once, at a rest stop in Greensboro, a longhaired surfer-type whose car sported California plates sidled up to Lucky, who was absorbed in the latest canine gossip. As the man moved closer, Lucky edged away. He hunkered down, beckoned to Lucky, and held out what looked like a piece of sandwich. Fixing him with a suspicious look, Lucky craftily padded back to my parked car. I quickly opened the rear car door, calling out Lucky's name. But there was no sign of Lucky. I went around the car and saw Lucky playing "hide-and-seek" with the man in between parked cars. Veteran hunter that he was, Lucky knew that predators stalk the prey first before launching an attack. Cannily he kept out of the man's line of sight. When I opened the car door on the side where he was waiting, Lucky bolted in. Safely ensconced in the car, he stared out, the tip of his tongue sticking out between his front teeth

"You got yourself a smart pooch there. I sorta like his looks. Sure would like to have him," the surfer said.

Yes, indeed, Lucky could seduce. Everyone, human and canine, fell under his spell. If there was a universal canine standard of beauty and index of cuddliness, Lucky was at the top. Even the insouciant Paris ET succumbed, habitually deferring to this country yokel ~ "Born Free," another one of Lucky's labels. Neighborhood canine Lotharios came to kow-tow. Every dog, especially the male ones (for a strange reason), wanted to mount him (without luck of course) especially when he was still a puppy. For example, there was Oscar.

It was late fall. I was tending a patch of lemon balm and pepper-apple-mints that threatened to take over my herbal garden. Lucky was peacefully dozing on the lawn. Suddenly a silver-gray Weimaraner wandered into our property, like a specter. I had never seen him before. Apparently he knew Lucky. Ears laid back, sleek body scraping the ground, tail tucked between his legs, he gingerly approached Lucky. Lucky lay unmoving, keeping one eye on the trespasser. Abruptly, out of nowhere a sausage body came hurtling, all twenty pounds of him, angrily cursing and hurling imprecations at this gatecrasher. The seventy-pound dog hurriedly fled, the feisty dachshund snapping and yelping at his heels. Tail up and proud, the black terror trotted back, heading straight for his "Lady Love." Once more, he had triumphantly championed Lucky from a dire threat to his honor and chastity.

That is Oscar, Lucky's faithful German squire. They have a curious relationship. Presumptuous Oscar compulsively tries to mount Lucky every chance he gets. Torso never far from the ground, stumpy legs wriggling, he struggles valiantly but vainly to get a good grip on Lucky's bulky back. Lucky usually indulges him. He is not so indulgent with others who try to mount him, treating them with nothing but scorn and withering insults. But after a while Lucky loses his patience, and tosses Oscar off with a snarl, sending him sprawling.

The impulse among male dogs to mount Lucky is amusing as it is intriguing. Perhaps it is nothing more than a canine ritual to symbolize friendship between particular dogs, or, as among Bonobo apes, to affirm harmony and cohesion in the group.

Oscar is Lucky's partner in delinquency. Everyday he comes to escort Lucky through the daunting hazards of the jungle outside. At exactly twelve-thirty noon, he comes waddling up our steep driveway in his usual swaggering way. His owners, good friends of mine, usually come home for lunch at noon and let him out their door. Thereupon Oscar heads for our house, half-a-mile away. In no time he is scratching on our front door, punctuating his scratches with an insistent, high-pitched bark. If I do not immediately open the door to him, he will keep up his ear-splitting yapping, and even bang his entire body against the door until, in exasperation, just to shut him down, I give in and let him in. For a small dog he has a singularly penetrating bark, so intimidating that it always gets him what he want ~ from everyone.

The two are a two-dog pack, roaming the woods together. Other times, when Lucky just wants to laze around, Oscar is content just to cozy up to him, huggin' n' kissin'. He hangs around, patrols the property from threats (real or imagined), shares our dogs' homecooked meals, demands body massages, car rides, or walks in the park. Of course, he has to have a bed of his own in our bedroom, cleverly burrowing into his blanket, sleeping unmoving, completely covered. Not only has he fallen in step with our dogs' sleeping habits, but he has also adopted our topsy-turvy sleeping schedules. Early the next morning he wakes me up to let him out, after which he heads straight for his home. If he feels I have not pampered him enough, he decides to sleep in ~ maybe two nights in a row. No one, not even his owners, can stop him from doing so when he makes up his mind. He has to either be bodily delivered by me or picked up in a Jeep by his concerned owners.

In fact, Oscar had become a privileged character in and around the entire subdivision. One day he was rushed to emergency for gastric dilation. As soon as word got out, his owners received an astonishing number of phone iquiries from concerned neighbors. After he recovered, Oscar resumed his snooping into everyone's affairs in the subdivision, human and canine. He acts alpha to the omega dogs, and acts omega to humans and my dogs. When I spot him at the cul-de-sac, surveying the lay of the land and getting set to come up the driveway, I say loudly, "Uh, oh.. here comes K 9-007 again."

Lucky's origins were always a mystery and why he happened to be where we found him. At the time I was searching for Chornley, I turned up a clue as to his genealogy. In the course of a wide-ranging sweep over the area behind our property, beyond the woods and a grassy dale that served as a small pasture for cattle, I stumbled on a backyard breeder in a trailer-home with a makeshift enclosure for dogs. The man who answered my knock was a tall, unshaven, and obviously inebriated denizen of the backwoods. This was my first encounter with the moonshine crowd, and despite an impulse to turn and run, my curiosity was piqued. Thirty- something, he looked and acted the stereotype of the mountain-man. His shoulder-length, rust-colored tresses were gathered together in a ponytail. He had the beginnings of a potbelly bulging out of his tight denim pants, his beltline way done below the bulge. To my relief he did not just mumble an excuse and shoo me off the premises. He listened attentively as I described my plight and promised to help find Chornley. But instead of answering my query, he began to talk about his own dogs.

He led me to a ramshackle kennel that held a pack of noisy Beagles. Picking up one of them by the ears and neck, he boasted with backwoods bravado about how he created this or that feature. Neither a breed fancier nor a breeder for profit, he was just experimenting ~ for fun I guess. He waxed ecstatic about all the wonderful results he was getting breeding dogs. I sensed an ebullience fueled by beer.

All of a sudden while we were talking, he excused himself, turned around, spat, and then did something else. As he stood with his back to me a powerful stream jetted out in an arch and started to form a puddle on the grass. Drunk as Cooter Brown, he was relieving himself in my presence!

Unexpectedly the following day he showed up atop an unhappy horse trotting all the way up our driveway, camouflage suit, boots and cowboy hat and all, obviously relishing the rough-hewn image of the woodsman and hunter he believed he projected. He was still, I noticed, "under the influence." He said he was on his way to hunt.

I couldn't help wondering why , in the name of sport, anyone would want to take the life of a one who wants to live.

Violence begets violence . A recent news item reported an incident involving two septuagenarians. The two friends had gone out early together to hunt for wild turkeys on a 200-acre tract of land, a few miles from where I live. While prowling the underbrush the two had gotten separated. In the dim light of dawn one of them saw something move in the underbrush that looked like the up-and-down movements of a turkey's head. He raised his gun and fired. It was his friend, perhaps bobbing up and down or nodding his head like an old geezer with a tic.

"Hey, ma'am, cain ah borrow 'im?" Mr. Moonshine-breeder-hunter shouted out, snapping me out of my reverie. He was pointing to ET, who was all fired up at the sight of a horse. What for? I asked. He did not answer. Then the suspicion came: to use him for breeding, what else! Thinking fast, and not wishing to offend him, I quickly announced that all my dogs were fixed.

"Naw. Shorely, ma'am, not dat burd dawg," he drawled in disbelief, now pointing to Lucky.

Nervous as a sore-tailed cat, Lucky whined softly , as if a dim memory was surfacing. He looked suspiciously at the man. Mr. Breeder got down off his horse. Swaying unsteadily on his feet, laughing and baring tobacco-stained front teeth with a big gap, he moved closer. Lucky took off like a cat out of hell. Not for him another close encounter with this kind. I had to think fast. Had Lucky's past finally caught up with him? I called back Lucky, scooped him up, and showed Mr. Breeder proof of Lucky's neutering. All the while Lucky struggled to get loose, thrashing his legs about.

"Ya shoud na done dat," he said, reproachfully. I showed him I had done the same thing to ET, who was eagerly wagging his stump of a tail, oblivious of a fate he just escaped. Disappointed, Mr. DUI climbed back on his horse and clomped away through the woods.

A bulb lit up. Eureka! Five years ago Lucky had escaped this man's slave camp! And fled through the woods, flea-infested and frantic, to where he found us. It was his flight to freedom. He and the rest of his litter were the result of Mr. Breeder's "experiments." Mr. Breeder must have "borrowed" the neighborhood's free-roaming studs and mixed their genes together in his backyard laboratory. I guess I'll never know for certain about Lucky's ancestry. Mr. Breeder was not telling, and I was not about to ask. I guess Lucky will take his secret to the grave.

Indeed, Lucky has a little bit of every dog that once lived or still lives in the vicinity. For instance, there was Pookie, a shy Basset hound; Gizmo, a cheerful Cavalier King Charles who was exiled four years ago to the country after a neighbor complained to Animal Control about his having chewed up his sneakers; Snickers, the high-strung Cocker Spaniel who was given away two years ago when the insurance company threatened to suspend his owner's home insurance policy after he had done something mischievous. Occasionally I see a couple of coon hounds, red ticks, and blue ticks in the neighborhood, one time a pair of Rottweilers. (Hunting foxes released from cages in a wooded area for coons and hounds to hunt down is still a favorite sport.)

The genetic experiment that produced Lucky gave him a wry mouth, a certain twist to his lips that made him look as if he was either happily smiling, or sneering in disgust. "Wry mouth" is a term used by vets to describe an upper jaw that is longer than the lower jaw, skewing the mouth to one side. Worse, also the result of indiscriminate mixing was a mutation in which certain teeth are missing. Lucky has no lower premolars. His teeth are gapped far apart, giving him a bad bite. This malocclusion problem causes Lucky to swallow his food often without chewing. Also, there is abnormal hair growth between his toes and under the pads of his paws which makes him slip on smooth surfaces, unless it is trimmed. All these make him the "highest maintenance" dog among all my dogs.

But Lucky always turns a bad thing into a good thing. His so-called defects give him an arresting persona and makes him indisputably the BIG BOSS. Whenever my husband and I square off on one of our petty squabbles, the sight of Tuatauke grimacing with disgust and looking disdainfully at us from a corner of the room is enough to stop us. By saying nothing, he manages to say everything.

And when he does not want to do something, no force on earth can budge him. I was eating, one time. I had put Lucky on a diet. My peripheral vision caught sight of him, his head down on the Tabriz in the breakfast corner, baleful eyes affixed at me with a dolorous frown. I stopped eating and looked at him ~ shamed by his wry smile. To appease him I gave him all the food from my plate.

Another time, I asked him to get up the couch to cuddle him. He obliged. But when he sniffed the soiled linen with its scent of other dogs, he quickly got down and refused to be coaxed back. Browbeaten, I promptly got up and replaced it with clean linen. I had to carry him back and let him sniff the freshly laundered sheets.

He goes through life knowing exactly what he wants, telling me exactly what he likes, having his way always. After Chornley's death, I began restraining Lucky from straying beyond the property lines. To appease him, one of my daily chores was to take him by car to various places where he could leave and read messages in canine cyberspace. They delighted Lucky with the details they contained, such as sex, moods, personality, when the dog was there last, and invitations to mating. These were the times he really came alive, sniffing every post, hedge, fence, and tree trunk. Nothing excited him more than getting E-Mail from mysterious sources. Travelling everywhere with me, Lucky was able to surf the canine web. Even after a long lapse, whenever he revisited one of these sites and downloaded messages, he wagged his tail in triumph and smiled his crooked smile.

Behind a laid-back façade is a brilliance, intensity, and complexity that never cease to fascinate me. He is quick to size up potentially dangerous situations, enabling him to always steer clear of them. Often, when I suspect danger, I turn to Lucky's instincts. One time, as I jogged on a lonely country road with Lucky as my scout, he suddenly jerked back, baying and booing scandalously and refusing to proceed. A mile away, I saw a man coming out of the woods. Hastily we made a 180 degree turn and sprinted as fast as we could in the opposite direction. As southerners say we were as scared as "dogs shittin' peach seeds."

His extra-sensory skills saved us from natural calamities. When Hurricane Hugo brought a tornado to our doorstep, even before it happened Lucky sensed a movement in the air and ground and vehemently refused to go outdoors to pee.

His adaptability makes him fit into any place, any situation. At my parent's home he is sensitive to house rules and never breaks any of them. He lies quietly in a corner or is quick to obey orders without much cuing. At Third and Fifth Sister's houses he knows how to play his cards well while fraternizing with his canine and human cousins. In contrast, at home he is unabashedly demanding.

When he was five years old, he was the only dog we took with us when we drove cross-country to the West Coast. Unlike in Europe where a pet is an accepted part of every entourage, travelling with pets in America is always an iffy thing. Lucky learned to discreetly slip in and out of motel rooms, unnoticed, quiet as a bird when a hawk flies over. During those trips, he learned to forgo his habitual morning runs. He did not need to be told; he simply kept out of sight.

In California, we stayed in a relative's suburban house where dogs were not allowed inside the house. Our car became his bed at night, windows cranked down a bit so he could enjoy the mild California breezes. He slept soundly with a sheet covering him, as if he was back home in his own bed, and never had a single toilet accident. During the day, he hobnobbed with California canines in the neighborhood park and awed them with his rustic, pastoral persona. When we visited another relative in the suburbs of Chicago, Lucky charmed everyone by putting on impeccable, big-city manners. He became a sort of role model for their two young sons in the matter of going to bed *sans furore*. As soon as I commanded Lucky to go to bed, he marched upstairs, unprotesting, to the guest bedroom and plunked himself down on his travel bedding. However, when alone with their doting housekeeper, he would sneak up onto their Queen Anne chair, then just as quickly step down as soon as we returned.

Lucky early on developed an uncanny ability to figure out connections between quite abstract concepts, to distinguish physical cause from effect and act appropriately. One day, at the expansive library grounds, a favorite trysting place, a younger but larger dog unexpectedly charged at Lucky. Humiliated, Lucky ran to me and looked me in the eye. I knew instantly what he wanted. When I got between them and moved toward the other dog, Lucky gathered himself together and went flying at the larger dog, sending him packing, all the while booing profanities. He was acting exactly like a kid who becomes more self-confident when superior force backs him up. Lucky was following the transitivity rule: if A dominates B, and B dominates C, then it is inevitable that A dominates C.

At a nearby school playground which is Lucky's favorite place for picking up the latest canine community gossip, a group of young girls and boys playing in the Jungle Gym caught sight of both Lucky and ET. Their squeals of welcome prompted ET to rush forward to greet them with his usual exuberance.

"Don't touch dem dawgs, " a hostile voice snapped out. Stretched supine on a long bench with her back against the stationary picnic table was an overstuffed woman, probably the children's grandmother. She was looking at ET with an ugly frown.

As if they are little boys themselves, Lucky and ET are instinctively drawn to children. Strangely, on this occasion Lucky was having second thoughts. He stopped, sat on his haunches and stared long and quizzically at this battle-ax, assessing whether this was friendly territory or a free-fire zone he was getting into. With the hostility unabating, Lucky got up, turned and walked away, deaf to the children's entreaties. Meanwhile, ignoring the bad vibes, ET continued cavorting with the kids.

And there is Lucky's instinctive predilection for hunting. When he was young, he was quite a hunter. More than once he would lay a dead squirrel, rabbit, or mole at my feet, proudly, as if to show off his prowess, or perhaps to gift me. At first my reaction was of horror and reproach. But when I realized he was after all just following his nature, obeying his primordial calling, I became more tolerant. Nevertheless, I could not help being dismayed each time. Along with this behavior he had a repugnant habit of rolling on his back over the carcasses of dead animals.

Was it perhaps to acquire the scent of potential prey and to disguise his own, to be able to get close to them? Or maybe, was he metaphysically uniting with the prey animals? Or, more mundanely, was he telling me to give him a bath, knowing how I would react to what he did? Lately he began taking delight at being bathed. Warm baths and all that grooming always turned him into a rural dandy, reeking of fragrant talcum powder. For days afterwards he would avoid going outdoors and soiling himself.

During his younger days, whenever let out he would sniff the air for intruders ~ he always pretended there were. Then he would take off, baying and booing, bounding through the underbrush, finally disappearing into the woods. He boos rather than bark or howl. Unless repeatedly called in, he would spend the whole day outdoors crashing through thickets after a mole or sprinting after a hare, or vaulting over the chaparral like a deer, up and down, left and right, the white tip of his bushy tail waving over the weed-tops.

In mid-life he could no longer go on the chase. Even if squirrels and hares were gamboling outside, he would just look elsewhere, acting as if they were not there. But cats appearing on the property rejuvenated him, restoring him in a split-second to his nimble old self and menacing hunting style. He would run them up a tree and sit under it for hours, waiting for them to come down. I doubted, though, whether he could hold his own with cats if they ever decided to stand their ground. With his rather irregular dentition, Lucky did not pose a real threat to any cat. But of course, neither he nor the cat knew that. It was all posturing. He was putting on a bluff and bluster act for his, mine, and the cat's benefit. He was just being faithful to what he believed was expected of a hound dog.

At night, he continued adventuring in his sleep. Lucky had a rich subconscious. Whenever he entered the REM state (I could tell by his snoring), I knew he was having himself a fine dream, running off toward elysian fields, chasing celestial rabbits. His hind legs, spread-eagled, would twitch and his paws move up and down as though he was running. His half-open eyes would roll, his tongue loll. He made little funny noises: high-pitched moans, suppressed barks, faint growls. No wonder he liked to sleep as much as he did. That was when he was enjoying himself most.

Now in the twilight of his life, Lucky has learned to come to terms with the passage of time. Recently, at my parents' backyard, I saw Lucky perk up and then just as suddenly freeze. Slowly, like in a slow-motion film, he lifted up his right front leg first, and then alternately, his left hind leg, all the while inching forward toward something. Uh..oh! I said to myself, trouble. However, he was not making as much noise as he usually did on the hunt. Actually, I thought he was trying to make himself invisible. All of a sudden, he made a mad dash, straight at his "prey." But what's this? His prey stayed put, immobile. Lucky put on the brakes in mid-attack, dumbfounded and chagrined. Then he turned away, not even bothering to check out his putative victim or give it a sniff. He simply walked away and never looked back. It was only a white terra-cotta rabbit!

This, to me, was another instance of a process of abstracting taking place in his canine mind. He had correctly checked out the visual markers of a rabbit, and started to behave appropriately vis-a-vis those properties. However, when other sensory inputs told him crucial characteristics were either missing or different, he concluded this was no rabbit at all. Hence the abrupt breaking off from the chase.

There are times when I wonder if Lucky had made that quantum leap to a higher consciousness as he remakes himself. Surely a primitive "lizard" brain is not capable of intricate feelings or abstruse thinking. How else can I explain why he can be respectful one day, irreverent the next ; altruistic one time, selfish the next; and tolerant to one person, but impatient with another? Why will he defer to Bertha, and then pee on Johnny's brown pants, Bertha's husband. Why is he gentle with one dog and gruff with another? Why would he refuse to go into the house unless a new friend, another dog of unknown breed whom we had nicknamed Thingamajig, was also allowed in, and then demand that I give the little beggar a treat. Yet when I take the initiative to "remake" Scruffy, a nondescript mutt I had rescued, Lucky cleverly sets him up by surreptitiously peeing on the ficus in the atrium and making me believe Scruffy did it. By hanging around the site and sniffing the crime scene, then looking me in the eye, he brings me around to disciplining the new dog. I finally caught on when I saw him doing it himself. After I had a stiff word with him, the scheming stopped.

To me only a convoluted mind can account for Lucky's docility to my husband and his indifference toward me despite all that I do for him. I take care of almost all his daily needs, but given a choice he makes a bee-line for my husband, lie or sit at his feet, and respond to his calls, not to mine. One afternoon, Lucky bolted out of the bar room like a bat

out of hell,   straight to the kitchen where I was preparing sushi. He
nudged me with his wet nose, making whining noises all the while.
Sensing his displeasure at something, I asked repeatedly "what?" Hearing
the commotion, my husband joined us, and gleefully admitted having
passed gas silently, the way Lucky himself often does. When the odious
smell permeated the room, Lucky jumped up as if he had just been
poison-gassed. He looked accusingly at my husband and scrambled out,
snorting in disgust. That was one of the rare moments when he came to
me. Tit-for-tat, I told Lucky, you're getting a dose of your own medicine.
Just two old farts; it takes one to know one.

Early on, Lucky learned to handle with panache different situations
in which he found himself. To get most-favored-treatment from everyone
he was able to bring deductive and inductive powers into play. If these
did not give him the results he wanted, he tried seducing, cozying up
and rubbing his soft body against the seducee, disarming everyone with
his bedroom eyes. And when this still failed, he resorted to "nuking",
that is, dropping the ultimate bomb. He would thrust his behind into
the face of the unsuspecting, and pass gas. But in a no-win situation he
simply ran away, following the 36th Chinese way to solve problems.
Indeed, Lucky was resorting to this the day we found him. Lucky for
him to flee; lucky for us to find him

Yes, Lucky is a real tease. But he is single-minded about his
volunteer work as pet therapist for retirement and nursing homes.He
takes it very seriously. Performing before a live audience pumps up his
adrenalin and affirms his mission in life. It gives him a raison d'être, and
is vital to his geriatric wellness. As he enters his second decade he has
begun to occasionally wet his bed. The first time, he woke up soaking
wet, visibly upset and embarrassed. Nowadays, he tries to cover up by
sniffing out the accident, not casually but repeatedly until I take notice
and clean it up. Is it candor, or simply saving face?

Not yet ready to retire, Lucky helped jump-start Leg-Up, a pet
therapy project organized by Joy for a nursing home in her community.
Joy, now sixteen, has acquired her own Oscar , which she brings with his
bag of tricks for this project. Oscar is a black toy Dachshund, which she
got after being smitten with our neighborhood spy Oscar, Lucky's
"consort." Joy's Oscar is her best friend now. He shares her bed as
Chornley used to once. She tells me that with Oscar by her side,

growing up as a Jewish-Chinese American in the South is not as confusing and chaotic as it used to be.

Recently, in my own county, a dog named Sophie became a resident therapist at the local hospital's Restorative Care Unit. She provides constant affection to elderly patients suffering short-term injuries like broken bones. Kindness ~ the canine kind ~ is the best medicine for the elderly. Her physical presence alone hastens recovery by taking minds off the aches and pains of aging, and reminding some of their own pets waiting at home. Now a tenured staff addition to the hospital's fifth floor, complete with her own bed and water dish at the nursing station, Sophie boasts a job description that includes being a stress-buffer for the doctors and professional staff. A certified mutt, Sophie was found by two staff members of the hospital's behavorial health unit at a parking lot of the Golden Corral Restaurant during one of their lunch breaks.

Most recently, Lucky's work in nursing and retirement homes touched another heart. Lisa, a local librarian, had heard of a Dalmatian who was about to be put down. The owner said he was too hyper; his neighbors said he was disruptive, and reported him to animal control. Or maybe, he was himself an innocent victim of backyard brawling among neighbors. Being a cat person, with Ali and Gallagher monopolizing her life, Lisa debated, long and hard, with herself whether she could put up with the inconvenience of caring for a behavior-impaired dog. For starters, she researched the breed; and then concerned herself worried with the genetic problems of inbred Dalmatians. Single, without children, Lisa decided to take the plunge. She kept the name given him: Alex.

I was gratified at the smooth and rapid transition with which Lisa accomplished Alex's move into her life, and how successfully she coaxed out Alex's good points. Alex in turn brought out Lisa's own hidden talents. One day, Alex set himself free and went haywire with a garter snake straying in from the nearby woods. Lisa was at work and learned about Alex's mischief from her neighbors. Though Alex was waiting for her when she returned home, Lisa decided to splurge on a chain-link fence.

Alex bounds energetically around, chasing birds and butterflies, with Lisa looking on like a doting mother. She videos and takes still pictures of Alex at different phases of his new life. Though Alex peacefully co-exists with the cats, Lisa has decided to provide Alex with a canine companion. After a systematic compilation of "free to a good home" ads, Lisa decided on a cocker mix puppy with a white nose. She named him Nicholas. "Nikki" sleeps on a bed rejected by her cats, and drags his toys to that bed, while Alex fondly looks on. Giving dogs a new lease on life has been empowering for Lisa. She quips that her family has grown overnight. As soon as Alex is completely socialized and Nikki is big enough, Lisa hopes to share them with senior citizens at nursing homes and with the children in her Sunday school.

An 11th Century Chinese poet likened life on earth to a flock of geese alighting on the snow, sometimes leaving just an ephemeral trace of their passage. But just the same, a trace.

Yesterday, I saw a white butterfly feasting on the ambrosia of dewdrops glistening on a calla lily. Lucky was gazing at it too. Somehow Chornley came to mind. Slowly I went inside the house to retrieve, fondle and sniff a lock of Chornley's hair, which I still have. I went back to kiss Big Boss on the forehead. He smiled a kind of Mona Lisa smile, lying on his side and peacefully inhaling the mist and cosmic ether of the land of his birth. He and Chornley shared many secret places of the heart in their field of dreams.

There are more things in heaven and earth, Master *Laozi*, than are dreamt of in your philosophy.

10

THE EXTRA TERRIBLES

The loudspeakers blared: "Medium-pony riders to the ring in five minutes!"

Hurriedly tacking her gelding Excel, eleven-year old Joy made ready to go. I was lending her a helping hand when Lucky jauntily sauntered in from his prowl in neighboring stables. All of a sudden I heard his familiar BOOOO...! almost spooking Excel. Lucky had seen something; he was not one to get much excited about anything. For the moment I didn't mind him. Joy needed all my attention.

Joy wanted my presence at the ring. An avid competitor in the hunter-jumper circuit of the American Horse Show Association, Joy regularly competed in regional shows to qualify for the nationals at Devon, Washington D.C., and at Meadowlands. Both parents were physicians with a thriving medical practice and were not always available. I became a "horse-show aunt," sometimes driving interstate with ponies in tow and my mascots Lucky and Chornley dozing on the back seat with Joy.

I had to make sure before leaving for the ring that Lucky was not about to launch into another of his daredevil exploits. Conceding to Lucky, Joy proceeded to the ring on Excel by herself without a fuss.

Ears folded back and head low, white-tipped tail slowly fanning the air, Lucky was directing my attention to a pile of dirty straw and hay on the stable floor.

Half-hidden in the straw, almost invisible, was a small dog with button ears, snippy muzzle, tan patch and black splotches on one side of the face, like the Phantom-of-the-Opera mask. It was lying on its side, breathing heavily. Calling in a groom from the next stable, I asked who its owner was. He had no idea. He had not even seen the dog before. Inspecting it more closely, I realized it was either sick or injured, I did not know how gravely. I had to act quickly. After getting directions to the nearest veterinary clinic, I put Lucky and Chornley in the Suburban and, wrapping the limp body in a horse blanket, gently laid it on the front seat floor. Throughout the drive the little dog's sad eyes were on me. Lucky and Chornley were unusually subdued.

At the clinic, the young veterinarian told me to leave the dog overnight, possibly a few days, for her to observe and run some tests. As the vet poked and probed him, the dog neither complained nor resisted. His striking brown eyes, circled by black mascara kohl like Cleopatra's, watched my every movement. Tears welling into my eyes, I entreated the vet to do everything possible to save his life. I had fallen under his spell.

Returning to the horse show, I found Joy back at Excel's stable. She was on her knees on the freshly-laid straw, giving her chestnut pony a massage as he lay on his side. She didn't notice me until I spoke and asked her how she rode.

"Blue ribbon, Aunt Betty!" she announced proudly and with a sigh of relief. "I was so nervous, but Excel was so good. She's such a sweet pony."

She continued to massage the pony, giving him full attention. Still thinking of the dog, I went to the other barns to inquire if anyone was missing a dog. Negative. Questions kept streaming into my mind: was he hit by a vehicle, kicked by a horse? Was he abandoned, or did he simply get lost? At horse shows, small dogs roamed freely. Together with Ferragamo loafers and Hermes scarves they were part of the horse culture.

Not finding any leads, I returned and hunkered down beside Joy. Sensing my preoccupation she asked, "What got into Lucky?" I told her about the dog in the straw. Joy jumped up and said, "Let's see how he's doing! I'm not riding again until later." I needed no persuading.

The X-rays showed no bone injuries. The vet suspected it was intestinal virus, or that the dog had ingested something toxic. The IV had revived him somewhat. Struggling to his feet he started licking Joy's face. Joy giggled as she usually does when overwhelmed.

"Aunt Betty, he's like ET!" she cried out. She too was smitten by the dog.

Calmer now, I agreed that indeed there were many similarities: the uncommonly large head, the short stumpy legs, and eyes that stared unblinking. But this one had a gay, not a ring, tail. More like a eunuch. A tailess dog is how the Chinese referred to a eunuch.

Despite a preposterous bill for $650 ~ no doubt due to the ongoing horse show ~ the vet was not quite clear nor forthcoming about what ailed the dog, except that he had so many intestinal parasites in him. I didn't fuss about the bill. I was just too relieved that the dog would live.

Back at the horse show, I found the dog's owner, a barn groom. The vet's bill made him stammer. Shrugging his shoulders and shaking his head, he said the dog must have blundered into something and that the dog was stupid; he peed when handled. He asked if I wanted the dog. He wasn't going to pay a bill like that. Anyway he was on his way back to Tennessee and was uncertain about his own plans.

That was how a Jack Russell terrier came into my life.

During the seventy-mile drive home, the terrier became restless, and started jumping from front seat to back, back seat to front, getting up on my and Joy's lap, bumping his nose against the glass windows. Lucky and Chornley just sat quietly, watching this uncouth stranger.

Developed by John Russell, a fox-hunting parson from Devonshire in the early 1800's, Jack Russells were bred to hunt vermin and to flush out foxes. With jaws that are deep and teeth that are punishing, legs that are bowed and powerful, paws that curve out, they readily go to ground, bolting at all sorts of rodents. Hardy and tenacious, they are indefatigable exterminators in farms and stables. Introduced to the United States in the 1960's, breeders avoided Kennel Club registration for the breed until very recently because of fear of in- or overbreeding. I was not familiar with the breed.

After a while I noticed the trademark butt-and-tail wiggle as well as the uninhibited high jumps of the Paris ET. This dog wagged his tail the same way, swaying his butt as if it were part of his tail. He communicated with the exact same type of eye contact, body signals, and bark. To get attention he also shook his body in progression from head to tail. Like the lecherous French mutt, he showed signs of being a lecher himself, trying to hump the nonplussed Chornley as he lay prone on the floor. Even after being neutered he never lost his sex drives.

All this convinced me that my irrepressible French mutt was once more insinuating himself into my life. So it was fitting that I named him ET. He was extra-terrible, even if he could not be an extra-terrestrial from another world as my first ET seemed to be.

Unlike the Paris ET, however, this ET did not suffer from an attitude problem. Instead, he had the sweet disposition, but not the serenity, of the original Kenneth, that *eminence gris*, my security blanket in Asia.

Daring, tireless and persevering, ET completed the hunting pack. They became a formidable team. Nothing in our vicinity escaped their attention, not even the lowliest mole. Lucky was the bloodhound, sniffing out the prey; Chornley the sight hound, waiting to get it in his sights, and ET, with his iron jaws, muscle-bound legs and perpetual-machine energy, ready to flush out the poor victim and run it to ground. With Lucky barking out orders, Chornley would stand by while ET dealt the *coup de grâce*. They enjoyed the chase even if it turned out to be fruitless. At times they tarried overnight in the woods, waiting under a tree for squirrels to make a dumb move and come down.

ET redefines the "working terrier" description of the breed. He does work hard to have fun. Life is one long, unending frolic. Give him an opening and his engine cranks up and never stops. He creates his own fun, whether by kissing up to a good-looking UPS lady-driver, barging into a soccer game with kids, intercepting a basketball at a school court, plunging into a lake to get into a water volleyball match, helping us spade up soil in the garden, or getting acquainted with a pet ferret. When he wants to play, he picks up his knotted rope and plunks it down at my feet. If I do not respond, he jumps onto my lap until I am conned into playing.

He learned to play soccer, jumping to intercept the ball in mid-air with his head and then rolling it on the turf with his snout, weaving his way through flailing children's legs, muscling the ball toward the goal with his body. He knew how to wrestle the ball away from an inattentive boy, scoring for his all-girls' team. In these games ET was fully absorbed, unmindful of fatigue.

He also figured out how to play water-polo and plunged in when a game was in progress to join the melee. At first he just barked and ran up and down the pool. Then he decided one day it wasn't fun enough to be on the sidelines. He took the plunge and after that could not resist any body of water. This was when he devised a water-polo game with Bandit, a long-haired Jack Russell of Fifth Sister. ET saw a beach ball floating in the middle of the pool. After some hesitation he dove in, dog-paddled his way to the ball and then nudged it with his nose toward his sidekick Bandit, waiting at the shallow end of the pool. Bandit then pushed the ball up onto dry land. There a rough-and-tumble game of soccer would ensue between the two Jack Russells, ET rolling the ball around with his snout, and Bandit trying to snatch it away by getting on top and holding it fast with two front legs, snarling and screaming. ET would try pushing the ball out from under Bandit's legs. It usually ended in a draw.

Children's parties galvanized ET into scene-stealing acts. One time he saw a balloon sailing up to the ceiling and then bobbing down. The instant it came within reach, ET leaped up and bumped the balloon back up to the ceiling with his snout. To the celebrant's dismay, one kid after another abandoned the party games to join ET. He timed his leaps right to keep the balloon up. When kids got in his way and it became a free-for-all, ET decided to end the game. The next time the balloon made it almost to the floor, he pounced on it and popped it.

It was amazing how focused ET could be. Once he got started on something, he would turn tireless and relentless; nothing could distract him. This quality would influence a five year old boy named Jared.

ET met Jared at the park near a local day-care facility. They hit it right off, boy and dog playing together. Thinking himself a kid like Jared, ET imitated everything Jared did. At the Jungle Gym, he followed Jared up the suspended tires, through the tunnel, ran, balancing himself on the swinging footbridge, and then slid down the toboggan after Jared.

The next day, after learning that ET played soccer, Jared brought a soccer ball. The minute he saw the ball, ET as usual went bananas. But quickly, Jared lost interest in soccer. He tried to make ET go play at the Jungle Gym. Now completely absorbed with the ball, ET ignored Jared. No amount of distractions could deflect him. Looking on, Jared's mother marvelled at ET's concentration.

Without our realizing it Jared was absorbing the example ET gave him of sticking to an activity, whatever it was, instead of hopping from one to another. He had found a kindred soul who, unlike him could pay attention He told me, ET was the "coolest" dog he had ever met; he told his mother, if a dog could pay attention, so could he.

The game that most engrossed the two was "guess which hand?" Holding out two closed fists, Jared dared ET to guess which held a treat. ET pounced on one and proceeded to pry it open with his snout. He correctly guessed 9 out of 10 times.

Jared and ET spent energy together in varied ways over several months. ET's hyperkinesis matched that of Jared, but he showed the boy it was more fun to funnel one's energies into just one activity. On my advice, Jared's mother gave him more fish and vegetables in his diet to increase the Omega-3 fatty acid intake. Soon, his mother was able to take him off Ritalin.

I was curious about the processing power of ET's brain. Biologists measure intelligence by concept formation, perception, recognition, problem solving, remembering, learning, and imitating. Could he make believe? By mock-menacing him with upraised arms, I made him pretend he was a guard dog. ET responded, wrinkling his brows, curling up his upper lips, showing his fangs, then growling. But straining to reach out and snap did a number on his nose. It set him to sneezing and wheezing uncontrollably. This Doberman Pinscher pretend-game became one of his show-case tricks.

To further test his awareness of self, I stood before a full-length mirror with ET in my arms to see if he could distinguish between a mirror image and the real thing. I had read that monkeys never could tell the difference between themselves and their mirror image, and will attack the image as if it were another animal. The first time, ET looked intently at his own image and growled at it. Next time, apparently realizing it was his reflection and not another dog, he looked briefly, then turned away, as if embarrassed at seeing himself. To further test his perceptions, I asked my husband to come up from behind in such a way that ET could only see my husband's mirror image approaching. Then my husband would raise his arms, threateningly. ET readily responded to the mirror-image, performing on cue. After a number of times, his brain made the connection. He figured that the mirror image of my husband behind us was a reflection, not the real thing. Realizing this, ET responded first to the mirror image, and then twisted and turned in my arms, trying to look directly behind me at my husband. Can't fool me no more this time, he seemed to say.

In the aftermath of Chornley's death my home became a sanctuary of salvaged souls and an impromptu behavioral clinic to repair damaged dogs. One troubled dog after another fell under my charge. Where did they all come from? Obviously they came not by coincidence. Many decided I needed to replace Chornley.

Scruffy, Maddie, Missy and others came in succession. While their advent caused drastic changes in my daily life, I had no objections. I got to know more not only about canines but also about human nature. Every dog had a story to tell. Know a person by his dog; it reflects his habits, manners, idiosyncracies, and attitudes. Dogs are never disingenuous.

While most of these dogs had difficult behaviors, nurturing them effectively resolved many problems and opened up hidden dimensions of personalities. Time and again I proved the power of nurturance to unlock the potential in any living thing, given the right stimuli. Like the cognitive abilities of children in their formative years, those of dogs get sharpened by positive reinforcement. Lavishing love and affection on dogs is a surefire cure for any damage they might have sustained by being chained and deprived of meaningful interaction with fellow-dogs or humans. The effects of being brutalized or neglected can be reversed.

These experiences more than ever convince me what a thin and diaphanous veil separates us from animals. Dogs are like children, except they never grow up.

The sun was not quite up yet that day. As if drawn by an unknown force, I got up and peered out of the bedroom window. I was impaled in the hypnotic stare of a dog, squatting high up the hill slope behind our house. He was looking down through the window into our bedroom, where Lucky and ET were still asleep. A few days ago, I had seen the same dog next to the compost pit behind the house, higher up the slope. When he saw me he cocked his ears, then as suddenly as I saw him, disappeared.

Black dog ~ could it be an omen? I tried to go back to sleep, but could not. Must be a free-ranging or feral dog, I thought. That afternoon, while tidying up the herbal garden, I saw him again, this time behind some bushes. The intruder had been quietly watching me. Being obssessive-compulsive about finishing the task of the day, I didn't pay much attention. Soon I saw him running around, frolicking with Lucky and ET. When the late summer light began to wane, I called in Lucky and ET. After cleaning the garden tools and putting them away in the garage, I stepped outside for a moment. Suddenly I sensed the dog's presence. I turned around and there he was, startling me by his proximity.

Scruffy, scrawny, he stood there, wagging his tail. He was a nondescript, medium-sized dog, about 20 inches at the whithers. He looked like a feist, a local word for a generic, backwoods breed of indeterminate ancestry. We made eye-contact. Moving forward, I petted him on the head and checked him out. He had no ID, no collar, but was clean ~ no ticks, no fleas. Must be a neighbor's dog, I thought.

The following morning, as I walked down the hill to fetch the newspaper with ET and Lucky at my side, the dog showed up again. My two dogs appeared to welcome him, soon he and ET were engaged in a rough and tumble game all the way back to the house. ET had found a new friend. As soon as the dog entered the house, he forgot all about ET, going straight for the food dish and proceeding to gobble up ET's Kibbles. I wondered if he was from the neighborhood; I'd never seen him around before. I proceeded to call all my neighbors who had dogs and posted a lost-and-found.

No one in the neighborhood claimed him. I had no choice but to keep him. Our relationship quickly segued from food to companionship. I named him Scruffy. He watched and observed every move we made. While at first he committed one faux pas after another he proved to be a quick study, absorbing house rules effortlessly from my canine teaching assistants.

One of my husband's garden sneakers one day appeared in the garden outside. After that his work gloves vanished. (About this time, another dog, a puppy, appeared on our property.) Exasperated, my husband, otherwise tolerant of their comings and goings because of the Chinese belief that dogs are bearers of good fortune, expostulated, "One more dog and out I go." Joking, perhaps, but in quick retort I said: "Out you go, then." Concluding Scruffy to be the culprit, I scolded him. The poor thing just hung his head ~ no baring of teeth, no growls, meekly accepting my scolding.

We reached an amicable compromise: ten days to find a home for Scruffy. Ten stretched to twenty. It wasn't easy. Scruffy was scruffy. A friend told a single mother of two boys, whose cocker spaniel had just been run over, about Scruffy. She asked to see him.

I spiffed up Scruffy with a yellow bow, and dusted him all over with talcum powder. It was love at first sight. When she opened her car door, Scruffy jumped into the car without hesitation and scrambled onto the back seat, where her two-year old boy was strapped into a child car seat, munching a sandwich. Scruffy quickly helped himself to the burger. Upset, the boy twisted this and that way to keep the burger away from Scruffy. Gwen laughed: "Gev it to 'im, honey. We' uns will hie us to McDonalds and git ya a burger each."

Scruffy and Gwen was a match made in heaven. There was nothing Gwen would not do for Scruffy, so loving was their relationship. He slept with her on her waterbed; her boys, owning few toys, played games of make-believe with Scruffy. Imagination can do wonders. For his part, Scruffy did household-duty by baby-sitting kittens that kept showing up in Gwen's property. Scruffy opened my eyes to the inherent nobility of the poor in America.

Scruffy had a protective attitude towards children. Gwen said that whenever she spanked one of her boys when he overstepped the bounds, setting him off to screaming, Scruffy would scurry to the boy's side and then growl at her. Not knowing whether Scruffy was just play-acting or dead serious, Gwen would go along and refrain from further punitive action. Taking the cue from him, Gwen decided to try psychological, not corporeal, punishment instead, like forbidding her boys from playing ball with Scruffy outside as the consequence of an infraction. She found this to be more effective at times.

Then one day I got a call from Gwen. She was crying. She had just moved to another trailer-home three miles away from her old home. That day, leaving for work she had left Scruffy outside her new home. When she returned home, Scruffy was missing. She looked everywhere for him, calling for him. Not a sign of him. She became desperate.

My heart skipped a beat when I learned he was missing. Then I had a thought. Gwen, I said, why don't you check out your old place? I had a hunch that perhaps, like cats Scruffy continued to be attached to the place where he had been very happy. Gwen jumped at my suggestion. I waited an anxious half hour. Then Gwen, laughing with relief, called me again. Driving there, half-hopefully and half-fearfully, she had found Scruffy sitting relaxed on the porch of the empty house with the two little kittens. Gwen had neglected to bring the kittens with her to the new house!

Before Scruffy moved to his new home, I intercepted ET one day heading for the woods with one of my husband's garden sneakers in his mouth. Before that incident I had also caught Lucky red-handed, burying my husband's garden gloves under a pile of leaves. The ugly serpent of suspicion hissed in my ears: the two were setting up the interloper Scruffy! It was different, though, with the puppy who showed up one ordinary summer Saturday afternoon.

Neighbors were on their John Deeres that lazy summer afternoon, knights riding out on their trusted steeds to do battle with the last solitary uncut blade of grass that was defying them. Up in the sky, a couple of rowdy crows were harassing a circling red-tailed hawk as it screeched defiance. But somehow its familiar, ear-splitting "eek-eek" lacked its usual belligerence, sounding more like a plaintive call. Likewise, the couple of red-plumed woodpeckers and the haunting "hoo-hoo-aw" of the barred owls that used to make the woods behind the house a noisy, lively place were missing. Wildlife in the woods seemed to be diminishing in number. I wondered if they were finding less and less to eat with loggers cutting down the older trees. Or perhaps they were succumbing to all the toxic chemicals pouring from all the well-groomed gardens and lawns around us.

I was on my haunches, weeding, with Lucky sitting like a gargoyle beside me. My husband was walking the push mower up and down the steeply-sloped lawn, with ET yipping at his heels. From my vantage point I saw a black pick-up cruising the subdivision, as so many teenagers do in their pick-ups on week-ends. But this one paused at the cul-de-sac, where our driveway began. Lucky got up on all fours and stared intently down the slope at the car, ears cocked, alert. The car revved up, turned sharply around, then drove off. ET stopped playing, looked towards the departing truck, at Lucky, then with a growl took off down the slope. Lucky dashed after him. Booing all the way, Lucky overtook ET and was soon way ahead Alarmed, I clapped my hands, screaming at them not to go past the property line. Dutifully, the two stopped at the cul-de-sac. As I came up, Lucky gave me a meaningful look on his ever-expressive face; ET madly wagged his stump of a tail, looked down and started licking a small black object.

My bare feet were burning on the hot asphalt as I bent low and made out a tiny, black puppy. She was so small ~ a mere handful. Picking her up, a hundred fleas assaulted my arms. Hyper-allergic to insect bites, I hurried back to give the fleabag a scrubbing in the garage's utility sink.

I called her Baby Girl. She had the sweet scent of baby's breath. She wasn't much of a looker, but like all puppies was exceedingly cute. Her coat was hard and wiry, her tail sickle-like, her ears flopped down half-way over a rather broad and plain face.

Like babies, puppies possess universal appeal. Old Fogie Lucky was immediately drawn to her, acting like a smitten adolescent. ET energetically competed for the puppy's attention, sometimes blocking Lucky from giving the puppy a fond lick. ET could not seem to have enough of her. In the morning, as soon as he got up, he would start to fuss over her. If she was still asleep on her stuffed pillow, he would sit and stare at her, sometimes for hours, flipping up his folded ears.

I wanted to keep Baby Girl, but a twelve-year old girl wanted her even more. A daughter of one of the old upper-class families in town, her mother had heard about Baby Girl from the veterinarian. The whole family came to my house ~ father, mother, the girl and her teenage sister. I knew that Baby Girl would be happier with this little girl. They renamed her Maddie.

Today, Maddie lives the life of a pampered "missy" in a plush Southern mansion, riding a cream Land Rover. They tell me that Maddie picks up the empty dish with her mouth and drops it in front of the puppy sitter whenever she wants a treat.

Maddie was not going to be the only "missy" in my life.

It was an icy gray night, New Year's eve. Thirteen inches of snow lay on the ground; the town lay paralyzed, just as a light snowfall immobilizes Paris. Grounded, lounging with a glass of Pinot Noir in my hand, watching the evening news, I was all set for a quiet evening when all of a sudden Lucky's baying and ET's frenzied barking jolted me from my chair. From the way they were barking and wagging their tails, I knew it was someone they knew. But there was no vehicle in sight. Then the doorbell rang. Who would come at this time in such weather? The doorbell rang again.

"Who is it?" I called out through the locked door.

I couldn't make out what the voices were saying, but they sounded like children. With some hesitation I cracked the door open a bit. Three young boys in heavily padded anoraks, cheeks flushed, were standing on the stoop. They were from different families in the subdivision. I did not know these boys personally, but had seen them around. The taller boy said that four days earlier they saw this dog hanging around. His mother warned him that feeding the dog invited it to stay.

I let the boys into the atrium. As they filed in I noticed the small dog in the arms of the smaller boy. He said with alarm that his mother was ready to take it to the pound first thing in the morning. There was a plea in his voice, in the eyes of all the boys. Please, he said, speaking for all of them, did I not want the dog instead?

I placed the dog on my lap, where she sat unmoving, her eyes misted over. She was coquettish, but no beauty. Nose upturned a bit too much, her lower teeth protruded from a prognathous jaw like that of a Pekingese. But her head and snout made her look more like a Chihuahua, with a coat the color of ground ginger. She had a slightly domed head, large bat-like ears, bulging eyes. As she curled up on my lap fleas hop-scotched up my arms. An unpleasant odor emanated from her, overpowering the flower scents in the atrium.

I coughed. This was going to be an even tougher one, I was sure.

After the boys left, I put her through spring cleaning, giving her a makeover. While shampooing her I noticed scaly, crusty-red patches where her hair had thinned around her neck. Noting a distended stomach, I pressed my fingers over the lower abdomen. There were small firm lumps. The nipples were hard and swollen. I squeezed one and a milky fluid oozed out. She protested with a piteous cry.

Despite her lack of looks, she was so prissy and lady-like I decided to call her Missy. She had a huge appetite and seemed otherwise well except for a certain edginess. That night, Missy pulled her blanket-bed under the telephone table. In a while she began scraping the blanket with her paws as if digging a nest.

Early next morning I took Missy to the veterinarian. He confirmed what I suspected and dreaded: she was pregnant. Worse, her pelvis was too narrow; the puppies would be too large for the size of her birth canal.

"She doesn't need another litter to fulfill her life," the vet joked as if to speak my mind.

My guess was that poor Missy had been on a chain and a bully dog came around and raped her. As I drove home with a Lucky who was all too thankful that the veterinary visit was not meant for him, I was fuming. What kind of human abandons a pet he loved and who no doubt loved him in return?

Two days later, I went back to pick up Missy. While waiting at the anteroom I saw a dog with a metal ring sticking out from under its chin. The lady who brought him in said she saw a white male in a pickup drop the dog outside the convenience store opposite the frame shop where she worked. The collar had become imbedded inside the dog's neck! It was a hideous sight. Shock and outrage welled up in me again. I couldn't believe that here, in the heart of America, something like this, so in your face, could happen.

Aghast, I asked the vet assistant what happened. She shook her head resignedly and told me that the metal collar had never been adjusted and the neck had grown around it as the puppy grew into a dog. She said, sadly, "I've seen it happen too many times. Good thing it didn't choke to death."

The sight of Missy twitching her ears when she recognized me was enough to gladden my heart. The vet told me I had brought her in the nick of time. Without help, she could have had a uterine rupture.

Missy did not have to undergo postpartum blues alone; she was immediately assimilated into our daily routine. Despite all the knocks she got, she did not lose spirit. My quick response to her needs and preferences opened up her personality. She was no longer insecure, instead, was now saucy and impudent, arching her butt up slightly like a southern belle whenever provoked.

"Missy must have thought she died and gone to heaven," the boys who brought her said when they came to visit her.

Soon I began looking for a permanent home for her. She had gone through finishing school with flying colors. A lady wanted to adopt Missy to breed with her Chihuahua; another wanted Missy to stand as a guard dog, of all things. No, no, I was not about to condemn her to the life of a slave again.

After a wide-ranging search, the right match came, in the same town where I lived. The local radio station had often helped to bring about pet adoptions. I decided to visit the station. There I introduced Missy to Bob, the local DJ. When Bob called out to Missy, she gave a pouty face, acting for all the world like the flirt that she was. Bob moved close to Missy and started using baby-talk to her, pitching his voice high, falsetto-like. Then he took her in his arms and put her on his lap as he worked the radio controls. She looked at him affectionately and licked his hands. There and then I knew the chemistry was right between the two.

A few days later, Bob phoned. He wanted to know if Missy had been adopted out. He had talked to his landlord and he had given permission for an in-house dog. He asked if he could come right over Missy had been on his mind since he met her.

Like a good Chinese matchmaker, I said excitedly to Missy, "This could be it. We have to get you ready." I dolled her up, powdering her all over with talcum. Missy greeted Bob like he was the most important guy on this planet. With Missy on his lap, Bob relaxed and opened up. He reminisced about a dog of his when he was growing up in Georgia as an only child, and then, about his Mother's cat.

"I wonder how Missy will relate to Hank."

Bob recounted the story of Hank. His parents had just returned home from Cooperstown, New York, when a black cat showed up at the back-porch. The cat sat on the picture of Babe Ruth on the Baseball Hall of Fame wrapping paper they brought back from Cooperstown. His Father said, "Name the cat Babe." His mother countered, "The cat's black." So they named him instead after Hank Aaron, who played for the Atlanta Braves.

Still unmarried, Bob dutifully confessed the new love of his life over the phone to his mother. "I have someone sleeping with me now," he said half-apologetically, half-boastfully. "And she's white."

The mother wanted to meet her. The following weekend, Bob drove home to Augusta. It was Bob and Missy's first road trip together. Missy traveled like a veteran. Upon arrival Bob sprang the surprise on his mother. This time, Missy was no longer the shy, self-effacing dog she used to be. Now she asserted her place in his mother's house, sitting on his father's lap as he sat in his bathrobe, coffee cup in hand, in front of the TV. She turned playful, picked up a towel in her mouth, shook and whipped it about, until Bob took the cue.

"At last, Bob, you've given me a grandchild," Bob's father joked.

Missy brings out the softer side of burly Bob. He gets up at 4 a.m. to go to work, gives her milk in a tupperware while she lounges on the mattress. She postpones getting up, however, until Bob has brought out the cheese from the fridge. At the precise moment she steps down daintily from the bed, then pads softly to the kitchen where Bob is already having breakfast. As soon as he leaves for work, she goes back to bed. When Bob returns home for lunch, Missy is at the door, leash in mouth, and dances about on her hind legs. She pouts when he is on the phone too long, nudges his hand when he gets too absorbed in the Sunday papers.

The two make a striking couple. The sight of a diminutive dog saucily looking out the window of a red sportscar with a two-hundred-fifty pounder in a reversed baseball cap next to her never fails to charm. Missy has become Bob's passport to a lively social life, just as my Paris mutt was a serendipitous key to the enchanted corners of Paris. At the walking park, Bob with Missy in his arms or on a leash invites many a friendly encounter. Missy is always on guard, and instinctively screens Bob's contacts, inviting some, turning away others. She always has the final word.

Once in a while I sit back and ponder on the directions my life had taken, why things happened the way they did. Then I think of the alternate possibilities if I did not plumb the depths of human-animal relationships as I did, and what were kept hidden from view: the slave-camps, the carnage, the killing fields. Were it not for the circumstances of Chornley's death, I would have remained mute and blissfully ignorant of the sad plight of many who share this planet with us. I most probably would continue a sanitized life, narrowly dedicated to the pursuit of popular goals, safe, materially rewarded, thoroughly dysfunctional. Cocooned and encapsulated in my human conceit, I would never have shared in the life of others on this space ship with us, whose fate will surely determine humanity's future as well. Or experience the wondrous and intoxicating feeling of transforming a debased creature, albeit different, into a free, fully functioning living being. Or feel the breath of God when animals cleave close to humans, as blind Ray feels with Iris, a seeing-eye Shepherd-mix, who runs a gas station with him.

I would have missed the exalted moments with the lonely dogs who sought sanctuary in my home, and taught me tolerance and forgiveness. I would never have gotten to meet the individuals in my community who share my views about animals, like the good ol' boy who turned from hunter to animal welfare reform advocate, a local sheriff who rescued a dog from the pound and made him into his drug-sniffing buddy, a college student who spent her weekends as a volunteer worker at the animal shelter.

The many synchronicities in my life began to have meaning when I was reunited with my parents and sisters. Exile had given me a sense of the Taoist reach toward eternity. The stoic calm, the existentialism, the unstinting love of which animals are capable, were part of that "gaze toward Paradise." They taught me that even if we cause each other pain, love should never be out of reach. These understandings enabled me to take family politics in stride. Lucky, ET, and their canine cousins were great moral teachers: they brought out the kind and generous impulses in all of us. They dispelled negative vibrations and brought laughter and serenity to Mother's house. The games we played ceased to be gamesmanship. As we learned to be more humane toward one another we grew taller in our humanity.

It was a Friday evening. The sounds of a busy kitchen reverberated throughout Mother's house, just as they used to do back in our old home in Asia. Mother had just returned from the hospital and was sitting at the breakfast table. Two sharp barks, a pause, then a long whining sound made me stop short. For a moment, I thought I was hearing Chornley's vocalizations, commanding me to let him in. Lucky and ET were whining, bugging me to do something. Rinsing off the sticky, vinegared *Kokuho* rice for the sushi I was preparing, I proceeded to the back door, opening it slowly.

A glossy, black Doberman Pinscher, almond eyes filled with anxiety, bounded into the house from the garage, stepping heavily on my foot. My dogs panicked, but she ignored them. Nervously sniffing the air, she circled around, searching. For a moment she didn't know where to go, but suddenly scrambled toward the restroom out of which Third Sister's husband was emerging. He had slipped into the house ahead of Third Sister, after an arduous five-and-a half hour drive. Having found him, the dog relaxed.

Third Sister's husband took a seat at the breakfast table where Mother was sitting, and as he did so Annie, the Doberman, slid under the table, put her chin contentedly on his bare feet, and watched his every move. He rubbed her head and neck with both hands and said to Mother: "Pets like Annie will drive us doctors out of business, maybe even drive down medical insurance." Laughing, he continued " Of all the women in my family, only Annie reduces my stress hormones."

Mother smiled, nodded her head, but said nothing.

As I got to know Annie, I became more and more convinced she was Chornley come back. Everything about Annie ~ except her breed and looks ~ was Chornley. Her whimpering when accidentally trampled upon and the way she slept ~ mouth agape, in a foetal position as if to make herself smaller ~ were Chornley all over again.

Fifth Sister came early the next morning with her three children. As we sat chatting around the breakfast table in an impromptu family reunion, I mentioned how much Annie reminded me of Chornley, how I believed Chornley had returned as Annie to be with Joy, who had given him the unconditional love that turned him around. As I talked Joy turned pensive. Remembering earlier times, we both wept. Fifth Sister's five-year old son, Chet, stopped his clowning. Clueless about what was making us so emotional, nevertheless his eyes reddened and he became teary. He never knew Chornley. That was how much we affected him. It was so funny we all laughed.

The three of us went over to Annie, who was lying supine on the floor, kissing and hugging her. Overwhelmed, Annie looked quizzically at me, at Joy and finally Chet. Then she dropped her head back down to the floor and continued her dozing.

Chet and his sisters had a dog too, a long-haired Jack Russell named Bandit. Skittish, feisty, he was often out of control. Slipping off his leash or dashing out a door inadvertently left open, he would take off, causing everybody to go frantically scrambling after him.

With all the attention we were giving our pets, Chet and his sisters picked up the cue and started sharing more of their daily lives with Bandit. The effect of this on Bandit was marked, even remarkable. He began to be less jumpy; his outbursts of wild, undirected energy became less frequent. The children, in turn, discovered Bandit's secret life. They watched him squabbling with gangs of rowdy crows who burgle his Kibbles from his feeding dish outside the house; they saw him cannily catching insects on the wing, leaping high to snatch them out of the sky; and relentlessly burrowing into the dirt in hot pursuit of a mole. They took note of the intensity with which he watches, along with them, the images of wolves on the TV screen on a Discovery Channel telecast, cocking his head as if he could see, hear and understand. They saw how he entertains himself by taking a tennis ball in his mouth and tossing it in the air, catching it on the way down; how he plays make-believe by pouncing on the pool vacuum as if it were a mouse; and how he kisses up to Ginger, the family tabby with an attitude, and defers to Ringgo, the ferret with a puckish streak.

Soon Chet and his sisters accepted that animals, too, had emotional needs, that they were capable of giving deep love and friendship, of experiencing shame and grief, fear and hope, joy and laughter, of being bored and even of being lonely. They began relating to Bandit as they never did before.

The never-failing power of love visibly changed Bandit's behavior. It ground down the rough edges and burrs in his personality, and honed his sensitivity to the temper and moods of the humans in his life, including myself. Aware of the consequences of bad behaviour, Bandit now makes a real effort to tone down his uncontrollable ways.

Bandit comes around often. His world has expanded to include many human and canine friends. Now he is one of the pack, and has imbibed dog decorum from Lucky. Whenever ET indulges in a bit of rough-housing with visiting friends like Oscar and Jackie, Bandit comes to me with an accusing expression on his face.

"I'm not extra-terrible; he is!" directing my attention to ET. The perfect clone of Frazier's Eddie, Bandit was fingering ET, Wishbone's clone!

And he has become presumptuous too. When he wants a body massage, he makes a big ruckus. When I get around to giving it to him, ecstasy is etched all over his face and body. First he lifts his head, looking blissfully up. Then, as the massage continues, his body drops down and he splays his hind legs to a kneeling position. I dare not stop, because if I do, he turns around to give me a reproachful look.

One day as he lay, resting his head on my bare feet, I began to chatter away in a multicultural mish-mash of English, Chinese, Tagalog, Spanish and French. It was my silly way of expresssing affection to dogs. The moment I paused he raised his head. Our eyes met; his had an unusual sparkle in them. All dogs responded to me the same way ~ including Jackie, the other dog in Chet's young life.

For the past two years I watched, fascinated and vastly amused, the life and loves of a neighbor's black-and-white female dog who at odd hours would show up in my property. She was a good-sized mutt with a trace of Border Collie. She would come all the way up my driveway, and invite my dogs out for a romp in the woods. Once, through binoculars, I saw her mating on my lawn with another dog. Then one day months later she came up the driveway with her family, a "husband" and a litter of three. They disappeared into the woods beyond. She never allowed me to touch her and her puppies. Her mate was more gregarious, always receptive to a dog biscuit and a pat that came with it.

One morning during the week that Chet was spending his vacation with me, Lucky, ET, and Bandit suddenly went completely bonkers. From their barking I knew the intruder outside was a fellow canine, coming to leave mail for them. My property was fast becoming the canine community Bulletin Board.

It was the female dog. She was alone. She looked pregnant again. I tried to befriend her but she scampered off. Chet watched from a distance. The following day, probably looking for food, she was back. Chet went outside to call her. She came to him without hesitation. We fed her. I found out her name was Jackie.

For some time she did not show up, neither did her mate, an Alsatian mix. It was New Year's eve this year when a neighbor telephoned me that a dog had been fatally shot and killed, in a fit of rage, by another neighbor. The shooting of the dog was the culmination of bad blood that had developed into open hostility between this man and his neighbors.

The dog who had been shot was Jackie's friend. He was chained at his doghouse when this neighbor walked over, rifle in hand, and executed him. I was outraged at the news. I remembered Chornley; it was the same neighborhood.

This time, armed with a better understanding of the workings of the criminal justice system in cases of animal cruelty like this, I informed the newspapers and a county commissioner who is also a veterinarian and animal lover, about what happened. Determined to use the full weight of the law, I helped the indignant neighbors with a plan of action to hale the perpetrator before the bar.

The upshot was, he was adjudged guilty by the court, but only of a misdemeanor, in accordance with the laws of the state. It was gratifying to see the press give it the publicity it deserved, although a felony conviction would have been more just.

This spring, Jackie began showing up again at my house. Maybe she was lonely, maybe Chet was on her mind, but for whatever reason Jackie came often to look for him. Chet took Jackie under his wing. A beautiful friendship began to develop between the two. To reciprocate her special fondness for him, Chet decided he would make Jackie proud of him. He began winning trophies in sailing and swimming competitions and dedicated them to Jackie. His successes taught Chet to persevere in a task, and to single-mindedly pursue an objective.

While Jackie inspired Chet, Chet expanded Jackie's world. At Chet's Lake Norman house, Jackie was, at first, reluctant to plunge in and swim, not being used to open water. Only when she saw Chet and ET cavorting in deeper waters and having a grand time goofing off did she wade in to follow them. Having taken the plunge, Jackie turned into a tease, swimming around the private foot pier, showing off to Bandit who kept to the shore. The taunting had an effect on Bandit, who hated to get wet. He ran from the gazebo to the water's edge, gingerly putting in one paw, then another, finally going all in. Paddling around, gradually he moved toward deeper waters. When the gang boisterously swam toward him, Bandit decided to swim towards the ducks sitting peacefully on a neighboring pier. The others, seeing the panic among the ducks, went after the cackling birds too. It was fruitless, of course, and soon everyone was back panting.

In the beginning, Bandit and ET bullied Jackie, despite her being three times their size. She ranked lowest on the totem pole. But not for long. She was to prove in many ways the supremacy of the alpha female to all the males, even to the alpha male. In her quiet, humble way she established dominance. Yet she remained thoroughly feminine, so demure I referred to her as *Baba-e,* Tagalog for woman.

Their owners, next-door neighbors, are cousins. Jackie and Oscar act like cousins too. As soon as they are released, Jackie joins Oscar at my place, and stay on, sometimes for days at a stretch. They have their own sleeping corners in our bedroom, properly laid out with fresh linen. What is more, they have adapted to our idiosyncrasies. They think life is one pajama party after another. Both shuttle between their households and ours, switching from one lifestyle to another with undisguised glee. But with a hostile neighbor quick to jump on the slightest misstep, there is always a threat looming in the background.

Jackie and Oscar's freewheeling lifestyles raise certain questions in my mind about human-animal relationships. Specifically, should we subject pets to the same restrictions and rules we promulgate for our own comfort and safety? Do the requirements of a human-structured environment justify drastically limiting the freedom and rights of animal pets? These are not simple questions, and there may not be a single and simple answer. But I am enough of a realist to expect that decisions about this planet and its creatures will be made almost entirely from the point of view of those who make them.

For the moment, all these questions are on hold in my neighborhood. Oscar and Lucky are buddies; but Jackie, ET, and Bandit together are a *ménage à trois.* When I drive by, Jackie and Oscar know it's my vehicle, even when they're inside the house. Their owners tell me that get excited and want to be let out, so they could hitch a ride with me. All jam together cheek by jowl in my utility vehicle for walks in the park. Whenever Chet is around, it is he who walks Jackie on a leash, while I take charge of three on separate leashes. Lucky, the privileged one, runs free.

At one park a middle-aged woman sitting on a bench called out: "Ah declaire! Y'uns got yer hands full, lady. Ya the dawgcatcher?"

I shook my head, smiled, but said nothing.

"Ah got ma own dawg. Cute as a button. But Ah don' wannit ennymore. D 'ya wannit?" she continued.

"Why do you want to give your dog away?

"It barks a lot. Ma neighbors complain, and Ah don' wanta git into trouble."

"Maybe your dog barks because he misses you. They get lonely too, you know."

"Aw shucks. Ah don' 'ave da time. Ah work two shifts, 'ya know,"

She got up and started walking away. "Weill, I guess Ah have to tak'it to da pound tomorrow. Mebbe someone'll take a liking ta it and take it off me 'ans. Baa baah now!"

Chet was all ears. Sometime later, we watched a story on Hard Copy about several teenage boys who lured a neighbor's Pomeranian, forced it into a black garbage bag, and set the bag on fire. He listened, wide-eyed, as I described in graphic detail other instances of animal abuse and neglect that I had personally witnessed. Telling the stories broke me up. Throwing his arms around me, Chet said in a big-boy voice, "Don't worry. When I grow up, I'll be a lawyer so I can put all those bad guys in jail."

His chutzpah warmed the cockles of my heart.

But I'll still be a *carnimore*," he said, taking a dig at my being a vegetarian.

I Ching, the Book of Change says, "Though you do not seek the innocent yourself, the innocent seek you, because your aspirations correspond."

11

PRELUDE TO JOY

Year after year for five years all was silence.

Then one day in the summer of 1995 I found a message in the answering machine. It was Father, speaking quietly in *Fujian*: "Mother in hospital...stroke." That was all. Cryptic and terse as ever.

My heart leapt to my throat, my mind began to churn. I had to immediately go to the hospital. But what hospital? Father did not say. And I did not even have their telephone number.

My parents had been living with Third Sister for eight years, first in Chicago and then in eastern North Carolina. Suddenly they packed up and went two hundred sixty odd miles across the State to establish residence near Fifth Sister. Fifth Sister was now living seventy miles farther south, her husband having relocated his practice there. My two other sisters stayed where they were: Fourth Sister, near Chicago; Eldest Sister, near Canterbury, Kent in England, having given up a promising medical career to devote herself entirely to home, garden, and husband. Fatalistically, she shrugged and said, in the greater scheme, we shall all die anyway, sooner than later. Like Fourth Sister and myself, she had no children.

Heart racing, mind whirling, I drove distractedly to the hospital where I guessed Mother would be. I was on a long and winding road I had never travelled before. Every two miles I passed red-brick churches; between churches country estates commingling with pre-fabs and mobile homes scrolled past. A traffic sign, altered by pranksters to read "pee Limit: 45 miles," momentarily piqued my curiosity about this town where the Ku Klux Klan once held sway.

Out of nowhere a bright-orange Kubota   tractor   suddenly lumbered onto the road. I jammed on the brakes, hurling ET from the back seat to the car floor. Lucky managed to keep his place on the front passenger seat, applying his "paw brakes." Turning his head, he gave me a quizzical look. I reached out to pet them. Both settled back and resumed their placid inattention. Unruffled, making no reproach nor comments ~ their manner reassured and calmed me.

As traffic ground to a crawl behind the tractor on this no-passing road, a line of pick-ups piled up behind me until the tractor turned into a dirt road. While waiting, my mind again wandered back to times past. Familiar strains of old melodies from the car stereo first jogged, then ignited, my memories. Image after image came flashing back, among them Mother in earlier and happier days. I tried hard to concentrate on the present, but the past kept intruding.

Past events revived needling questions about the family. What had gone wrong? Where was the vaunted rock-solid unity, the harmony and Confucian order? Was the family really this fragile, or was it shredding to pieces from the twists and turns the family had taken?

In Southeast Asia our family had been solid in the teeth of severe pressures from having to live among "barbarians." In America we were also living among "barbarians." But not only was there buffeting from outside, within the family there also reared up newer and more virulent contradictions. The safety net was tattering to shreds.

Father and Mother had come to America with soaring hopes. Father was to be the empire-builder of a family corporation of medical doctors making money by the ton. There were now seven doctors in the extended family. Three of my sisters had persevered back in Asia on the long march to medical degrees, graduating with honors from a top medical school before coming to America. In our new adopted land Third Sister became   a   gynecologist   and   married   an anesthesiologist;   Fourth   Sister   and   her   husband   became anesthesiologists as well. Fifth Sister, who like myself, was not a physician, married an orthopedic surgeon. In England, Eldest Sister became an immunologist and married a microbiologist-doctor. Father had indeed many aces with which to parlay the cards toward an empire.

The cards never got to be dealt: the game-plan never took off. The pool did not hold any water at all: there were just too many leaks. From the start it became clear the extended family could never get together to become a corporate body. Indeed, even as a family it had become a house of cards, ready to fall apart at any moment.

The paradox was that wealth and prosperity, instead of strengthening, weakened the collectivity and threatened its dissolution. The seeds for the family's break-up, having been sowed, began vigorously to sprout.

Perhaps the disarray in the family mirrored what was happening around it. This was not the best of times to be in America. America was agonizing through a moral crisis of its own. Sleaze replaced the morally correct, compassion gave way to "entitlement," self-esteem took precedence over social responsibility, dysfunction became more chic than family solidarity. Altruism, community *esprit*, family values, the "all-for-one, one-for-all" mind-set, the "strain towards consistency" ~ such American standards were going by the board. Antagonisms festered: between racial and ethnic groups, between churches and faiths, between interest and advocacy groups; among disparate centers of gravity, within corporate boardrooms and halls of Congress, in every corner and nook of America. The *zeitgeist* no longer favored playing by the rules. Greed, unbridled and wholesale, had become democratic, equally distributed, pervasive. Everyone wanted more and more of everything: money, power, sex, at the expense of the gullible.

Dissonance in America's ethos made for discordance among us. The crass emphasis on material success was largely to blame. But it was an obsession that resonated well with us. Like many first- and second-generation immigrants, we were caught up in this single-minded pursuit, but not simply for survival's sake. One needed money to discharge kinship obligations both in this life and in the other. One needed more money to honor ancestors with *guanxi* ~ the wherewithal with which to bribe the gatekeepers in the afterlife. One had to burn gilt paper money at funerals and *Qing Ming* festival, to provide ancestors with pocket money in paradise.

Among us the values of individual autonomy and group consensus-making clashed with a feudal, authority-centered mind-set. In China, ancestors are venerated like gods and elders obeyed without question. In America, such ideas are deemed fossils or extinct, like dinosaurs. We sisters were constantly torn between tradition, i.e. putting our own lives on hold, and modernity, i.e. getting on with our own lives. Choosing to do the latter *ipso facto* made us unfilial.

A quandary like this made filial piety not only a social, but also a personal problem. In Asia it was what kept the family together, drawing a definitive boundary between us and other families; in America, not only was it supposed to keep us together but also to keep us Chinese. If we were unfilial, what happened to our Chineseness? If the family broke up, what became of our Chineseness?

For the short haul, one could continue being blindly filial. After a while the buffeting from pressures became unbearable. Tradition had largely become an illusion: clinging to it was bound to do everyone a real disservice. The only way to maintain the illusion was to live in a state of denial. A state of denial only delayed a much-needed redefining of relationships and remaking of the family structure. My lone, foolish attempts to "democratize" family relationships incurred everyone's ire. Reform from the bottom was unthinkable. I was being presumptuous, disruptive and arrogant.

Despite its dysfunctional effects, filial piety continued to persist among us. The past had crossed the seas with us. Although each lived apart, some with children, economically self-sufficient, we sisters remained locked in bondage to our parents and indeed to one another. Our parents continued to solve problems as they always did: by passing them on to their daughters to solve. The "biggest chair" went to whoever did it.

When we were young, sibling rivalries were quickly resolved and soon forgotten. In America, rivalries became acrid. More potent "weapons" were at hand to use, such as money, cleverly used. Unity suffered frequent melt-downs in the white heat of personal agendas running wild. Parents pushed buttons to escalate the competition for top-dog position among us. Beneath the surface we were stepping on each other to move up, each trying to do more for our parents than the other. The synergy among us was no more; the whole was now only a meaningless sum of its parts. Differential abilities no longer complemented each other or contributed to a collective solution; instead they became sources of conflict.

Interracial marriages made for frequent clashes between filial piety and sororal solidarity, often degenerating into a *casus belli*. Except for Fourth Sister who married a Chinese, all married "barbarians": a Filipino from Manila, a New York Jew, a Dutch-German Lutheran from Minnesota, an Anglo-Irish Protestant from Limerick, Ireland. Diversity in origins brought differing cultural compulsions into play that collided noisily with one another.

Mixed marriages are inherently flammable, quick to ignite, primed to explode. Great-Han Chauvinism regard such marriages as anathema and scorn the "half-breeds" they produce. Strenuous efforts are made to keep the Han blood "pure" ~ though southern Chinese like us were once disdained as "barbarians" by the northern Chinese in Qin and Han times. When I was young, I heard Father contemptuously refer to a business competitor as a mix "of ten races." This is the mother of all Chinese insults.

Now we were in America, a land that proclaimed all races to be "equal" before the law. There ought not to be any cultural barriers between different races, especially within the extended family. But the melting-pot never came about, especially in the South where most of us had settled. Racial and even ethnic divides were just too high a barrier. America was proclaimed to be the birthright of those who came down the gangplank of the Mayflower and of their descendants, of those who wrested the land from the Indians, in accordance with the rights of conquest. The most recent immigrants, especially the non-Caucasians, are interlopers. Possession is nine-tenths of the law.

The incessant drumbeat involving differences of values, perceptions, lifeways, allegiances, church affiliations, philosophies made for a Tower of Babel. Often we were just talking past each other. Speaking a potpourri of languages did not help: English among sisters, and with parents, Fujian, spiced with an occasional Tagalog expression.

The climb up Gold Mountain was nerve-wracking, strewn as it was with boulders and razor-sharp rock. Complex issues and baffling questions relating to our new life in America were never even discussed. Instead of threshing them out, we acted them out, with little thought of consequences. Like most children of first-generation Chinese, we were discouraged from, even punished, for attempting to address a problem discursively. Perhaps for this reason second-generation Chinese excel in non-verbal skills like math, computer science – the sciences where verbal skills are not crucial. Talking makes the problem bigger. Thinking made it worse.

At the root of the problem was a fundamental difference in the nature of the family. In America when a person marries she starts her own family and her primary obligations are to her new nuclear unit. Not so in the traditional Chinese family. In it the original family simply absorbs the new families into a single, extended grouping. Relationships and obligations continue pretty much as before. The new members have to get in step.

Therein lay much conflict. The seamless fabric that once united the sisters tattered to shreds when marital obligations collided with sororal solidarity or parent-daughter dependencies. Nuclear plus extended family was a highly combustible mix. Not only was peace at risk within the nuclear family, but also peace between one nuclear family and another, and between daughters and parents.

Notwithstanding, some of the sisters did get together as before to indulge in fun and deviltry, regressing to childhood ways. Not used to the power of filial piety, husbands stood on the sidelines as spectators. Their own parents had either passed on or were no longer significant others in their lives. However, if the noise level became too disconcerting, they would weigh in with ultimatums, serving only to raise the decibel levels of the cacophony. It was a situation rife with captious confrontations.

When nuclear family went head-to-head with extended family, the sister had only an unchinese choice to make. But the cost was high. She faced heavy counter-pressures that made having to make a choice excruciating. Of course one could always stitch together a compromise, at best a temporary one, because it was always like riding a bucking bronco in a rodeo. Some took the practical way out: through perfunctory rituals – greeting cards, gifts, yearly visits – but otherwise kept a distance. This was performing the li but only in form, not substance. Going with the flow, preserving harmony and rhythm of things according to the Tao was probably the wisest. But at this time I was Cartesian, with an inclination to take the bull by the horns.

Trying to reconcile opposites did not often work. Even as the family stayed together, it did not stay well together. Attaining material goals did not make for success. Luxurious residences, lake homes, jet skis, sail boats, European holidays, equestrian hobbies and show horses, German luxury cars, and so on. None brought a sense of fulfillment or of euphoria.

The ambiguous, nebulous character of our self-image was at the root of our problems. The games we incessantly and mindlessly played with each other were really to fill a vacuum. The lack of clarity about our identity could not be dispelled by either staying   together or keeping apart. It was a real dilemma, one that reflected the ambiguity of our Chineseness.

Marginality was the albatross around our neck. It started in Asia and came to roost in America. Indeed, our marginality was two-fold. We were half-in and half-out of both American and Asian communities ~ misfits in the culture from which we came; misfits in the culture into which we ventured.

To be sure, lack of success in identifying with any group was not entirely voluntary on our part. There are barriers to joining or identifying with other groups. Such barriers in America are not meant to be permanent. Actually, some are.

Adrift, we had no place in which to drop anchor. Living at the margins of society, without a viable support system, indeed without a community to connect to except ourselves, we leaned on each other more than it was safe or sane to do so. Far too often we gnawed on each other, as if in frustration.

Everyone wanted control but in reality no one could be   in control. As the extended family faced complex problems requiring technical expertise as well as a consensus on a solution, the habitual way to address an issue was to look for someone to blame. The knee-jerk reaction to a situation gone bad was to personalize, even demonize. Never mind if the problem was not solved, so long as someone got blamed. Saving face, escaping blame was what mattered. Someone else, usually the lowest on the totem pole, had to be thrown into the doghouse for the "mistake." Alienated, the family was alienating its members in the quest for control. In such a disorder everyone begins to feel terribly alone.

In its microcosmic way the family is reenacting the whole gamut of contradictions in Chinese society: between autocratic control and freedom to express oneself; between feudal bondage and liberty; individual and group; uniformity and diversity; ancestors and descendants; male and female; youth and old age; present and past; tradition and modernity; between a stable but stagnant social order and material progress; between western and eastern values.

Mao Zedong made a historic, valiant effort to correct China's dysfunctions, by instituting his own version of order. For the sake of a more equitable and stable social order, he replaced unquestioning obedience to parent and elders with unquestioning obedience to the Communist Party and its Great Helmsman. Under Mao, filial piety was re-oriented toward country and state, away from ancestors.

What Mao did was to replace the Confucian leash with a more implacable iron chain, a choke collar that squelched diversity, dissent and innovation. Worse, he shut the Chinese people in as he shut out the world with a xenophobic chain-link fence. For three decades, China was in self-denial until he died. His demise unleashed pent-up frustrations that came to a head in the 1989 *Tien An Men Square* uprising. Was this a premature, still-born initiative, or a foretaste of rebellions to come? Will there be room for new beginnings in China's search for a modern identity? Can a hundred flowers bloom as China redefines itself? Or will they wilt in the heat of gunfire? Or be squashed by tanks?

A thousand years before Machiavelli, the Chinese philosopher *Han Feizi* said that humans are essentially evil, requiring force to make them good. His advice to the ruler: to maintain one's rule, foment division and confusion. To divide is to pre-empt conspiracy, to ally is to conspire, to isolate is to form coalitions. To win, one must engage in gamesmanship, play one against the other, spin the truth. Being honest and candid is to be weak, naïve, or a cop-out. Oppose a countervailing force quickly in order to stand a chance of winning.

To maintain control, the sovereign must be supreme in all matters. And let no one contest the correctness of his decisions. Toward this end, the First Emperor ordered 460 Confucian scholars to be buried alive, for he alone should possess all the wisdom and knowledge the people needed. Everyone, from the Grand Councilor down to court astrologers, ministers and officials afield, accepted his

primacy and authority in all matters. In the task of unifying a
fragmented China, he brooked no dissent.

Two millenia later, another ruler came full cycle. In 1966, feeling
threatened by "counter-revolutionary" forces, Mao Zedong instituted
the Great Proletarian Cultural Revolution. In the name of socialist
purity, he launched an internecine and fratricidal convulsion that
pitted Chinese against Chinese, brother against brother, sister against
sister, parent against children. It went on for ten years, inflicting
grievous injury on the Chinese psyche, and setting back China's
progress.

But there was a Confucian precept that lurked in the background
A leader enjoyed the mandate of heaven *only* when all was well in the
land under heaven. Although the elders and the powerful had all the
privileges, they could not escape reciprocal obligations to those under
them. Often, it was easy and convenient to ignore such obligations.
When this happened Mencius' prescription came into play: exercise
the right to rebel.

Mao Zedong rebelled against his own father. It was his first act of
breaking free from a Confucian leash.

As the road twisted and turned I wondered what effect this
crisis would have on the family. I hoped it would lead to the resolution
of many issues; indeed I looked forward to magical changes. Now that
we are in the West for good, is this the fabled Western Paradise, or
should we keep looking?

As I went up the elevator to the intensive care unit, memories
flashed through my mind as if in fast-forward: darkened room,
beeping monitors, labored breathing... I was eight then. The image of
Yama came and comforted me once more. Then my mind shifted to
the insistent ringing of the telephone at our Paris apartment one early
morning in 1985. It was a call from a Chicago hospital, where Mother
had just had an emergency hysterectomy.

Crunching the numbers, I winced at the coincidence. This year
Mother had turned sixty-nine. The first crisis was when she was
twenty-nine, the second she was forty-nine. I recoiled. (The number
Nine is unlucky for the Chinese.) I said aloud, "No, Mother is
seventy." It was a ploy to trick mischievous spirits that lurked in the
dark, waiting to snatch my frail mother away.

Anxiously, I looked for the intensive care unit. I hesitated for a moment at the door, then slowly peered in. The fragrant scent of roses mingling with the pungent smell of Tiger Balm wafted to my nostrils. Potted chrysanthemums, various flower arrangements, and children's hand-painted cards plastered on the walls filled the room, poignant markers of life events I missed for five years.

A thousand griefs assailed me. Mother looked so fragile, so diminished. Her face, once rosy and powdered, was now pale; her hair, once shining and black as ebony had turned a sickly gray.

Mother did not recognize me at first, mistaking me for Fourth Sister. When I identified myself, she cried and tried to sit up. But needles stuck into her were like fetters that pulled her back. Tears bathed my eyes as I stepped forward to enfold Mother in my arms. If only I could turn back the hands of time...

It was arteriosclerosis, an embolism or blood clot in the cerebellum that paralyzed her left side. Her family doctor had made light of a sudden impairment of Mother's vision as a matter for the optician. He did not notice her slurred speech and unsteady gait; neither did he order diagnostic tests when she complained of a heavy head and of neck pain. Why was he so dismissive? Was it because Mother was elderly, a minority, and on Medicare? Would additional tests cut into the HMO's bottom line?

In fact Mother was having a "stroke in progress." Third Sister, who had assumed the responsibilities of a son was present, in one of her almost-weekly filial visits. She immediately suspected something was not right. Without delay she rushed Mother to the hospital. It was in the nick of time. Had she not done so, Mother could have suffered irreparable brain damage.

Again, Third Sister's training and gut feeling saved Mother's life. The first time was when she made an eleventh-hour decision to fly Mother out of the Carolinas to Chicago, despite negative lab tests, for an emergency hysterectomy at MacNeil's, where she had spent her residency. There they found a malignant uterine tumor.

All during the crucial six months after the stroke, the five sisters took turns ministering to Mother's needs, without neglecting Father's usual prerogatives of course. Despite our own overburdened lives, we performed our filial duties as if nothing had changed.

Unlike Father, Mother was never sedentary. When she came to America, the vast selection of consumer goods created in her the habit of painstakingly picking out the best and the cheapest. She would spend agonizing minutes deciding which was the most perfect peach from a basket of perfect peaches. Now, her sudden infirmity threw her into despair: she had lost control. For a long time she refused to leave the confines of her home, resisting ambulatory aids such as a wheelchair or even just a walking cane. In the China of her memories, the handicapped and disabled were despised, reviled, and humiliated in public for being useless. So she thought it was better to hide away from others. During one visit I saw her weeping as she had never done before. She even spoke of just letting go.

To boost her morale and empower her, I told Mother the story of the miracle of the brain. Doctors had removed half the brain of a three-year old because of a tumor. Despite the odds, the mother never gave up. She kept providing all sorts of stimuli to the child. She invented ordinary mental exercises like making the child repeat as fast as she could what she just saw, heard, smelled, touched, and tasted. Eight years later, her untiring efforts had astonishingly succeeded in creating numerous new synapses in the remaining half of the brain. Miraculously, this half had taken over all the functions that originally were performed by the hemisphere that was removed.

Mother listened attentively, her eyes shining bright. I told her that most people go through life using only ten percent of their brain cells by being creatures of habit.   By accepting new challenges and changing attitudes, her brain can recreate lost functions and create new connections, much like the three-year old. She too could produce new brain synapses as if by magic.

"But I'm too old and sick to change," Mother said, shaking her head slowly.

"Mother, we change all the time. When we go to sleep and wake up, we have already changed."

Mother stared at me blankly and said nothing.

"Mother, what are we 'Luung' for?" I said with a challenge in my voice. The character for our family surname "Luung" stands for dragon.

"It's not too late to be a xien," I continued. Then teasingly, "Which one of the eight immortals do you want to be?"

She perked up and scrolled through her memory banks. After a
prolonged silence, she started to speak with some effort, "The ...last
immortal. That one..."

"Is it the street-singer who claimed to be a man and not a man?"
The most colorful immortal, he was dubbed by many Chinese to be
insane because of his complete apathy toward money.

"Not that one," Mother said. She forgot that her speech and
thought patterns were not in sync. "The last one...the woman..."

"Oh yes, the maiden with the ladle, floating on a lotus leaf, whose
stepmother starved her. When she fled to the forest, subsisting on
moonbeams and mountain dew, the other Immortals took pity on
her and carried her away with the kitchen ladle still in her hand," I
said.

Perhaps because Mother was starting to get intimations of
mortality, she also began to be more flexible. The No! became less
frequent. It was gratifying to watch her opening up. With her
tenacious will, I was sure she would not remain disabled for long.
When she set out to do something, there was no stopping her.

I saw the opportunity to share with her the ideas of holistic
healing through a vegetarian diet, exercise, yoga breathing, the use of
herbs and natural products, as well as unconventional healing
approaches such as the companionship of pets. I thought of restoring
health   through   *feng   shui*,   achieving   spatial   harmony,   and
strengthening the *chi*, the universal energy force.

Following Chinese geomancy practices in balancing wind and
water, I installed mirrors on walls facing entrances, to channel *dragon
chi* into the house. I put plants along proper lines to maximize the *chi*
flow throughout the house, a screen before an unprotected opening to
serve as a spirit wall to block troublesome *gwei*. The belief is that
ghosts travel in straight lines. To this, Mother shook her head
skeptically but did not comment. In her desire to get well, she allowed
me to do what might lead to her recovery.

Eldest Sister concurred strongly with the notion of alternative
natural paths toward recovery. "Less medication is better than more. A
healthy body and strong spirit is its own best medicine. The body
will naturally heal itself. The common cold for instance will peak and
then go away."

I do not know if my ministrations did any good, but Mother's speech and muscle functions came back faster than her doctors and physical therapists thought possible. Everything went well until a second, gross misdiagnosis by the same family doctor brought Mother close to a diabetic coma. It unleashed conflicting "second opinions" among the seven doctors in the family, ranging from medical management to the choice of specific medications, between *Ticlid* and *Coumadin*, glucophase and glynase, and so on, *ad nauseam*. Debates waxed bitter, and as before, personal agendas ran wild. It was like walking through a minefield.

It was obvious most were still fettered by the parental leash. Some used the occasion to once again assert the pecking order. Emotions swung between highs and lows, like a wild ride on a choppy stock market day when the Dow oscillates irrationally from plus to minus and vice versa in a matter of minutes.

Mother's recovery was at stake. Disheartened and confused, I sought refuge again with my dogs. I sat quietly with them at my side, and collectively we meditated, our way of praying. They shared my thoughts, my fears and pain. Once again, C.S. Lewis came to mind. It was as if he was reminding me to see with my mind and listen with my heart.

In the past, I was the proverbial bull in the china shop, succeeding only to exacerbate the disorder. In the authoritarian Confucian mind, the problem of opposites can only be resolved by the triumph of one or the other, not both. Like water and oil, they do not mix. But in other dimensions of the Chinese mind, there is the middle way.

In the way of *Tao*, yin and yang are complementary parts of a whole; together they form an integral unity. In this view oil can mix with water as in an emulsion. Either the contradiction or opposition is ignored or both are taken into account. Thus harmony is preserved.

Fortunately, the intimate human-animal interactions I experienced in the period of my isolation expanded my mind and enriched my spirit. I gained insight not only into myself but also into others. Knowing myself better made me try to understand why people are what they are and do what they do. Understanding them makes me get to know myself even better.

My parents were steeped in a tradition that made tyranny, exploitation and arbitrary laws a daily fact of living. They grew up at a time when a weak China was being savaged from within by bandits, contending warlords and, from without, by a rampaging Japanese army and predatory foreign imperialists. It was a cruel time in a cruel world.

They raised us the way they were raised, in the only way they knew, albeit in an alien social environment that diametrically opposed their values. They were always absolutely certain theirs was the correct way; I never enjoyed that certainty. My neuroses probably caused them pain too. Were the family dysfunctions the consequence of historical circumstances, as in most immigrant families? Would there be a question of choice, if an Anglo-Saxon, Christian education had not intruded? What I am certain about is that my parents tried to be the best parents they could be and that is what really matters.

Today's neurosis, nevertheless, need not become tomorrow's legacy. The uncertainty and insecurity of one generation need not be passed on to the next. That generation will have its own contradictions to grapple with, why haunt it with ghosts of the past? They don't have to grow up leashed as I was, as we all were. They had to be, and had the right to be, socialized in an entirely different way.

For this task of socialization I turned once again to my dogs. By deliberately juxtaposing their lives with those of my sisters' children, I managed to begin instilling the unity of biogenic existence into the children's consciousness ~ and conscience. The children learned to connect with the inner lives of their pets and, treating them with respect, unleashed their own hidden potentials. They discovered that animals are singular and complex in their own right, and can relate passionately not only with each other but with humans as well. For the children it was a crucial first lesson about commitment. Carried through life such a commitment should ultimately become a spiritual bond with all of nature. It opens up the infinite resources of nature, fortifying and properly equipping them as they start on their journey through life. Not until I am assured they have internalized this commitment can I consider my task done.

Mutualism, and the lifelong commitments it entails, is the rock-basis of family and community relationships. There should be recognition and respect for the unique needs of each other. This is how exploitation in all its forms can be abolished. Not only should this be true among humans as it is among other primates and non-primates, but it should hold between humans and non-humans as well.

All the coincidences in my life were falling in place. Mother's stroke was another turning point. It was not a coincidence that at every turn dogs were there to guide and heal me. They were the link to my sweet-and-sour childhood. And they will be the link to joys and rapture in the days and years to come.

They heal in more ways than one. About this time, the usually spotless Lucky started to develop a large skin rash around the neck, and to vomit in spasms. In Mother's house he and ET were confined by the rules of the house to the utilities space which served as the back entrance. It was the only door kept unlocked, for convenience. Here my dogs stood guard, like the stone guardians at temple gates in China. Perhaps Lucky was repelling trickster spirits with his body. Or perhaps he was deflecting to himself negative *chi* away from Mother. To the Chinese, dogs have this mystic puissance. ET was not to be outdone.

One morning, while I was busy cleaning the oven, I heard Mother chuckling. She was seated at the breakfast table, doing hand exercises prescribed by an occupational therapist. Since Mother rarely showed any emotion, I looked for its cause, turning to where she was looking. It was ET, madly wagging his little stump of a tail, peering stealthily at her from the passageway. He was squinting comically at Mother as if imploring her to waive the house rules and let him in to make her acquaintance.

Mother blurted out, in slurred Fujian, "Betty-ya, why did you get a dwarf dog, fat like a hotdog?" She seldom spoke after her stroke, so this was unusual of her.

"Mama-ah, my friends say he looks like me."

"*Aiya*," Mother shook her head slowly. "Why didn't you get something prettier like that." She pointed to their neighbor's white furry Bichon Frise on the deck next door.

"Mama-ah, since Paris, I take whatever dog comes my way. You'll love ET when you get to know him."

"*Aiya*, get something you can sell.. make money.. pay expenses."

I could have told her Jack Russells were in high demand, too, but that was beside the point.

"Mama-ah, that would make me 'an old tick gettin' fat off a hard-working dog,'" I cracked a Southern quip, ready to burst out laughing myself. Switching to dialect, I said "I don't engage in slave trade, selling dogs like hot dogs."

Mother didn't like what I said.

"Betty-ya, don't be foolish like many Americans. Don't waste your time and money."

I hid my discomfort and said nothing. I did not realize the subject of dogs could provoke such strong feelings. Nonetheless I was relieved to see any sign of recovery. The moment she was her old plucky self again, I knew she was well on the road to recovery.

In no time Mother waived the house rules and allowed all the family dogs to roam in liberty inside her house. She even cooked special meals for them, the way Grandmother *Ama* used to for Cinnamon and her "running dogs."

One day, with Lucky and ET underfoot, I tried to stimulate Mother to talk, as part of her speech therapy. While massaging Mother's face with an electric massager to stimulate the blood flow to where her face felt numb, I asked casually, what gift she had given to her family doctor, who had afterwards misdiagnosed her stroke.

"A Burberry tie and wool cardigan from Harrods," Mother said.

Suddenly Father's voice roared from the passageway. "NO! You are wrong." He had just returned from his morning round of supermarkets.

"We gave him a big basket of expensive English foodstuffs from Fortnum & Mason!" he went on as he emptied the brown bag of skim milk, fruits and other items on the kitchen counter.

The bright Carolinian morning sun highlighted a stubble of white hair on his shaven, well-scrubbed pate. In America, he had to shave his head himself, afterwards splashing on English Leather. Out of necessity he learned to drive a car. After breakfast and a forty-minute session on the treadmill, he would hop into his Benz 500 SEL and disappear until lunchtime. After an hour-long siesta, he would drive off in his 750 BMW, and show up only at dinner time.

"No!" Mother retorted, shaking her head as vigorously as she could. "How could you know? You disappeared in Harrods when I was picking out the gifts!"

When we were young, Mother had always been afraid to speak up, much less contradict Father in his face. In America, she saw the chance to finally assert herself. Every chance she got she turned the tables on him with a vengeance. While it was Father who regularly read both English and Chinese newspapers ~ Mother preferring to watch her favorite TV re-runs "I Love Lucy" and "Bonanza," she was the more adroit and agile contender in their verbal jousts.

"You always insist, so stubborn. That's why you had a stroke," Father blustered.

"And you slept the whole afternoon that day while I was weeding the garden," Mother riposted.

"I told you to come in, it was very, very hot. But you are so bull-headed. That's why you had a stroke!" Father repeated, storming all the way.

"And you are so lazy! If you were not so lazy, I would never have had a stroke. Anyway, it's you who likes to eat the *ku-tsai* I plant!"

"Silence, woman!"

"Give me the telephone," agitated, Mother commanded Fifth Sister, who after watering the dendrobiums and cattleyas, was compulsively re-arranging the family photos on the rosewood table brought all the way from Manila.

Mother dialed Third Sister. They talked for a few minutes, after which Mother began to sound more cheerful. Mother knew that telling on him to his moneyed daughter served to cool Father's choler.

"*To-sha*. I love you too," Mother sang out and hanged up. Her parting words were new to me.

I do not remember ever hearing the words "I love you," or its equivalent, spoken among us until after we moved to America. Some of us automatically adapted this American speech habit as casually as we drank Coke. As for myself, love was too precious to be expressed so often and so openly this way.

"Tuna was 31 cents at Bi-Lo; the Charmin toilet paper only 90 cents at Winn-Dixie, the Harris Teeter muffins only 39 cents," Father reported proudly, knowing that bargains and discounts pleased Mother. He avoided her eyes. She merely nodded to acknowledge what she knew was an olive branch.

Stiff from degenerative arthritis, Father stooped with difficulty as he measured out a handful of raw semi-glutinous rice into a pot to make *congee,* his specialty. Cooking rice was a chore he used to regard as a woman's job or a servant's duty. Now he could even make yogurt, taught him by Eldest Sister in one of her annual visits. He made it a regular part of their breakfast. Cooking and preparing a meal, no matter how simple, was now the most important ritual of his day, next to driving to supermarkets.

Eating soft rice ~ gleaming white and fragrant ~ was Father's way of maintaining authority; for us sisters it was a symbolic act to reaffirm our Chineseness. Even the children, all four of them, eventually developed a liking for congee. Their American fathers stayed away from the pickled radish, fermented bean curd, salted cabbage, soy-sauced Chinese shitake ~ various dishes taken with congee. They stayed faithful to their hamburgers and pizza.

To help Mother in her recovery, Auntie *Phang-ti* flew in from Hong Kong with Cousin *Ayen,* now twenty-seven, a graduate from an Australian University and already a Registered Nurse. Her brother *Ati* drove from the University of Michigan, from which in a couple of months he expected to get a Ph.D. in electronic science. To enable his son to do full-time study without having to work summers, his father financed his undergraduate studies at North Carolina State. He graduated at the top of his class and collected a slew of graduate fellowships.

Brother and sister sat beside each other, silently dispatching a Western breakfast of ham and eggs. They had not seen each other for years, but there was little talk between them. Auntie *Phang-ti,* peach flannel pajamas still on, happily and animatedly sorted out two big boxes of Chinese herbs and foodstuffs while squatting on the pickled-oak kitchen floors. She was identifying elixirs and immortality-guaranteeing items: seaweeds, sea cucumbers, black fungus for blood thinning; bird's nest, ginseng roots for rejuvenation. She fleshed out the inventory with a running commentary in Fujian.

She had not changed at all. Brooding eyes, coarse black hair cut in a layered bob made strands hang out in all directions. No rouge, no Chinese face powder, no lipstick. She was sure of her own identity and was comfortable with her standing in life, habitually deferring to her older sister, my mother.

I joshed Auntie *Phang-ti:* "Did you get these black fungi from the Isles of Immortality in the Eastern Paradise?"

Laughing, she said "If I went to *Peng-Lai*, you won't see me now here with you. The people the First Emperor sent there never came back."

"Ah.. of course they won't return, that was their chance to get away from Chin Shi Huangti, like when you escaped Mao!" That should have clinched it, I thought.

"No, *Meiling*, they were young men and women. When they found *Peng-Lai*, they decided to stay and have children. I'm too old!"

"Auntie, you still have many years to find all three Paradises promised to the Chinese. You can stick to the Western Paradise here, in America. Better than *Tien Shan*, in the Kun Lun Mountains."

"Who wants to live in America? Everything is the same, all food taste alike. People have nice, big, clean houses but they give parties in their garage, cooking what? Hamburgers and hotdogs! Everytime the same. Make you bored and sick."

"Better Western Paradise than Heaven Paradise in the sky, where you go when you die, still looking for immortality."

Auntie *Phangti* ignored what I was saying. She was more concerned with the lotus seed congee I was preparing. It was a Chinese home remedy for diarrhea, one of the side- effects of Mother's anti-platelet medication. *Ticlid* was one of the eight drugs her doctors prescribed for her stroke, high blood pressure, and diabetes. Taking all eight caused side-effects that required her to take more drugs.

"*Meiling*, stir more slowly so lotus seeds stay crunchy. That way, you will be filial," she said. "In China, when a mother has lost her teeth in old age, the daughter should nourish her with milk from her breasts. When a father is sick, a daughter should slice her flesh to make nourishing soup with it. A daughter should not drive the mosquito away from herself because the mosquitoes might go to her parents. That is being most filial." She seemed serious.

Retorting, I declared: "In America, children have no such obligation to their parents. Their obligation is to their own children. Here in America one looks to the future, not to the past."

"You are lucky. You have good fate, good life. You know, in our village in China, First Aunt told me they still drown baby girls because they want a son and families are allowed only one child."

"In America, things are different. I live in America now," I said.

"*Aiya*, but you are Chinese." Her tone was one of dismay.

"Auntie, must I stick to a tradition that enslaves? The Chinese need to get out of the time warp they are in..."

Unlike Mother, Auntie *Phang-ti* kept close contact with all her relations: those who remained in China, and those who escaped to Hong Kong, Canada, Australia, and America.

Sitting at her usual place at the breakfast room facing the kitchen, Mother was curling her hair in rollers. I did not notice her presence until she exclaimed: "Betty-ya, we *are* Chinese, don't forget."

"But we are not in China," I immediately replied. "Though someday, I'd like to live in our ancestral village."

"*Tiento.* You don't know what you are saying," Mother said, her eyes flashing. "Your father and I visited China in 1993. We know. China has changed, but it's still China."

I was eager to ask what she meant.

"Going back to live there? I don't think so," she said, with a knowing look in her eyes. "The way to love China is from a distance."

I began to understand why Mother always seemed so detached from most everyone including her fellow-Chinese. Although China continued to be an emotional pole, she accepted her being a sojourner for the rest of her life. Like me, she was ambivalent about her identity. Unlike me, she accepted marginality as a permanent way of life. She never anguished on account of it.

Today, all is well under heaven. Mother looks healthier and is more alert than ever. She had beaten the medical odds with the help of medical science and alternative healing. All these had the effect of reversing the adverse effects of her stroke. Her pancreas, in fact, was now producing its own insulin. Her doctors now counted Eldest Sister and Third Sister working in close consultation with her new family doctor.

Recently, I overheard Father proudly tell his friends at the mall, "You know I would never exchange my five baby girls for boys."

EPILOGUE

A Tibetan folktale tells about an old frog who lived all his life in a dank well. He refused to believe, when told, that there was something better and bigger than his well. When a young frog challenged him to go with him to see *his* well, the old croaker agreed to go. When he saw the ocean, it literally blew his mind.

Like the old frog, I was stuck in my own dark well. I had no insight, no strength to pull myself out and see the light. My inchoate Chineseness made me withdraw into a black hole; a hollow self made me ill-equipped to cope with the larger challenges of life. At odds with things as they were, I was completely alienated from everyone, even from my own true self.

A succession of extraordinary dogs sparked the mind-expanding experiences I needed to fashion a sense of self and purpose, to bridge the chasm between me and others. The Master Plan, I am now certain, was for me to cross paths first with one dog, then others, to lend me the power to keep going as I emerged. It could not have been by pure chance, the synchronicities were just too remarkable. At every crossroad and byway a dog was there, waiting for me. I had to fully live out my part of the Plan.

A dog's eyes probing into mine had a strange, unexpected and wondrous effect: it made me question my certitudes; it put backbone where all was jelly; it made me look for the true, turn my back on the false. Astonishing how a dog's steady, unblinking stare can unleash one's mind! Inspired to seek insight into the whys and the wherefores, I scoured every nook and cranny of my mind for meaning, especially of psychic suffering.

How could I look a dog in the eye if I was not honest about myself, how could I deceive in the face of that trust, and return honesty for honesty if I refused to see things as they were? In their presence I began to stitch together the separate threads and strands of a discordant existence, to weave a truer image of myself. I was ambivalent and raw, impaired in my ability to make informed choices.

Yet I had a legacy out there from which to draw strength. But where was it? I could no longer linger in the realm of shadows and ghosts, luxuriating in angst; I had to emerge into the light of day. It was time to fashion Joseph Campbell's " antithetical mask" ~ the true self. Lacking such an identity, I could not begin to respect myself or others, to escape my prison and lose myself in the larger whole.

Agonizing through the process, I realized I was in danger of being imprisoned by my skin color and by my construction of reality. I was behind a wall that kept me in a virtual limbo, a wall of cultural misconceptions ~ high-sounding, noble, but false. It was much like the Great Wall that Chin Shi Huangti built to protect China from northern barbarians. But those Chinese had a firm identity to protect. How could I lose an identity I did not fully have?

Every religious, racial, age, ethnic and gender group builds a wall to protect what it believes sets it apart from other groups and make it superior. Unfortunately, such *verities* and myths not only exclude, but often demean those who are different.

In this vein, humans erect a wall between themselves and other beings by calling them "just animals." They are supposedly without "rational" souls ~ a typical human myth ~ consequently without feelings, emotions, consciousness, or a sense of identity. But how do we really know that? The bottom line: only myth and prejudice make us deny such attributes to animals. Montaigne said we refuse to communicate with animals because we want to keep them in their place. *To despise the victim, to consign it to an inferior status, is a precursor to abuse, neglect or worse.* This frame of mind lies back of many acts of human violence and exploitation, including slavery, child labor and medical experimentation on the mentally impaired.

I wanted to demolish this wall.

We deny animals their rightful space because they do not speak in a language we understand. Yet we have found out that dolphins are able to communicate with autistic children; scientists "converse" with apes in Ameslan, such as Koko the gorilla; seeing-eye dogs warn their charges of impending danger; therapist dogs pick up, then communicate, advanced signs of seizures in the neurologically impaired; animals, even insects, anticipate typhoons, droughts, earthquakes and communicate warnings to farmers; pets sense fire or break-ins and warn their masters; dogs detect drugs for law enforcement agencies; dogs sniff out trapped survivors of bombings and earthquakes; and that any pet, feathery or furry, scaly or slimy, easily bond with troubled children and even with hardened criminals.

When humans communicate in a language like English, can they really be sure they are communicating the same thoughts or feelings to each other? Are we not all prisoners within our own skin ? When we say we understand one another, can we be sure we are talking about the same thing? When an eyewitness swears to state "the truth and nothing but the truth," why does another eyewitness' truth often differ ? Don't we all wear differently tinted eyeglasses ? Don't they put us all in a *solipsistic* predicament?

Why is it that when we do not like somebody we say "she/he is like an animal." Or, when we like an animal, we say "it is very human." Are not animals more human than we thought, just as at times, humans are more animal than they think? To me the fact that animals respond to us in our terms, in human terms, makes them superior empathizers. But it does not speak well of our vaunted ability to empathize unless we respond to them in their own terms.

Animals are a mirror to our souls.

In every phase of my life each dog was a defining element for that segment. What I wrote about each dog reflect the changes that took place in me. By sharing their lifetimes with me, these dogs helped to connect me ~ to myself, to my own kind, to ancestors, human or animal.

More than ever, I became convinced that animals and humans are together on earth to help each other in their spiritual evolution, so that at death, the individuality and character of each, improved by mutual contact, survive. All animals can help us this way if we but let them.

I saw what a thin and brittle barrier divides us from non-humans. We may all look different from each other, but together we make up one continuity, united by the indissoluble tie of moral causation. In fact, we have the same DNA as animals. The Chinese say all creatures are different: some wise, others foolish; some noble, others base. But in the democracy of existence we are all alike. No one escapes the inexorable convergence.

Thus I broke free from complicated leashes and began recycling my heart and mind, turning back to first principles. I decided to restructure and simplify my life. I found out that the less material baggage I had, the less I desired. It did not impoverish me; on the contrary, life became more ample, existence more tranquil, my world much more expansive. I became more alive, my sensibilities more keen, more attuned to every nuance of existence. An earlier but vanished sense of wonder, a more profound awareness of the Creator's hand came welling back. It made me fervently try to break through the barrier between species in the hope of being able to share consciousness ~ of euphoria perhaps, or even of pain. It came: a magical experience, a sense of fullness of joy where there was none before, an ascent to new planes of existence.

Like the monk *Da Mo*, who found refuge in Shaolin for nine years and learned about life in solitude, all creation conspired to enlighten me. Every earth spirit became an ancestor, guiding me. I was filled with the vitality of nature. It was natural healing.

Healing uplifts, makes whole in spirit. To be healed is not to be in a Buddhist Nirvana, for that negates yearnings; not Tao seclusion, for that withdraws from human affairs; not a slave to Confucius, for that constricts in a box of conformity; not enmeshed in institutional Christianity, for that affirms human primacy and dominance over all of creation.

One needs to be empowered, not hobbled by mindless leashes. One has to be proactive and make changes, take decisive action. One day, listening in shock to *"Lament of a Swan on a Spit"* from *Carmina Burana*, I was precipitously impelled towards a new turning point: I became vegetarian. It was a long drawn-out struggle because as a Chinese gourmand, I used to eat everything edible, and to a Chinese very few things in this world are not.

Certainly the decision to be a vegetarian did not render me malnourished. Instead, I felt replete; my sense of physical well-being was never better. I had an intimation of immortality, of being alive because everything else was alive. Any life is immortal while it lives.

Being a vegetarian made it easier for me to connect deeper with other sentient beings. From them I learned to be a peace with myself as well as with those who caused me pain.

Creatures who injure one another can also heal one another. By giving an unwanted animal a new lease on life, by assuaging the pain of an abused dog, I palliated my own pain. Because no matter how much pain we caused them, they give back nothing but pure love. Giving voice to their muteness silenced my own inner screams.

Saving one dog after another is like falling in love over and over again. To love is to heal. This is the ultimate therapy.

In the beginning, dogs were just a substitute for humans. With them it was unnecessary to expose myself to the prevarication and artifice that make living so unedifying, so enervating. They were my escape from a difficult reality.

But today, they are not an escape. They *are* my reality. They make it possible to attain to the serenity previously beyond my reach. By accepting my whims and idiosyncracies and even my subconscious impulses without judgment, they satisfy my need for acceptance. By being sensitive to my feelings, even at subliminal levels, they nourish my self-esteem. By accepting my roller-coaster moods, be they manic high or deep blue funk, they make it easy to manage such moods. Being mute and seemingly uncomprehending, dogs were my salvation, for they forced me to make the effort to comprehend.

As I now suffer the hormonal flip-flops of aging, I have no need for Provera, mood pills, or estrogen replacement hormones. Dogs help me come to terms.

To what end, then, was I healed? Making dogs my ever-present reality gave me a new, refurbished portal to my own kind. They became for me the greatest gifts I could ever get. I realized they were more than a crutch; they rebuilt my bridges to family and community. For dogs, no matter what type, can break down cultural, racial, gender, economic, religious, and even political barriers around people. Dogs taught me to be as sensitive and tolerant as they are, to peel away masks people wear to disguise thought and feeling.

Now when I look in a mirror I do not get back a forlorn image, but a whole community, myself among them, striving to close the primordial gap between humans and non-humans. Sharing a universe of meanings with all of creation I no longer feel alone. Walking together we leave our footprints on the sands of time.

I have taken the first step in the fabled journey of a thousand miles to repay the karmic debt I owe to my companion dogs, who played such a large part in the healing of my infirmities. I now wear proudly and fondly a new leash. It binds me to every sentient being on this planet.

I shall keep it on for as long as I live.